Europe, a Leap into the Unknown

A Journey Back in Time to Meet the Founders of the European Union

P.I.E. Peter Lang

Bruxelles · Bern · Berlin · Frankfurt am Main · New York · Oxford · Wien

Victoria MARTÍN DE LA TORRE

Europe, a Leap into the Unknown

A Journey Back in Time to Meet the Founders of the European Union

"Memories of an Evolving Europe"
No.5

The book was subject to a double blind refereeing process.

© P.I.E. PETER LANG S.A.
  Éditions scientifiques internationales
  Brussels, 2014
  1 avenue Maurice, B-1050 Brussels, Belgium
  info@peterlang.com; www.peterlang.com

ISSN 2032-5843
ISBN 978-2-87574-173-8
D/2014/5678/41

Printed in Germany

CIP available from the British Library and from the Library of Congress, USA.

Bibliographic information published by "Die Deutsche Nationalbibliothek".

"Die Deutsche Nationalbibliothek" lists this publication in the "Deutsche National-bibliografie"; detailed bibliographic data is available on the Internet at <http://dnb.de>.

Acknowledgements

I must give special thanks to Pamela Stewart and Tony Robinson for their invaluable help with the editing of this book. I would also like to thank Iris Ontavilla for travelling with me to the houses of all EU founding fathers; and to Etienne Deschamps, Josette Torres and Giuseppe Zorzi for their input on the characters and their assistance in finding the photos.

Table of Contents

Foreword 11

Preface 13

May 1948. A New Europe Is Born in The Hague 17

Jean Monnet. Seller of Dreams 33

From 1948 to 1950. Towards the 9 May Declaration 49

Robert Schuman. A Minister with a Tonsure 71

1950-1952. The European Coal and Steel Community 85

The Old Chancellor, Konrad Adenauer 107

1952-1954. The European Army fiasco 125

Alcide De Gasperi. Husband, Father and Leader 147

1954-1957. Benelux Breathes New Life into Europe 163

Paul-Henri Spaak, a Master on the Political Scene 181

1957. The Signature of the Treaties in Rome 201

Bibliography 207

Foreword

Javier SOLANA[*]

This year we mark the one hundredth anniversary of the outbreak of the First World War, a war that – like the Second World War – began as a European conflict and became global. The project for European integration was born from determination never to relive the horrors of war and to reconcile those who until then were sworn enemies: France and Germany. By delegating crucial areas of sovereignty, a formula to bring about peace and prosperity was found. Today, more than 60 years later, the European Union is the most innovative and successful integration process in the history of humankind.

The spirit that drove the first pro-Europeans was to tear down borders and unite peoples. They exploded the myth that the balance of power is the basis of stability. Europe has succeeded in creating a community of law, a community in which we have freely chosen to live together, to know each other and to build a better future together.

The peace, freedom and prosperity that we enjoy today, and that we want to protect, are no accident, but the result of Europe's integration. Today it is more necessary than ever to be aware of this reality. With the crisis, the globalisation process and worldwide uncertainty in this multipolar world, we see how political messages that we considered extinct are reborn. They take advantage of citizens' fears to throw up new barriers between us. But nationalism and turning inwards on ourselves are not the right answer.

Even though the first generation laid the foundations for our common house, the building work is not yet finished. Those leaders, with their vision and their genius, set out on the adventure of European integration and left an open end. It was – and still is – 'a leap into the unknown'. But they had a clear aim: to unite peoples through common values. The rule of law, respect for difference, solidarity, freedom, multilateralism or social justice, are all the identity signs of modern Europe. However, in the face of new challenges, these values must be set out in a different way. This is the gauntlet thrown down before the new generation of Europeans.

---

[*] Former Secretary-General of the Council of the European Union and High Representative for the Common Foreign and Security Policy.

The attraction of Europe for those outside remains magnetic. There is a demand for a European voice in the world, and globalisation will be better if there is a solid, coherent, strong and united European vision. Now that peace is ensured, it is time to look to the future and find the stimulus that can make the young dream again and regain enthusiasm for a project that has always been synonymous with hope but is now coming into question.

The crisis has placed us in front of the mirror. And now, as in previous crises, we must find a new dose of imagination and confidence in our values to launch a new integration process. From the founders we can learn about determination and courage, but also about flexibility. They knew how to read the signs of their times and adapt. Today's Europe is bigger, more complex and faces the great challenges of a world changing at breakneck speed.

The Union must export its experience to the international scene. If an international community based on law, and a multilateral order that respects all, big and small, is feasible, the European model will be its flagship. We have learned that our strength is not the weakness of another -- and we have achieved an unprecedented reconciliation in record time.

The new Europeans will have to bring up to date the ideal for which so many worked before, solving the new problems and making this Europe their own; this Europe for which so many have fought so hard, over the years.

Preface

This book is the fruit of a 12-year process. It all began back in 2002, when I took a year off from my job as a journalist in Spain to do a master's degree in European policies and administration at the College of Europe in Bruges. For the first time I wondered who had come up with such a tangle of treaties and institutions that, from my point of view, did not quite gel.

That was the year of the Convention for a "Constitutional Treaty," a *sui generis* name half way between Constitution and Treaty, like so many other hybrids produced by the European Union. The former French President Valéry Giscard d'Estaing spoke at the opening of the academic year and very soon all the students dived into the debates: Does Europe need a Constitution? Is it possible to have a real European government beyond the coordination of member states in the Council? The birth of the euro as the single currency had the federalists dreaming again, and the lessons learned in the Balkan wars fed the idea of a true Common Foreign and Defence Policy.

The other issue that unleashed passion and "clashes" was the mention of the "Christian roots" of Europe in the preamble to the "Constitution." Should the European Constitution refer to Christianity? As I heard the arguments for and against I could not make up my mind. I wondered what the founders of the European communities would have said and if this question had come up when they drafted the first treaties. I did not research it much at the time.

After graduating I went back to the newsroom of the weekly *Tiempo* and I continued covering EU news. I had to write about the "fiasco" of the "Constitutional Treaty" and about the disappointment of the federalists – which many then considered too utopian – and the subsequent crisis caused by the unexpected setback.

Europe rescued as much as it could from the "Constitution" to draft the Lisbon Treaty – again a hybrid between reality and aspiration –, and then the euro crisis broke out and the questioning of the whole European project began. Is this the end of Europe? This financial crisis affected me personally: I quit the magazine and was lucky to find a job in the press team of the Socialists and Democrats in the European Parliament.

For the first time, I could see the institutions from within: the bureaucracy, the multiple seats, the imaginative solutions to reach consensus even if it means giving up a clear goal for Europe's future. And being inside the cold EU's civil service I understood why Jacques Delors believed that Europe needs a soul.

So I wondered again what the so-called "Fathers of Europe" would have thought. I began to read their memoirs and biographies, and then went on digging into the digital archives of Europe's institutions. I found a treasure of official documents, meeting minutes, letters, photographs, videos and old newspaper articles.

Little by little the characters came alive in my imagination. I was captivated by their personalities and life experiences. I chose five "Founding Fathers" as the main characters, even if there were many others who opened the way for the building of Europe. Without the contribution of intellectuals, philosophers, businessmen, trades unionists and the different citizens' movements for the united Europe, the political leaders would have never succeeded and would have lacked a solid basis of values and thinking on which to build the political structure. This is why I start the book with the Congress in The Hague.

Then I was confronted with the narrative difficulty of combining two objectives: to tell about the life experiences and the thinking of the five characters and at the same time see them alive and acting: I wanted to open a window so that the reader can enter the meeting room, listen to their discussions and arguments, see their happiness and disappointments, witness their failures and celebrations. The solution I found was to write a sort of "zipper book", where after one historical chapter reliving in the present tense two years of European construction – beginning with the Congress in The Hague in 1948 and finishing with the signature of the Rome Treaties in 1957 – the reader will find a biographical chapter for each of the characters, from birth to the point in time converging with the chronological story. This is why the odd chapters are written in the present tense and the even (biographical) chapters are written in the past tense.

Precisely because I wanted to let the characters act and speak, there is no interpretation, judgement or conclusion from the author in the story. I hope that each reader will come up with his or her own conclusions. There are subjective points of view, but in each case I tried to get inside the mind and heart of the protagonist. It may sound risky, but I thought I could go that far after having read their memoirs and private letters, and also after having spoken with people who met them. I travelled to their homes – most of them are now museums – and I feel that we even became "friends".

Despite their very different personalities, what they had in common was the ability to combine the ideal they aspired to for our societies with a very pragmatic and realistic vision of the shortcomings of all human beings. They also had the flexibility to keep adapting their immediate decisions to the long-term vision. They shared the experience of having lived through two world wars, and a real desire to leave a legacy for future generations. And they did not want this legacy to depend on the will of those who would come after them: because good will is not enough. While building takes enormous effort and lots of patience, destruction is often sudden and dramatic. This is why they were so keen on having strong institutions.

What about the "Christian roots"? I would say – and my interviewees agree – that the three Christian Democrats (Robert Schuman, Konrad Adenauer and Alcide De Gasperi) never thought about mentioning religion in any official document, even if they spoke publicly about the Christian values inspiring their political action. They did not find it necessary. And yet, both Jean Monnet and Paul-Henri Spaak (who were agnostic and atheist respectively) acknowledged that throughout history, Christianity has played a positive role in the cohesion of the peoples of Europe.

The main achievement of these five "Fathers" and all the other pioneers was to identify that peace and the common project was above any personal or ideological differences between them. They managed to build trust in order to engage in the most audacious political adventure of all time.

May 1948

A New Europe Is Born in The Hague

Congress of The Hague. European Movement in presence of Winston Churchill
(© European Parliament)

7 May, 1948

"Europe is threatened by its own suicidal tendencies," writes Salvador de Madariaga in the tiny notebook he carries in his pocket. As he gazes through the car window at the streets of The Hague he recalls the darkest chapters in the recent history of the Netherlands – and Europe. Three years have passed since the German occupation and the end of fighting, but the wounds of war still hurt in the buildings of the Dutch city and in the hearts of its citizens.

Still alive in their collective memory is the "friendly fire" killing of 500 people in March 1945, just one month before liberation. As the car passes through the once densely populated Bezuidenhout neighbourhood, the ruins confirm the tragedy. That day the British Royal Air Force intended to neutralise a V-2 missile launch pad set up by the Nazis in a nearby park. But a miscalculation meant that the bombs fell on the local people instead.

Travelling in the car with Madariaga is his friend Josep Trueta, a famous surgeon from Barcelona whom he met when they both left Spain for exile in Britain. The two men teach at Oxford University: Madariaga is a professor of literature and Trueta of medicine. The Catalan doctor invented a celebrated technique for healing bullet and shrapnel wounds, which spared many lives and amputations, first during the Spanish Civil War and later during the Second World War.

The two Spaniards are picked up by a driver at The Hague port who will take them to the Dutch Parliament. In the rear-view mirror he observes his passengers, who are the mayor's special guests. Madariaga and Trueta remain silent while the streets pass by. This continent, shattered by two wars, is still unaware of its own identity, thinks the writer. It is still not conscious of itself, the rich diversity of its peoples or the need for them to unite in order to put an end to brutality once and for all. Against out-dated voices that want to use an iron fist with the Germans, some intellectuals argue the importance of avoiding the same mistakes as were made after the First World War and call instead for a true new order.

On this sunny spring morning, the main individuals and groups who advocate a united Europe will come together in The Hague. It is time to move from words to action. Madariaga himself is one of the organisers of the meeting, and he has asked his friend Josep to accompany him. Since working as chairman of the League of Nations' Disarmament Section in the 1920s, the Spanish diplomat and writer has gained a reputation as a pacifist. He promotes his ideas in the pages of his books, as well as through politics, and that is why he holds meetings with other Spanish exiles and opponents of the dictator Francisco Franco. At European level, he has founded the Liberal International, a federation bringing together all liberal parties across the continent. He hopes that today's gathering in The Hague will lay the foundations for the future of Europe, a new Europe free from wars and from hatred passed from one generation to another.

Much hope has been invested in this conference that will draw leading figures from all over the world, including American observers. The main personality is undoubtedly the former British premier Winston Churchill. One year ago he asked his son-in-law, the Conservative MP Duncan Sandys, to coordinate all the pro-European movements and to establish a permanent organisation. The outcome is the Joint International Committee of the Movements for European Unity, chaired by Sandys. It encompasses, among others, the United Europe Movement founded by Churchill; the

Union of European Federalists; Madariaga's Liberal International; and the New International Teams (*Nouvelles Équipes Internationales*), a Catholic European organisation. They will later be joined by the Independent League for European Co-operation set up by Paul Van Zeeland, former Belgian Prime Minister, to promote economic cooperation.

Almost 800 leading policy-makers, intellectuals, businessmen, trades unionists, scientists and artists have confirmed their attendance. The logistics need considerable imagination: with post-war shortages and so many shattered buildings, the Dutch senator Pieter Adriaan Kerstens, chair of the organising committee, has been struggling to find food and lodging for everyone. The Business donations cover most of the expenses and the goodwill of the people of The Hague and its surroundings makes up for the shortages: restaurants and coffee-shops offer cheap, fixed menus and sandwiches. Given the lack of hotel rooms, many families are opening their doors to delegates.

Local people have thrown themselves into this summit, and they eagerly await the arrival of the first guests, hanging out of their windows opposite the parliament, or leaning on the walls of the streets around the historical *Ridderzaal* (the Knights' Palace). Buildings are festooned with banners and flowers, the colourful flags of the participant countries alternating with the flag containing the new symbol for the United Europe: an enormous red 'E' on a white background.

At noon the first guests show up. After picking up their badges and discount coupons for local restaurants, delegates grab lunch before the opening, scheduled for 2.15 pm. The young activists already look impatient as they begin to take their seats at the back of the spacious room. On the second floor, a room equipped with typewriters and telephones will allow journalists to cover the event. In the basement there is also a lounge with cool drinks, a tourist information office and a post and telegraph counter.

Shortly before 2 pm, Princess Juliana and her husband, Prince Bernhard, walk into the already full Knights' Hall. Most delegates are men but here and there one can see a woman. Despite her personal commitment to the congress, Queen Wilhelmina has decided not to take part because of her great age. She has handed responsibility to her daughter. The impressive room, decorated with the coats of arms of the Counts of Holland, reminds us that this castle was built by an ancestor of Queen Wilhelmina in the 13th century.

The prince and princess ceremoniously greet the public and step on to the podium. The royal couple are joined under a canopy by the organisers of the event: Salvador de Madariaga; the well-known intellectuals Hendrik Brugmans and Denis de Rougemont; and Paul Van Zeeland and

Paul Ramadier former prime ministers. The elderly and stocky Churchill enters the room to a standing ovation. He has become the grand liberator of Europe from Hitler, and is admired everywhere. Following him is his son-in-law Sandys, who sits next to Madariaga.

The mayor, Willem Adriaan Johan Visser, formally opens the session and welcomes the participants. Churchill lights his cigar and looks around. He is satisfied that he has managed to organise the event on the scale he wanted. Despite the enthusiasm that he raises among the people, not all leaders honour him. From the front row, the Italian Foreign Minister, Carlo Sforza, looks annoyed. He doesn't appreciate the prominence Churchill has gained. Aged 73 and after a life fully dedicated to diplomacy, Sforza is a key figure in the government led by Alcide de Gasperi. Together they have designed post-war Italian policies, with the aim of bringing Italy back to Europe as a democratic and stable partner. Sforza knows that Italy cannot lead the construction of a new Europe for it must yet overcome its dark episode of fascism. At least Churchill has the political charisma to carry the audience in the room with him, even if his long-term plan will never coincide with that of Sforza and De Gasperi.

Nor do Hendrik Brugmans or Denis de Rougemont go along with the leadership that Churchill has assumed, but their reasons are different. These two intellectuals fear that the European integration project may be hijacked by a mistaken Atlanticist view. With that approach, Europe would have to choose between one of the blocs, American capitalism or Soviet communism, as if there were no other option.

Brugmans and Rougement would like to base the European project on a different notion of the human being, along the lines of "personalism". Half-way between the self-sufficient individual proclaimed by liberalism and the masses in collectivist Marxism, the so-called "personalists" place the person, with a social and spiritual dimension, at the heart of political action. Brugmans and Rougement want this model for Europe. This is why they would rather work for a purely European initiative, not one designed by the Anglo-Saxon axis.

However, with Europeans apparently incapable of acting rationally, it is left to the Americans to bring order to the old continent. By offering financial aid to those countries that voluntarily coordinate their recovery plans, they have managed to establish a permanent framework for cooperation between former enemies. General Marshall has promised generous funds to restore buildings, streets and roads, and to get farming and industry back in production. Without that help, European nations would fester in hunger and ruins. Through their financial aid, the Americans succeeded in obliging the Europeans to set up the Organisation for European Economic Co-operation (OEEC).

Both Churchill and the American delegation attending the congress in The Hague would be pleased to see the OEEC as the basis for a united Europe: a permanent forum for cooperation linked to the US. The Conservative and Atlanticist agenda that Churchill promotes is opposed to the personalist federalism advocated by Sforza, Rougemont and Brugmans. It also faces criticism in the UK, particularly within the Labour party, which even asked its members not to attend the congress.

This explains the absence of Paul-Henri Spaak. Following the advice of its "sister party", the Belgian Socialist leader did not come. Despite his personal admiration for Churchill's stand during the Second World War, Spaak does not wish to offend his left-wing friends in England. However, many Labour activists and even MPs disobeyed and have come to The Hague because they are convinced that most participants have a true European dream and do not really share Churchill's political views.

Once the mayor finishes his welcome speech, Churchill, with his characteristic plump silhouette, approaches the podium to sustained applause from an expectant audience.

He greets the royal family, all the authorities and, above all, the German participants. The German delegation is not very large and does not include any leading politicians, so they are pleased by the courtesy of the British. The leader of the delegation is the former mayor of Cologne, Konrad Adenauer, who smiles when Churchill mentions his country.

"Since I spoke about this in Zurich in 1946,"[1] says Churchill, "and since our British United Europe Movement was launched in January 1947, events have carried our affair beyond our expectations. This cause was obviously either vital or merely academic. If it was academic, it would wither by the wayside; but if it was the vital need of Europe and the world in this dark hour, then the spark would start a fire which would glow brighter and stronger in the hearts and minds of men and women in many lands. This is what actually happened."

He invites all governments to work together for economic consolidation of the 16 countries of western and northern Europe members in the OEEC. He also praises the military alliance recently signed in Brussels between five countries, underlining that this alliance does not consider Germany to be the enemy.

He adds: "Europe requires all that Frenchmen, all that Germany and all that every one of us can give. I therefore welcome here the

---

[1] Churchill delivered a speech at the University of Zurich on 19 September 1946 that became a turning point in European integration: "The fighting has stopped. But the dangers have not stopped. If we are to form a United States of Europe, or whatever name it may take, we must begin now."

German delegation, whom we have invited into our midst. For us, the German problem is to restore the economic life of Germany and revive the ancient fame of the German race without thereby exposing their neighbours and ourselves to any rebuilding or reassertion of their military power."

At 4.15 pm sharp Churchill finishes his speech and the conference breaks for 15 minutes. At 4.30 pm Paul Ramadier struggles to bring everyone back into the room and to have the silence he needs for the session he will chair. The former French prime minister is a historical figure of the Resistance and one of the fathers of the Constitution of the Fourth Republic. He had led the government until only a few months ago, but he had to step down in November because of strikes and demonstrations. Now a Conservative government is in place headed by Robert Schuman, a member of the MRP (*Mouvement Républicain Populaire*). Ramadier's passion and enthusiasm are unchanged, and he lights the room up with his impassioned speech, ending with the cry: "Europe or death!"

After him Count Richard Coudenhove-Kalergi takes the floor. Like his wife, he is a member of the French delegation. He is so well-known that he could be a delegation on his own. Aged 54, he is probably the most respected voice of the European cause. He became a symbol back in 1922 when he launched his call for the creation of a "Paneuropa" with a manifesto. Coudenhove-Kalergi recalls the long years of work with a common purpose. "This congress marks the 25th anniversary of the Pan-European Movement, that is to say 25 years of fighting for peace and freedom in Europe. In terms of history this is not much, but for the human generation it is."

And then a word of remembrance for the pioneer Aristide Briand: the French president's speech at the League of Nations calling for a European Federation on 5 September, 1929, was his personal attempt to translate Coudenhove-Kalergi's manifesto into politics. But he did not succeed, and their worst fears came true. "If he had succeeded, there would have been neither a Third Reich nor the Second World War," says the count. "It is about time to make that dream true: I call for a Continental Constitutional Assembly, with European members!"

Brugmans agrees. It is indeed fundamental to open an assembly that could draft a constitution for a federal Europe with a shared democratic basis. He stresses this in his speech when he says that Europe is the prerequisite, the ultimate objective, greater than any ideological divide, any economic interest or national supremacy. "European unity on a supranational basis is a prerequisite for all efforts towards international understanding," he says.

22

"What do we want? Beyond treaties, which can always be revoked, beyond secret meetings that can always end in stagnation, we want to create European federal institutions; institutions with strength and authority, capable of crystallising into a new society of the peoples of Europe. We should state it clearly to a world with reasons to be sceptical: we are not interested – absolutely not at all – in diplomatic constructions like the former League of Nations or a sort of European United Nations, paralysed by the right of veto," concludes Brugmans.

Madariaga nods. He lived through the failings and fiascos of the League of Nations, since he was one of those who launched the institution in Geneva after the First World War. He approaches Brugmans at the end of the session, and together they walk back to the hotel for a quick rest, a change of clothes and dinner.

The Dutch government is holding a reception at the Wassenaar Palace, and from here the participants can take a tram to the seafront. It is there, in the magnificent Scheveningen Kurhaus Palace, that dinner will be served every evening of the congress.

Built in the late 19th century on a former bathing resort, the Scheveningen Kurhaus has become one of the most exclusive hotels in Europe. The big hall with its grand staircase and ornate chandelier welcomes European guests whose names are announced by loudspeaker as they cross the hall towards the dining room. Churchill and his wife are staying at the Scheveningen, as is Anthony Eden, who was foreign minister in the Conservative government. The handsome Eden, with his trendy Clark Gable-style moustache, attracts admiring looks from the ladies.

The French delegation is put out by the special treatment that the mayor has lavished on the UK representatives. They complain that while the British are staying together at the best hotel, the French have been scattered about, many of them several miles away from The Hague.

The receptions and banquets and the etiquette of the congress annoy Konrad Adenauer. The mayor has always been austere, not keen on socialising and much less on luxury. He is still mourning his wife Augusta, who passed away only two months ago. If he is here in The Hague, and at this spectacular hotel, it is just for politics, or more precisely, because of his sense of duty: he feels responsible for leading his country out of the crisis and the shame of nazism. This meeting gives him a great opportunity to rub shoulders with the most important European leaders as their equal, not as victors meeting the defeated.

When he hears that Churchill has already arrived, he goes to the lounge to greet him before the prime minister takes his seat at the main table. Adenauer thanks the British for their efforts to avoid the partition of Germany. Before the end of the war, a plan to divide Germany into four parts circulated among the allies. The Morgenthau plan, developed by the US and backed by many in the UK and France, intended to change Germany's productive model and transform the country from an industrial into an agricultural economy. It also proposed giving the western part of Germany to France and the east to Poland, with the rest split between north and south. That way there would be no more expansionist claims by Prussia. The plan has now been abandoned, despite the insistence of some of its backers – because of the severe criticism it aroused, the most vigorous being that of Churchill.

Churchill accepts Adenauer's words of gratitude and wishes him well. He had heard about him and how he had been banned from politics first by the Nazis and then by the British authorities. The UK, as one of the four victorious powers that took charge of Germany after the war, is still responsible for Adenauer's region, North-Rhine Westfalia. The British then changed their mind, and two years ago allowed him to be active in politics again. But since his brother-in-law Suth had replaced him at the city hall, Adenauer has spent the last two years travelling around Germany to form a new political party: the Christian-Democrat Union (CDU), which he now leads.

Since the death of his wife Gusie, as he used to call her, on 3 March, he is entirely devoted to his work and a single thought occupies his mind: becoming chancellor. His children are already grown-up, because Gusie was his second wife and much younger. It actually never crossed his mind that he would outlive her.

The final weeks with her were very tough because he could hardly see her. When she first fell ill, he would spend hours at her bedside. Later on, the British authorities restricted his movements and would not let him live with his family. He was allowed to see her for just a few hours. Despite her weakness, she would stand up and prepare sandwiches and a flask of coffee for him and the driver. Together they were travelling around Germany and eating whatever they could at the roadside. Adenauer could spend only a few hours with her, even when she was no longer able to get out of bed. This will be the hardest part to forgive the Brits. At this moment, however, he must swallow his own feelings and work for the future.

Over the last two years, Adenauer has endeavoured to become the partner of the allies. Now the personal meeting with Churchill will give him an advantage. He also wants to speak with the leader of the French Conservative delegation, the MRP. Although its president, George Bidault, is not at The Hague, he has sent his right-hand man, Robert Bichet. Bichet is a Member of Parliament and has been a close friend of Bidault since they fought together in the Resistance. Adenauer's goal tonight is to round off his strategy to neutralise the other candidate supported by western

Conservative parties to rule Germany: Joseph Müller. Fortunately, Müller has not come to The Hague, a good omen for Adenauer.

The story of the Bavarian Catholic Müller won the hearts of the Americans, who made him their preferred candidate. Aged only 50, he is one of the main figures of the Catholic resistance and this role gives him a bright future in the eyes of the Americans. He is trusted by the US, the French Conservative MRP, the Italian *Democrazia Cristiana* and even the Holy See![2] The American Army freed him from Dachau concentration camp at the end of the war, and the secret services flew him to the Italian island of Capri for interrogation. Before going home in May 1945, he stopped in Rome for an audience with Pope Pius XII and an interview with the President of the Council, Alcide de Gasperi. The Italian head of government was impressed by the Bavarian and told his friends in the MRP that they should work with him.

The French followed De Gasperi's advice, and two years ago Müller was the only German guest to be invited to the MRP congress. Both Georges Bidault and Robert Schuman liked him and expected to see him thrive in German politics. But luckily for Adenauer, Joseph Müller discredited himself: in recent months he has called for rapprochement with the Soviet Union as a strategy for German reunification. Neither Washington nor London appreciated his comments. Adenauer believes the opposite: for him, a democratic Germany cannot expect anything from Moscow.

Now the MRP seems glad to accept Adenauer's leadership and tries to open new ways of dealing directly with him and building trust. This is why Robert Bichet also wants to speak with Adenauer in The Hague. After dessert, when some guests go out on the terrace to enjoy the fresh air, Bichet goes to the table where the Germans are eating. Adenauer chats with two other members of his delegation, the lawyer Heinrich von Brentano and professor Walter Hallstein.

Other delegations sneak a look at the odd couple, as Bichet and Adenauer shake hands amicably and stroll out to the seafront. Curious observers are unaware that they already know each other. They met secretly last March in Switzerland. Even if French public opinion rejects any formal contact with Germany, Bidault thinks that informal exchanges must begin as soon as possible. This is why he has established a system of secret meetings between Conservative leaders in Europe. It is known as the "Geneva Circle", based on the city where they meet, thanks to Bidault's friend Victor Koutzine, who lends them his apartment in Geneva. Their goal is to coordinate the action of Christian-inspired political leaders in Europe.

---

[2]   The Holy See is the episcopal jurisdiction of the Catholic Church in Rome. The bishop of Rome is the Pope, the leader of the universal Church.

The MRP contacted Adenauer for the first time two months ago to invite him to one of these meetings. Müller and Bidault were also among the participants. Adenauer accepted without any conditions. However, now that they have already scheduled the next meeting for October, Adenauer wants to be the only German representative. He firmly rejects any talk of getting closer to Moscow, while both Bidault and Bichet have come to realise that the old mayor, with his long political experience, is the person they need in Bonn.

During their walk, Bichet asks Adenauer about a project he discussed with Bidault in Geneva: the possibility of jointly managing coal and steel production in France and Germany. Bidault showed interest and they said they would talk about it. When he left Geneva, Adenauer gave Koutzine a message for Bidault: he should find a group of French experts to study the feasibility of the project, and he would find a group of Germans to do the same.

For his part, Bichet brings to The Hague a message from Bidault: the experts are already studying the project. However, he also has a request from his boss: Adenauer must decide whether he wants to be part of the *Nouvelles Équipes Internationales* (NEI). This grass-roots organisation is Bidault's personal initiative and he wants the German CDU to be involved.

Even before the end of the war, Bidault has been active in creating a grass-roots network of "teams" linked to Christian-Democrat political parties. The original idea is not his own but that of the Italian don Luigi Sturzo. This Catholic priest founded the Italian People's Party in 1919 and in 1926 he encouraged an International Secretariat of Christian-inspired Democratic Parties (SIPDIC) following the example of the Labour and Socialist International, created in 1923. But he did not succeed. Sturzo first escaped Italian fascism, then the Second World War, taking refuge to begin with in the United Kingdom and later in the United States.

In 1944, Bidault visited him in New York. They agreed to hold a congress of all Christian-Democrat parties as soon as the war was over. The Italian promised to support Bidault with his ideas and his contacts. So in 1945 the French took the lead and invited other Christian leaders to the congress the MRP was holding in Paris. Bichet was put in charge of building the new organisation's network.

Over the last two years Bichet has been working quietly on this project, called *Nouvelles Équipes Internationales*. He travelled to Belgium, Austria and Italy in 1946 to meet among others Van Zeeland and De Gasperi. In general, he found open willingness to participate, but every one of them had in mind a different kind of organisation.

At last, the NEI was officially constituted in Liège (Belgium) in March 1947 and Bichet is its president. However, its structure and aims are still unclear. Unlike the newly established Liberal International, the NEI does not represent political parties but the individuals who want to join in a personal capacity. The "Christian" label is the cause of all misunderstandings and the reason behind the lacklustre name that was finally chosen. The Italians and Austrians want an open Christian-Democrat International, whereas the French and Belgians cannot accept the name "Christian" in a political organisation. They say that it limits the scope and is against the secular principles of the French Republic. They see a clerical turn they dislike. The Dutch, meanwhile, feel closer to the French and Belgians.

When they met in Geneva, Bichet had asked Adenauer to appoint a German delegation to the NEI, but so far he has not heard back from him. The French leader does not know that Adenauer is just trying to buy time until he has stronger control of his own party. He is not really interested in the NEI or in the Byzantine discussions on the name of the organisation or the role of religion. But he is greatly interested in the secret meetings of the Geneva Circle because they open a door to direct contact with France. These conversations could discreetly pave the way to Germany retaking full sovereignty over its territory and to him winning the international legitimacy and political support to become chancellor.

Saturday, 8 May

The delegates begin to arrive at the Ridderzaal around 9 am. This time speeches are replaced by three round table discussions on specific issues: one on economics, one political and the third on culture. The corridors are full of policy-makers, businessmen, professors and trades unionists trying to find the right room.

It is bizarre to see General Confederation of Labour (CGT in French) unionists chat with businessmen from distinguished families like the Italian manufacturers Adriano and Massimo Olivetti. Several bankers, representatives of various European chambers of Commerce and renowned professors try to find the economic and social committee. Paul Van Zeeland, who is supposed to chair that meeting, leads the group. They ask the organisers, who wear a blue card on their lapel, to show them the way to one of the rooms in the Ridderzaal building.

To the cultural committee will go Rougemont, Brugmans and Madariaga, along with artists, musicians, architects, intellectuals like Bertrand Russel, and acclaimed writers like the British T.S. Eliot or the American journalist Walter Lippman. Together they go upstairs to the room next to the economic committee. In the meantime those attending the political committee leave the building and go to a bigger room outside, next to the botanical gardens.

The French fill the political conference. There are many historical figures of the Resistance, including Paul Reynaud, Leon Blum and Edouard Daladier. The latter was tried and handed over to Germany in 1942, spending almost three years in prison until the liberation in 1945. Others are not so famous, such as the young minister appointed by Council President Robert Schuman to be in charge of veterans and war victims, François Mitterrand. Schuman did not attend but sent Mitterrand on his behalf, accompanied by Pierre-Henri Teitgen, Minister for the Army. The prime minister likes Mitterrand and trusts him fully.

Among the Italians there are two key figures: Minister Sforza and the unsinkable Altiero Spinelli, who is as prominent in European circles as Coudenhove-Kalergi, but much younger. He has emerged from radical socialism – for which he was sentenced to 16 years in prison by the Fascist regime – to become one of the main advocates of a European federation.

He speaks and writes extensively about a united Europe: united politically, financially and socially, and well-rooted in freedom and parliamentary democracy. His manifesto for Europe, written while he was imprisoned on Ventotene Island with his friend and comrade Ernesto Rossi in 1941, was a watershed in pro-European literature. It provided practical material to federalists to defend a viable political project.

It has been five years since Spinelli regained his freedom, and he spends all his time on the federalist ideal through the organisation he founded: the European Federal Movement. His influence in the political committee is significant.

The three committees work on draft resolutions that were prepared by the organisers and circulated among the delegates before they arrived. The most ambitious one, tabled by Spinelli in the political committee, would create an assembly to represent the citizens of Europe and be a counterbalance to national governments.

There are many who think that it is premature to draw up plans for any common form of government before overcoming more urgent and potentially explosive issues, such as the question of the Ruhr and the Saar. This is the really hot topic of debate because it goes to the very core of the conflict on the borders of Germany after the war, and its steel and industrial capacity. The Saar has gained independent status – and as such its representatives participate in this congress – while the Ruhr, so far, is administered by the allies. But the status of the Saar and the Ruhr are not yet defined.

The Member of Parliament and MRP strong figure Maurice Schumann openly calls for the annexation to France of the German territory up to the

Rhine, so that the river will act as the natural border. On this he is backed by the Gaullists, who still favour partition of Germany.[3]

Adenauer must bite his tongue. He cannot stand the arrogance of Maurice Schumann and his patronising attitude on "the German problem", or when he quotes the special edition of the magazine *L'Esprit* that was entirely dedicated to Germany and how to "re-educate" the German people before the country can be accepted into the European family. Adenauer knows that he must not give the wrong impression or look aggressive. In the corridors, people say that Germany's participation in a European federation could be the solution for the Ruhr problem.

At 1 pm delegates go for lunch nearby. Heated debates continue over the tables of the small restaurants. Madariaga, Brugmans and Rougemont choose the New Literary Society and its simple but attractive menu. They use the lunch break to discuss a project they have been thinking about for a while: a university for European studies, where the young will learn the common roots of the continent, far from nationalistic feelings and from the history taught as a series of military battles and homeland heroes. They will also experience friendship and comradeship with their fellow students. There is neither funding nor a seat yet. This will come. However, Rougemont has another request: a cultural centre where the common history will be researched and cherished: from Homer to Victor Hugo, almost three millennia of bricks in the construction of Europe that no one should forget.

This little trio is not the only group procrastinating after lunch, driven by passionate conversations, so it is inevitable that the afternoon session begins a bit late. Unable to complete the agenda, they must go back to the meeting room after dinner at the Scheveningen palace. The night is long, but at long last the draft resolutions are ready for the final debate and vote the following morning.

Sunday, 9 May

Ahead of the vote, the presidency gives the floor to those participants who do not belong to an official delegation because they represent non-democratic countries. The Spanish group is led by the Socialist Indalecio Prieto, who calls on Europe not to turn its back on Spain. In a moving speech, he asks participants to isolate Franco, who had collaborated with Hitler and Mussolini. He speaks on behalf of many Spaniards who fought for a free Europe with the firm belief that Europeans would then help free Spain from the dictator, and who now find themselves facing pure indifference.

---

[3] In 1945, after the war, Germany west of the Oder-Neisse line was divided into four zones temporarily administered by the four victorious powers: the United States, the United Kingdom, France and the Soviet Union.

The Conservative José María Gil Robles was also invited, but Franco prevented him from leaving Portugal, where he now lives in exile along with the Spanish royal family. When everything was arranged, the Portuguese dictator Salazar warned him that he could leave the country but would never be allowed to return – so he stayed.

After all the guests have spoken, a coffee break gives them the chance to replenish their energy before the mass outing to Amsterdam, where crowds are expected to publicly support the newly-born Europe. At 2.30 pm a special train departs from the Staatsspoor station in The Hague.

The demonstration begins at 4 pm leaving from the Dam square, near the royal palace and commercial core of the seaside city. Hundreds of flags from European countries decorate the streets and private houses opposite the canal and the city hall. More than 10,000 people are here to listen to the leaders and to see what they look like.

Speeches by the mayor of Amsterdam, Ramadier and Brugmans are followed by Churchill's closing remarks. The honorary president of the congress condemns "all forms of totalitarian tyranny", which sparks an ovation. To the accompaniment of the local band, participants sing a hymn composed in Dutch for the occasion: *Europa Één.*

The huge logistic operation now resumes to bring everyone back to Scheveningen for the final banquet. The train leaves at 5.45 pm to allow for some rest at the hotel before the black tie dinner that will be attended by 1,200 guests.

Huge tables are covered with red tulips and little flags with the red 'E' on them. The mayor has struggled to finish every detail and also to overcome the shortage of wine. With outrageous post-war prices, a bottle has become a luxury product, so it has been impossible to bring wine for all. Many will have to toast with water.

When dessert arrives, as is the custom at big weddings, waiters offer cigars to the participants. Churchill's broad smile shows his pleasure at this tradition – and he invites everyone to toast the future of Europe, which of course they all do with great enthusiasm.

Monday, 10 May

The first resolution voted on in the morning is from the economic committee chaired by the Belgian Van Zeeland. Some still insist on negotiating in the corridors. The Liberals try to impose their market vision, while trade unionists search for support for minimum social standards. At the end they manage to include an article on the right for workers to be involved – through their representatives – in the economic management of Europe. The text is adopted unanimously.

The political resolution calls on European states to transfer some of their sovereign rights to a higher institution so that common economic and political action is guaranteed. It also wants a European Assembly, a Charter of Human Rights and the establishment of a Court of Justice to implement the Charter and impose sanctions when necessary.

The closing ceremony opens at 6.35 pm with the reading of a poem written by one of the participants. Then all the resolutions are read aloud. Salvador de Madariaga can't stay for the reading. He apologises and explains that he is about to miss his boat.

Denis de Rougemont reads a declaration: "Human dignity is Europe's finest achievement, freedom her true strength. Both are at stake in our struggle. The union of our continent is now needed not only for the salvation of the liberties we have won, but also for the extension of their benefits to all mankind."

Almost an hour late, the Congress closes at 8 pm. Some leave fully satisfied. Others, like Spinelli, have disappointment etched on their faces. The result is just the compromise between the cautious realism of the British and Nordic delegates and the enthusiastic idealism of Italian and French federalists.

Duncan Sandys and the European Movement vow to push for the resolutions to become concrete measures binding governments. They propose that the national committees of the European Movement contact each foreign ministry and prime minister in their home country to lobby them on the need to go forward.

Jean Monnet

Seller of Dreams

Jean and Silvia Monnet in Chappaqua, New York
(© Fondation Jean Monnet pour l'Europe, Lausanne)

Sitting in his armchair at home in Houjarray, Jean Monnet reads in the newspaper about the resolutions adopted in The Hague. He was already aware of the content, of course. Over the three days of the Congress he had spoken on the phone with some of the participants: one is the American journalist Walter Lippman, and two others are the Conservative British MPs Harold Macmillan and Anthony Eden. Monnet has been friends with Lippman for more than two decades, since the 1920s, when he was in banking and spent his life between New York and San Francisco.

He met the two Brits in London in 1940. Monnet had convinced Churchill of the need for France and the UK to coordinate their response to the Nazis. He used to calculate how many planes and weapons they would need, jointly, to defeat the Third Reich. Then he came across Macmillan again a few years later in the most unexpected place, Algiers. The French government had sent Monnet to the French territory where a part of the government-in-exile was established, and his friend was the highest British official in North Africa.

Monnet is truly keen on the integration of Europe. At the same time, he is very pragmatic, and since hearing about plans for a summit in The Hague, has questioned its chances of success and shown little interest in attending. For decades he has been thinking about how to unite the continent. He is one of the few who actually has some experience, because he has worked on all the transnational projects tested in Europe to date. Several integration theories have been circulating in Europe for some time, but they have neither been fleshed out into a political project nor been able to prevent two wars. "Good will is not enough", says Jean to his wife Silvia, who is sitting next to him in the living room, at the window facing the garden. She has always shared his deep desire to bring about lasting peace, and his frustration with each step backwards.

As the military threat disappears, so commitment from governments fades away with it. He, more than anyone, knows how politicians' convictions fluctuate – or at least the will to turn those convictions into concrete measures. Were not Winston Churchill and General Charles de Gaulle about to announce the total fusion of France and the United Kingdom a few years ago? Monnet witnessed the events. He had drafted the declaration of "total union" that both leaders were going to communicate by phone to the president of the French Council, Paul Reynaud, on 16 June 1940. If Reynaud hadn't stepped down that very same day, and Marshal Henri-Philippe Pétain assumed power, who knows what would have happened. But Pétain chose to sign an armistice with Hitler instead of fighting him, and that was the end of the fusion plan.

Once the war was over and Nazism defeated, neither Churchill nor de Gaulle ever wanted to be reminded of that crazy project into which they were driven by Monnet. And despite Monnet's efforts, he could not persuade them to maintain some sort of permanent mechanism for bilateral cooperation. At last, thanks to the Marshall Plan proposed by the Americans, European nations have committed themselves in the

Organisation for European Economic Co-operation (OEEC). It is a first step, Monnet believes, but not enough. It will allow each country to know its neighbours' resources and goals and will go no further than to facilitate the design of efficient economic policies. One cannot ask more from a system in which states do not surrender a shred of sovereignty.

At The Hague, grand words were spoken, and Monnet respects those who pronounced them. He knows them all, and he does not question their sincerity. What is needed, though, is political action, not more words. His experience in launching the League of Nations – where he met in his youth with Salvador de Madariaga – taught him that in any association of countries the common interest remains dim, imprecise, and the obligation to implement decisions is almost non-existent. That is why he is convinced that the OEEC, as well as any organism born in The Hague, will in no way be the ground on which to construct Europe. One must begin with more pragmatic achievements, going straight to the core of national sovereignty in a very limited area.

He leaves the newspaper on the table and puts on his jacket. He needs a walk to clear his mind: how to move ahead and give substance to the beautiful words of the resolutions? He cannot count on the leaders of the congress: Churchill is a smart politician who masters both the momentum and the speeches. He is capable of lighting up hearts and mobilising people. He made many young students dream with his speech at Zurich University at the opening of the 1946 academic year, when he called for the creation of a "sort of United States of Europe".

However, for those who knew how to read between lines, it was clear that the wonderful project was not meant to be for him. The United Kingdom is already committed to the Commonwealth and the former British prime minister thinks that the world should be organised around associations between states sharing common values and history. Churchill still thinks in terms of international diplomacy while Monnet wants to establish a new layer in relations between countries: between national and international levels, a new "supranational community", a new type of relation between peoples and persons; but where does one begin?

At the end of the war, General de Gaulle charged Monnet with an important mission: to come up with a plan to modernise the French economy and therefore to make the most of the funds from the Marshall Plan. Overall, there were 17 billion dollars to be used before June 1952. Monnet has four years to renew the French economy from its very roots. This is the moment to find common solutions to the financial and social problems that all citizens in Europe face. Monnet is in permanent contact with Robert Schuman, the president of the French Council – head of government – since his election in November, as well as with his foreign minister, Georges Bidault. He is confident of receiving their political support to launch a serious plan to unite Europe.

Unlike many of his contemporaries, Monnet does not care about popularity or power. If he so desired, he would probably find strong support for a political career. He certainly doesn't lack contacts or influence. It just happens that it's not his style. He would have to become a member of a political party and then follow the decisions of the leaders, and always communicate keeping public opinion in mind. This was definitely not for him. He would not be able to back other people's ideas. It would be almost like letting others think and decide for him. With his personality, he would not fit in a political party. When he was younger he wanted to become a boxer. Later on he realised that his greatest qualities were persistence, his shrewd way of dealing with problems and, above all, his ability to act discreetly and to draw up large-scale plans capable of raising to the top those politicians with the courage to trust him.

At the same time, he is very aware of his own limitations. He is not a good speaker, even though he can convince anyone over an amicable lunch with three or four guests. His persuasion can even bring British and French to accept an army under the same flag. Maybe this is the reason why – along with his international contacts, from Shanghai to Ottawa, from Washington to Moscow – some in France suspect that he is a CIA spy. He never went to university, but the school of life has been very productive in his case.

As long as he lives he will never forget the advice his father gave him when, at the age of 18, he decided to leave and explore the New World, the then inhospitable lands of the United States and Canada: "Son, don't take any books. No one can think for you in your place. Look out of the window, talk to people, and pay attention to what's next to you." It was not hard to follow this tip because, in any case, books were never his strong point.

As a child he hated school. He had a hard time trying to focus on learning those long texts, dates and names by heart as was expected in the French education system. He was not attracted by books and his parents already knew from his teachers that he had problems with writing. The curriculum, based on humanities and rhetoric, did not help, and his grades were mediocre. His father, Jean-Gabriel, did not lose any sleep as he saw in his son the qualities that had helped him in life: tenacity, capacity to observe and pragmatic intelligence.

Monnet grew up far from the Parisian bourgeoisie, in a family of farmers with ancient roots in Cognac. The local 'eau de vie' had been a highly-appreciated drink in neighbouring countries since the 18th century. Located 50 kilometres from the Tonnay Port, which opens to the Atlantic

Ocean from the Charente River, the city of Cognac flourished in the 19th century thanks to the flow of English and French boats trading in the artisan liquor.

After several generations, Jean-Gabriel managed to bridge the gap in a society clearly divided between peasants and land-owners. When Jean was only nine years old, his father became the manager of a wine cooperative and he persuaded the other small owners to re-name the cooperative, known ever since as J.G. Monnet & Co.

Their ancestors also had strong links to the vineyards. Jean's grandfather was a cooper at the winery owned by the mighty Hennessy family. His mother, Marie, kept to the simplicity of country life. She was a woman of faith, used to hard work, who taught her children the value of effort and a great sense of fairness.

The couple and their four children (Jean, Henriette, Gaston and Marie-Louise) were never alone. At dinner they would often have guests; travellers from New York, Moscow or Berlin. Jean-Gabriel loved to continue the discussion long after dinner, over a glass of cognac, enquiring about their lives, about news from their countries and the latest political events.

This is why Jean-Gabriel Monnet was not surprised when at the age of 16 Jean said he wanted to drop out of school and work in the family business, travelling around the world to promote their product. Yet at first his father tried to convince Jean to finish high school and then engage in the family business. Finally, his mother stepped in to support Jean's longing for freedom and his father gave in. He prepared a programme to introduce Jean into the world of cognac and its exports. Jean would first spend two years in the UK, where he stayed in London with Mr Chaplin's family. He was an old client and friend of the Monnets. Jean would have the chance to learn English and also to have his eyes opened to the world. Only then would he be ready to engage in the long commercial trips.

The young Monnet was fascinated by London. He was not used to big cities, and the few times he visited Paris he found it elitist and straitjacketed. London was something else; it was a lively city where one wanted to get lost. He shared Mr Chaplin's office in the City. He used to go with him on errands and was thus gradually immersed in trade circles. The British man introduced him to his acquaintances at the gentlemen's clubs and the restaurants where the big business of the empire was carried out over cigars and brandy.

By the time he returned home, two years later, it was clearer than ever that this was his world. After a brief stay in Cognac, he asked his father if he could already represent the firm abroad. He foresaw new markets and saw great potential for expansion for the liquor his father cherished so much. So Jean-Gabriel gave his blessing for a long trip to Canada. His mother agreed, although she feared the perils in those wild lands, still without laws and expanding frenetically to the west. The railroad to the Pacific was under construction and Canada seemed to be the promised land. Jean was eager to undertake the adventure and it did not cost him a lot to follow his father's advice: he left the books behind to invest his five senses in the people he would meet.

In Canada he found a new world, or rather, his eyes opened to the world's complexity and diversity beyond old Europe. In this young continent where the most diverse cultures converged, everything seemed possible. Immigrants from all corners of the globe had arrived, attracted by the search for gold, and many Asians were working on the railways. At first, he felt strange in the exclusively male environment, where women were barely visible.

The local first population lived in its own communities and had no right to buy alcohol. Monnet signed major contracts to sell cognac to the Hudson Bay Company, the state monopoly giving alcohol to Indian hunters and trappers in exchange for animal furs. Then from Canada he crossed into the US. He became friends with some families in New England and in this young society, halfway between Parisian conventionalism and the disorder he had found in the west, he felt at ease.

In 1910 the family business began to decline. Technological advances meant that artisan production was no longer profitable. They lacked cash, and Jean had to ask for a loan. Despite his father's insistence on continuing with traditional methods, Jean began to introduce changes and to rationalise the production chain. He continued to devote himself body and soul to the family business, but he craved his independence. He decided to create his own food brand, *La Bordelaise*. He went on travelling to promote the family cognac and from then on his own products as well. Sometimes his younger brother Gaston would accompany him.

In June 1914 he was in Canada when he read about the assassination of Archduke Franz Ferdinand and his wife in Sarajevo. The conflict between Serbia and Austria broke out immediately, but other European governments did not see any danger of the conflict spreading.

A few days after the attack, he began his journey home. When he arrived in Paris in July, the news from Vienna and Belgrade was alarming. The summer was exceptionally hot and Jean took a few days for long walks in the Alps, one of his favourite hobbies. As well as enjoying the exercise and the landscape, the altitude was good for his lungs. He knew that even if France went to war, he would not go to the front because in 1908, when he was called up for military service, his lung problems made him fail the medical examination.

Back in Cognac, he and his father followed events through the press. On 3 August, Berlin declared war on France. The president of the French Republic, Raymond Poincaré, seemed puzzled. The general opinion was that the conflict would be short and that the Germans would be defeated. But very soon it became crystal clear that it would go on for some time.

Monnet thought that problems of supply would soon arise. Although they were allies, London and Paris were suspicious of each other. Due to French demand, prices of wood, coal, wheat and copper rocketed in England. France and Britain started competing for goods. British ships would arrive full in France and leave empty and the same was true of French ships going to the UK. Jean, who was always very pragmatic, was bothered by this unnecessary waste of energy.

On 2 September, the French government was forced to leave Paris and moved to Bordeaux. On 6 September fighting broke out in Marne along a 200 km front. Confusion reigned in Bordeaux.

Still in Cognac, unable to join the army, Monnet wanted to contribute in some way. Aged 26 and without any official position or contact in government, he was determined to do everything in his power based on his international experience. He asked his father to help him to contact the French government. A friend of Jean-Gabriel's arranged a meeting between Jean and the Minister of War, Alexandre Millerand. The young Monnet convinced him of the need to coordinate the supply of food and fuel and to purchase equipment jointly with the British. He subsequently travelled to London with the minister.

The Armaments Minister, Louis Loucheur, was not happy and complained to President Georges Clemenceau: "It is doubly inconceivable that a young man who is not even mobilised can hold an important position in our civil service." But after an interview, the president confirmed Monnet in his position.

Back in the British capital, Monnet learned that there was a national commission for supply, which was in charge only of weapons, not food. With the French government's permission, he proposed to the British to set up a common procurement system in order to avoid competition in the purchase of steel, oil and coal. The UK and France paid for everything with gold and analysts soon began to warn that in three months the two countries would be ruined. Monnet then used his contacts in the United States and Canada – in particular in the Hudson Bay Company – to obtain a loan of nearly one hundred million francs for the Bank of France.

Meanwhile, the situation at the front improved, and the government was able to return to Paris. The front line moved east, cutting through the Vosges. Analysing the war strategy, Monnet thought that the key to victory would be at sea and in 1917 proposed that the London and Paris governments unify their navies to counter-attack and defeat the German submarines. This contributed to the final defeat of Germany by the allies. However, to Jean's deep disappointment, the allies dismantled their common structures as soon as the war was over.

Another high-level structure for peace was shaping up, and President Clemenceau believed that its French representative should be Monnet. This is how in 1919 Jean became deputy secretary general of the League of Nations. The organisation was born with the entry into force of the Treaty of Versailles on 10 January 1920 and established its headquarters in the neutral territory of Geneva. Monnet's brother and cousins took charge of the family business while he moved to Switzerland.

His sister Marie-Louise, who was 14 years younger, went with him. She helped him settle down and enjoyed organising dinners with diplomats. She particularly loved those informal suppers with the group of friends who soon entered Monnet's circle. They were enthusiastic and cosmopolitan young men and women, convinced that they could make the world a better place. Among them was Madariaga, who thought he had found in Jean an exceptional man, who stood out for his positive intelligence, selflessness and sense of public service. Another young woman he met at that time was Louise Weiss, who in 1918 had founded the journal *New Europe*. Monnet enjoyed discussing his ideas for peace in the continent with her.

But the great friend with whom he would share many adventures was the Pole Ludwik Rajchman, director of the hygiene section of the League of Nations in 1921. This doctor came from a Polish Jewish family of intellectuals. As a result of his political activities, he was first imprisoned and then fled to London. After the war he returned to Poland and launched a National Institute of Hygiene. In 1920 he set up a sanitary cordon along the border between Poland and Russia that protected Western Europe from typhus. His methods were unconventional but effective, which is why he was hired for the League of Nations.

After a few months, it became clear to Jean and Ludwik that there would be many obstacles to progress in the change they expected from the League of Nations. The new institution was born with a defect originating in the Treaty of Versailles: discrimination against peoples. All power was in the hands of the three victorious states, while Germany was humiliated by punitive reparation payments and territorial concessions.

The organisation was already lame when it began its work, because despite the original idea for the League coming from US President Woodrow Wilson, the United States refused to participate. The first task of the League of Nations was to put an end to territorial disputes that remained unresolved after the Treaty of Versailles, such as the Saar and Upper Silesia, both major mining regions. If the "property" and the use of these rich mining areas were shared between neighbouring countries, everyone would gain. That is what Monnet proposed to Poland and Germany to resolve a dispute over Upper Silesia, but neither of them agreed. In the end it was four countries with nothing to do with the issue (Belgium, Brazil, China and Spain) that decided where to draw the new border, for that was all Berlin and Warsaw seemed to care about. Nor was the Saar conflict resolved, because of the refusal of the neighbours to share resources as well as the harsh peace terms imposed on Germany. In Geneva, Monnet understood that equality was essential in relations between nations, as it is between human beings.

After three years in the League he resigned, a disappointed man. In 1923 his father died and his siblings asked him to go back because the family business was sinking, providing the perfect excuse for him to leave Geneva. Monnet again invested all his energies in updating production and opening new markets.

He managed to revive the company, but he was unhappy. He needed new adventures, so he got in touch with an investment firm in New York, Blair & Co. He was working in the United States at the time of the 1929 stock market crash. The system had serious flaws that led to a crisis of spectacular dimensions. The government took harsh measures to restore the credibility and soundness of banking, such as banning banks from using deposits and savings to finance investment, so that savings would not be put at risk by investors. This seemed only logical to Monnet. How come no one had thought of that before? Monnet learned a great lesson that year: "As always, wisdom and reform come into play only after major difficulties have run their course. Would a few simple measures, taken earlier, have prevented the crisis? Asking the question means being unaware that men accept change only in a time of need and they see need only in a time of crisis."

He was 41 years old and so far his plans had not included marriage. He was a well-established bachelor, no one knew of any romance or adventure. However, against all the odds, his life changed overnight when he went back to France in 1929. It was love at first sight. When he felt the stab in his heart it seemed an impossible love story. But in love, as in business, Monnet was determined never to give up, no matter how long it took.

It all happened one August evening at his home in Paris. He had invited a few businessmen for dinner. Among them was a young Frenchman, René Pleven. He was 28 and had just been appointed director for Europe of the US multinational Automatic Telephone Company. Another guest was the Italian Francesco Giannini, who worked for Monnet. When the butler, André, opened the door to Mr Giannini and his companion, Monnet was dazzled. He was captivated by Giannini's wife, a tall, dark-skinned, passionate young woman with a piercing gaze. As they sat at the table, both Jean and Silvia Giannini forgot about the others. Their eyes met with an intensity that neither had ever experienced before. It was a moment of shared and indestructible love, as Monnet himself would later tell his friends. Silvia was 22 and Jean was 42. He knew what he wanted: to spend the rest of his life with her, and the fact that she was married was just a minor inconvenience.

He needed to know if she felt the same and was ready to take the risk. André, the butler, was aware of the effect that Silvia had had on Monnet. Once the guests had gone, he dared to encourage his boss: "She is the one, she is the woman you need". Jean wanted to see her the following day. Early in the morning he sent a dozen red roses along with an invitation to dinner again that evening. He hoped with all his heart that she would accept his invitation and take the step of having dinner with him, the two of them alone. When she showed up he knew that all would go well: Silvia was wearing one of the red roses in the buttonhole of her dress.

It took time for her family to accept this relationship and their irregular situation. There was no divorce law in Italy and it was socially unacceptable to break up the marriage. She suffered but was clear in her heart: she had never been in love with her husband, a womaniser she had married to escape a difficult life and unstable family situation.

Silvia's father was an Italian journalist who had made a career in Constantinople as director of a French-language newspaper *La Turquie* and her mother was a Serbian citizen. At home they spoke French, Italian and Greek. After the First World War, the family moved to Belgrade. When the father died her brother became a Franciscan friar. Silvia and her mother were left alone with few resources and decided to move to Rome. They were struggling to make ends meet when she received Francesco's marriage proposal. He was a successful businessman and marrying him appeared to Silvia and her mother as a solution. They married on 6 April 1929, just months before she met Jean. From the beginning she felt unhappy.

Giannini was a senior banking executive at Blair and Co. in Italy, and Monnet was his boss. Gianinni often had to travel to the United States, and would sometimes go with one of his mistresses, leaving Silvia at home in Rome. However when he found out about the relationship between Silvia and Jean he was beside himself. Full of jealousy and rage, he accused Silvia of abandoning her home. Then a baby, Anna, was born in 1931, and Gianinni filed a suit claiming that the child was legally his since the marriage had not officially been dissolved.

For five years, Silvia and Jean lived in hiding, often far from each other and fearing that Giannini would kidnap the girl and gain legal rights to her custody. They established their home in Geneva, where Marie-Louise joined them to help Silvia with the girl. From the outset, she felt sincere affection for Silvia. An order to find "Ms Giannini and her daughter" was circulated around the world's foreign ministries. Monnet spent a fortune on lawyers. Through his friend Rajchman he contacted China's Chiang Kai-shek, who hired him in late 1933 to undertake a programme of reforms. He left Silvia and Anna back in Geneva.

In Shanghai, he drafted a plan for banks to finance the economic programme of the Chinese National Council. But his heart and mind were in Geneva and he did not stop in his diplomatic efforts to find a way of marrying Silvia legally. From China, he took the Trans-Siberian express to Moscow. He knew the American ambassador to Russia, and Rajchman had also given him the contacts of some people in the Russian government who were willing to help. There was a divorce law in place in Russia allowing women to act on their own to end a marriage.

With the Russian authorities' promise to grant her a divorce, Silvia requested and obtained Soviet citizenship. They had no guarantee that the plan would work, but it was their only chance. The couple met in Moscow on 13 November 1934, and in the strict privacy of a Kremlin room she first got the divorce and they then sealed their civil marriage. Silvia would have preferred annulment by the Catholic Church so that they could also celebrate a religious marriage, but it was not possible at that time.[1]

Monnet went back to Shanghai, now bringing his family with him, and worked on the country's modernisation plan. Although they were already legally married, they could not drop their guard against Giannini's threats. He once tried to kidnap the girl, but Silvia took refuge in the Soviet consulate in Shanghai. The demand for custody of little Anna had not yet been resolved, so they still worried. In the spring of 1937, a New York court granted custody to Monnet. However, they preferred not to travel to Italy in case the police and the Italian courts did not recognise the American ruling.

In the late 1930s, once he had legal guarantees to protect his family, he moved back to France. He had heard the worrying news about the advance of nazism and fascism when he was still in China. He felt Europeans were making the same mistakes he had already lived through: the German advance and lack of coordination between the allies.

---

[1]   In 1971 Giannini passed away and at last she and Jean celebrated their religious wedding. It took place at the Lourdes sanctuary and the local bishop Monsignore Donze married them, as he was a friend of Jean Monnet and his sister Marie-Louise.

In December 1939, Monnet was appointed chairman of the Franco-British Economic Co-ordination Committee in London. It covered the coordination of supply capacity for a broad range of items, from raw materials and oil to weapons and air and maritime transport. He developed a joint inventory of goods and established the combined import needs. He knew that this time, the key to military victory would be in the air: this is why the allies placed an order for airplane engines from the United States.

When the French government moved to Bordeaux, Monnet went to London to meet General de Gaulle, René Pleven and Winston Churchill on 16 June. It was then that the two statesmen had already agreed to a complete political union between the UK and France, and were ready to call the president of the French Council, Paul Reynaud, and dictate to him their "Statement of Total Union". Of course de Gaulle did not like the idea of creating a single country with the Brits, but he saw no other solution. He had just arrived in London; he was hounded by the Nazi offensive. Monnet's suggestion seemed the only way out. In the end, de Gaulle and Churchill were saved from going ahead with the plan because Reynaud resigned that very same day and was replaced by Marshal Pétain, who signed an armistice with the Germans.

In the afternoon of 17 June, de Gaulle was invited to dinner at Jean Monnet's place. The two men were so different that they saw the situation from opposite angles. De Gaulle considered that it was urgent to mobilise the army to liberate France, while Monnet thought it was essential to ensure the support of the allies. Dinner was tense despite Silvia's efforts to make their guest feel welcome.

The next day, de Gaulle addressed the French people on the BBC, calling on them to join him in defending the freedom of their homeland. Against Pétain's submission to the Germans, he offered honour and hope.

Monnet resigned from the Joint Committee, and immediately offered his services to Churchill. He became the British envoy to the US, and his mission was to convince the Americans to help France and the United Kingdom to acquire more weapons. The United States produced an enormous amount of weapons they were not using for the war. President Roosevelt had pledged to Congress that he would remain neutral and was reluctant to help one side. Following intense lobbying by Monnet, he agreed to make more planes and have them ready to sell to the allies when the time was right. As Nazi troops advanced, and especially after the invasion of Denmark, the American public was ready to accept US involvement in the war, or at least its explicit support for the allied troops.

When the British and French ran out of money, Monnet raised the issue with Roosevelt. By then, London and Paris were unable to buy more planes, so Roosevelt and Monnet came up with the formula of "leasing".

The Americans would lend the aircraft for a small fee. From the American point of view, it was better that the British had the weapons to win the war by themselves rather than to send American soldiers.

As the conflict went on, Monnet believed that the Americans would end up having to fight. This did happen in 1942. At that point, he began to calculate the joint Anglo-American needs to beat the Germans. To his pragmatic mind, a rapid Anglo-American victory was the quickest and most effective – albeit indirect – way to free France from the invaders. However for many in France, he was a traitor working for the British instead of helping France.

Those years in the US were joyful for the Monnets. They were far from Silvia's ex-husband and from the European war. The arrival of their second daughter, Marianne, added to their family happiness. The home was often enlivened by fascinating visitors. One of the most special was Antoine de Saint-Exupéry, whose spirit of freedom and adventure seduced Jean and Silvia. He had settled in Washington a few years before, having fled the Nazis. He was rejected for military service because of his age and now spent most of the time writing. When he visited the Monnet's home he would entertain the ladies with card tricks while the men discussed politics in the living room.

The Europeans who fled in exile to the US and to the UK had taken the lead in championing freedom and a European federation. A frontrunner was the French philosopher Jacques Maritain one of the first in Europe to criticise growing antisemitism in the 1930s. In fact this was the main reason he left Paris with his wife Raïssa, who was from a Russian-Jewish background having converted to Christianity. He was travelling with her as part of a lecture tour in the US when he learned that France had given in to Nazi Germany in 1940 and he never returned. He was committed to democracy and human dignity through his weekly radio addresses to his fellow Frenchmen and through the books he wrote both for American and French readers.

A visit to Monnet and Maritain became obligatory for all European leaders who passed through Washington. At his home in Foxhall Road, Monnet again met his friend Louise Weiss. Many Europeans were their guests. One of them was the Belgian minister-in-exile Paul-Henri Spaak. He was in Washington DC in 1941 and was invited by Silvia and Monnet. He would never forget that day. The food and the wine were outstanding – it was not in vain that Monnet had taken their cook from France to DC – but the conversation was even more remarkable than the culinary delights. They discussed post-war Europe and how to ensure long-term peace. Monnet explained his idea of common management of energy resources in Europe.

Another famous visitor was the Luxembourgian minister Joseph Bech. In the summer of 1942, before the Foreign Affairs Committee of the US Congress, he delivered a speech on the need to reconcile and unite Europeans when the conflict was over, with the full participation of Germany. By then the United States had already decided to go to war following the attack on their naval base at Pearl Harbour.

But it was not in Monnet's plans to stay there forever. Once he had achieved his target of ensuring US military support, he quit his job as UK representative and offered himself to the government of free France. He was asked to go to Algiers as commissioner for arms and provisions of the French Committee of National Liberation, the *de facto* government in exile. He accepted and left Washington on 23 February 1943, after he had also convinced his acquaintances in Washington that they should help finance the French Army.

This time it was even harder to be far from Silvia and the girls for an uncertain period of time. After several days' travelling, he landed in Algiers on a Saturday afternoon, with a suitcase and many questions on what his life would be like, surrounded by military men. Fortunately at the airport a familiar face was waiting for him: John McCoy, an American official with whom he had formed a friendship in Washington.

He settled in a small apartment, decorated with pictures of his wife and daughters, and small objects including Marianne's booties. He wrote almost daily to Silvia asking about the girls and telling her about his routine. It was hard to relate to the military but he had to get used to it while he managed to restore the republic and return it to civil government.

In the meantime, he worked to bring the two French military leaders closer: de Gaulle in London and Henri Giraud in Algeria. If they did not present a common front and clearly declare themselves in favour of a civilian government as soon as the war was over, they would never get the political and military support of the United States. Finally the two generals came together in the French Committee of National Liberation in June 1943.

The peace between the two generals made his professional life easier, and his private life also became more pleasant with the arrival, in the summer of 1943, of another Frenchman: Étienne Hirsch, a 42-year old engineer who had until then been fighting with the Resistance and with whom Monnet felt a connection from the first moment. With Hirsch he could share his hopes and fears about the future of Europe. Soon other young Frenchmen joined their discussions: René Mayer, Hervé Alphand and Robert Marjolin.

One morning in that hot Algerian summer, Monnet showed them a map of the Ruhr, Lorraine and Luxembourg. The origin of the two great wars lay in the coal and steel disputed by France and Germany. "We must take this region from the two states, one way or another," he confided to his friends. "There will be no peace in Europe if states are reconstituted on the basis of national sovereignty, which involves the policy of prestige and economic protectionism."

After the landing of US troops in Normandy and the liberation of France, in the summer of 1944, Monnet returned to Silvia and the girls. His American friends had watched out for them in his absence. The stay was brief. This time his destiny and that of his family awaited him in Europe. A huge task of reconstruction began for the continent, on the same scale as the challenge of forging a lasting peace.

General de Gaulle became president of France and asked Monnet for two things: first, to persuade President Roosevelt to recognise his government, and second to return to France and take charge of a plan to modernise the country. Monnet accepted both missions. He left Washington DC after a successful meeting with Roosevelt and then established himself in Paris, undertaking the responsibility of an economic plan entitled "Modernisation or Decline".

Although de Gaulle resigned after one year and a new government took power, Jean was confirmed in office and all his conditions were respected: he wanted to work directly with the head of government, without having to be accountable to the ministers.

Of course the ministers complained. Monnet's insistence on being above them has been interpreted as arrogance; it hurt sensibilities and caused more than one fit of rage. However, all Council presidents after de Gaulle – Félix Gouin, Georges Bidault, Léon Blum and Paul Ramadier – confirmed him in his post and his autonomy, including the latest head of government, who took office in November 1947, President Robert Schuman.

To Monnet, this freedom of action is essential to end the inertia of big institutions and officials who by nature tend to maintain the *status quo*. Things do not progress. From his privileged position Monnet wants a new dynamic to the government, one that an institution as bureaucratic as a ministry cannot provide. He is convinced that the traditional methods and slow bureaucracy will be unable to inject the dynamism that France needs or to find the resources so desperately needed for investment in renewed growth and industrial recovery. Whenever necessary, he calls his international friends, especially Americans, to secure funding for his modernisation plan, which has nearly been wrecked on several occasions because of lack of money and natural resources.

The Marshall Plan aims to bring the German economy up to the level of all other European countries by 1952. But this goal requires significant consumption of mineral resources by German industry. Monnet has some documents – given to him by Marjolin in August 1947 – showing that the German steel industry alone would consume all the coal from the Ruhr, meaning that steel production in France and the rest of Europe would be limited.

The fundamental problem in France – and hence in Europe – is still lack of energy resources. The same story repeats itself over and over in this old Europe, thinks Monnet. The war is over, but if each country starts competing again with its neighbours for scarce resources, we will end up making the same mistakes.

In Algeria he had discussed with Mayer, Alphand, Hirsch and Marjolin the possibility of an economic union of the bordering regions which are rich in mineral resources. However, he has not found the time to really flesh out a plan. The only long term solution is a European federation that will be born not from good intentions but from common laws and institutions.

From 1948 to 1950

Towards the 9 May Declaration

Robert Schuman at the *Salon de l'Horloge*, recreating the 9 May Declaration
(© European Parliament)

Summer 1948, France

Two months have passed since the participants left the Congress in The Hague, and their enthusiasm has not materialised into any concrete action. Good words, as in the past, seem destined to remain just that: words. After the passionate speeches, no government has submitted a proposal, and to top it off, the movements are now entangled in internal disputes. Duncan Sandy's European Movement questions the legitimacy of the European Parliamentary Union led by Coudenhove-Kalergi, who in exchange accuses the Brits of torpedoing continental integration.

Were they right, those commentators who said that the resolutions approved in The Hague were utopian? Georges Bidault, the French Foreign Minister, takes political leadership and looks for a formula to create an assembly of the peoples of Europe. After much reflection, he concludes that the best way to launch political integration is from an already existing organisation: the Brussels Pact.[1] Although the five member countries have agreed mainly to military cooperation, it could definitely be extended to other areas.

As the signing of the Brussels Pact is very recent, loose ends remain to be resolved. For that reason the leaders of the five governments have scheduled a meeting in Paris on 20 July. In his capacity of host, Bidault sent a letter to his partners announcing that he had added a new point to the original agenda: the creation of an assembly representing the citizens of the five states. No one complained.

However, a few days before the meeting is due to take place, a sudden governmental crisis in France jeopardises Bidault's plans. In mid-July, the Socialists break the unstable coalition chaired by Robert Schuman. Constant protests and demonstrations reflect social unrest. Post-war France is suffering food shortages and lack of raw materials for the industry; the franc has lost 80% of its value and so social tension leads to political instability.

The new government, formed by the Radical Party, replaces Bidault and appoints Schuman as foreign minister. This unexpected change unleashes uncertainty among members of the Brussels Pact. Will the newcomer uphold the meeting and the plans announced by Bidault? Bidault's interest in Europe is well known in diplomatic circles, and also that he is a heavyweight in the Conservative Party, the MRP. Schuman, on the contrary, is a lone voice in the wilderness. He comes from Lorraine, a peripheral region, and for the time being no one knows his approach to foreign policy.

Without delay, the new minister confirms that the meeting is still on and that he will also take on his predecessor's agenda. For him it is a priority to bring together the governments and the peoples of Europe, and he already has some ideas in mind. When they all meet he just outlines his vision for Europe as he needs a few weeks to settle into his new position and to prepare a proper strategy.

One of his first decisions is to see Paul-Henri Spaak. He wants the Belgian prime minister to convince his counterparts in the Netherlands and in Luxembourg to go even further than what they had agreed on in July. He intends to expand the Brussels Pact's Assembly to other countries and turn it into the assembly of the peoples of Europe, following the political resolution of The Hague conference.

---

[1]　The Brussels Pact, signed on 17 March 1948 by the UK, France, Belgium, the Netherlands and Luxembourg, is an international cooperation treaty by which the members commit to military assistance to the other partners.

It is a very ambitious plan, and Schuman thinks that having the support of the Belgian will pave the way to success. He enjoys an international reputation and the trust of the Americans. Spaak was also the promoter of the customs and economic union dubbed Benelux. Since it came into force, Belgium, the Netherlands and Luxembourg enjoy excellent relations and coordinate their policies not only in the economic field, but also in their external relations.

"The French government just decided on a step to which it would be highly desirable for you to associate," Schuman writes to Spaak. "It is about presenting a draft prepared by the International Committee of the Movements for European unity to the five governments who signed the Brussels treaty, in order to convene a conference to institute a European assembly."

Spaak's response is immediate: a resounding yes. In early September, he travels to Paris to discuss a common strategy with Schuman. Spaak believes that Luxembourg will be easy to bring on board, whilst the Netherlands, and especially Ernest Bevin, the British Foreign Minister, will be harder to persuade.

Even though Schuman promises his full cooperation, Spaak wonders how far their relationship can go. The two men stand on the antipodes, both in personal and political grounds: one of them is socialist, atheist, extravagantly dramatic and a bon vivant, whilst the other one is conservative, Catholic and extremely shy. Spaak has heard of the proverbial austerity of the French man, who is still a bachelor who lives with his housekeeper in a countryside cottage two hours outside Paris, devoted to books and prayer.

In their first meeting, the Belgian notices his timidity and that thin, nasal and sharp thread of a voice, with which he seems apologise whenever he talks. None of the qualities one would expect in a leader. However, his simplicity exudes such honesty and conviction that Spaak is not surprised that his placid smile and that halting speech, as if time had stopped, ends up dazzling his interlocutors.

Schuman and Spaak propose to the other Brussels Pacts to create an assembly with real powers, composed of representatives from various countries. They would decide by majority. The UK reaction is swift: Ernest Bevin will under no circumstances accept an assembly positioning itself above the British Parliament.

The reaction is positive in Italy. It is not a member of the Brussels Pact but it would be invited to this new assembly. President Alcide De Gasperi supports the initiative although he would like to fine tune it. He would rather see the OEEC as the core engine of integration instead of the Brussels Pact. In fact, Italy turned down the invitation to join the Brussels Pact because De

Gasperi did not want to be part of a defensive organisation still regarding Germany as a potential threat. According to the Italian, Europe's unity cannot be built on this ground. The French government did not appreciate his rejection. Italy is a former enemy and a defeated nation. Their willingness to invite him to join the Brussels Pact was an act of generosity from the winners, and they found his refusal quite rude. Luckily Robert Schuman does not share the mainstream vision of the French government. He agrees with De Gasperi, but he doesn't dare to say it out loud.

All his life Schuman has yearned for an understanding between French and Germans. This quest gives meaning to his existence: trying to overcome once and for all the inherited generational hatred between French and Germans. This is a hatred that he has never experienced because he has spent his life crossing the border between Luxembourg, Germany and France. Born in the Grand Duchy to a French father and a Luxembourgian mother, he went to school in Luxembourg and then studied law at a German university. His passport is French, but his accent unveils a multiple identity which is not highly valued in the wake of the war.

Actually he engaged in politics in an effort to build bridges between the French and the German-speaking in Alsace and Lorraine after the First World War. He accepted to stand as MP for Lorraine when asked to do so by both communities.

The bottom line for French politicians – and also for the rest of Europe and for the US – lies in how to bring Germany back into the international community. The fear of a German military and economic revival is the backdrop of all discussions, and yet no one has asked the Germans about their intentions, at least not in public.

Autumn 1948, Germany

At the end of the summer, Konrad Adenauer becomes the president of the Parliamentary Committee charged of drafting West Germany's Constitution. Adenauer must inform the three military governors of the United Kingdom, France and the US about each step, but he would also like to have direct contact with Schuman.

Adenauer met with Georges Bidault, the former minister, in the secret gathering held in Geneva last March, and then he strengthened ties with his team in The Hague. However, he has never met Schuman, who does not belong to Bidault's circles and does not participate in any of the secret meetings to create a Christian Democrat International alliance. It is common knowledge that Schuman is a fervent Catholic, but he has no interest in cliques.

Schuman accepts Adenauer's invitation without informing anyone in the ministry. On 10 October they meet in Bassenheim, a German city in the Rhineland-Palatinate region, near the western border. From the first moment Adenauer feels the closeness of a friend rather than a statesman. The conversation flows easily, not least because they both speak German. Schuman is sympathetic and shares the suffering Adenauer confesses that is caused by the terrible image that Germany has given to the world with Nazi crimes.

In the course of this lovely afternoon, while drinking coffee, they find out that they have many things in common. They remember their university days, where they maybe even coincided in the classroom or in one of the student associations. Both had also attended the events organised by *Zentrum*, the German Catholic political party.

By the time they say goodbye they feel comforted to know that on the other side there is someone they can trust, someone who shares the view of their historical responsibility to bring a lasting peace to Europe. They will keep in touch by personal correspondence, so that none of their decisions at the national level can be misinterpreted by the other and they avoid any possible manipulation by nationalists.

October 1948, Italy

Despite being one of the defeated countries, Italy found it easier than Germany to be reaccepted into the international community. The Second World War put an end to fascism, but abuses perpetrated by Mussolini are not comparable to the Nazi concentration camps and the campaign to exterminate the Jews. However, the Italian refusal to enter the Brussels Pact has created uncertainty over the will or the capacity of Italy to take part in the new European structures.

In mid-October, De Gasperi and his Foreign Minister Carlo Sforza meet in Rome with George Marshall, the American Secretary of State, to discuss the participation of Italy in the Atlantic Pact. The Americans want to replace the Brussels Pact with a broader alliance: a North Atlantic Treaty Organization (NATO). The US will be a member and the Americans want to know if Italy would join. The president of the Italian Council is an unknown on the European scene, having been banned from politics by the Fascist authorities for 17 years. He wants to show Marshall that he is a reliable partner. When the Brussels Pact was proposed he was not quite sure about its aims and he was in the midst of a tough electoral campaign. So it was better to reject it. Now he feels stable in the government and he understands that the Americans want to get closer to West Germany and also that their proposed military alliance aims to protect Western Europe from any Soviet threat.

Meanwhile, Sforza seeks the US complicity to the European federal project. He tells Marshall about the Italian plan – which so far Schuman has kept in the freezer – to change the OEEC from a mere economic-cooperation organisation into a "strong political and military front against the Soviet threat if it has support from the US". However, Marshall prefers not to get involved.

Some weeks go by and Sforza loses patience because Schuman does not respond to his formal proposal. Given the insistence of the Italian, Schuman explains by letter that, for the time being, it is impossible to advance through the OEEC. So he announces that he will continue with his plan to advance through the Brussels Pact. The Frenchman promises Sforza that he will keep him updated and that the new organisation will be open to Italy. Frustrated, Sforza sends a memo to all OEEC countries on 27 October inviting them to initiate a process of political integration through the OEEC.

When De Gasperi finds out about this outburst, he fears that Schuman may get angry. To minimise any potential damage he decides to lead the European issue personally. He needs to have Schuman and Spaak on his side because he knows that the British do not like Italy's joining the Atlantic Pact.

He finds an unbeatable opportunity when he receives an invitation from a cultural organisation to give a lecture in Brussels. De Gasperi accepts, but only once he has confirmed that he will be received by Spaak in the Belgian capital and then a few days later by Schuman in Paris.

Winter 1948, Brussels

On 20 November, De Gasperi delivers a memorable speech on freedom and justice as a prerequisite for peace. He claims that a friendship between peoples must be established in Europe, and a common action based on shared convictions must be launched. That joint effort must include Germany, and it should also overcome any peace treaty that could again feed the feeling of injustice and revenge. He encourages all to work for a free and democratic Europe, which all European peoples will willingly join.

The next day, De Gasperi's speech appears in the international press. Spaak reads it carefully ahead of his personal encounter with the Italian. There is no doubt that he shares De Gasperi's diagnosis and his thoughts on the cure. But he still wonders about something: is De Gasperi in favour of or against the US having a role in the new European defence system?

Over a friendly chat when they finally meet, they discover that they share the same Atlanticist vision. From their point of view, giving a role to the Americans in the security of the continent does not go against the building of a new Europe. On the contrary; it complements the European integration process. If faced with a Soviet threat, the Europeans would not be able not defend themselves. They need the US and that is not necessarily a problem for De Gasperi or Spaak. This approach collides with some sectors of the Belgian and Italian society, and even within their own political parties: it disappoints the Belgian Socialist Party but also the progressive sector of the Christian Democrats in Italy, because they don't want Europe to take sides with one of the two large blocs of the cold war.

De Gasperi explains why Italy rejected the Brussels Pact, and apologises for Sforza's impetuosity. Perhaps his minister was too abrupt, but only because he is determined to achieve the ultimate goal: to build a true European federation, which should not be limited to a military alliance. This is why they insist on the OEEC.

Spaak understands, but he warns De Gasperi: there are many interests and sensitivities at stake. Before De Gasperi leaves to his next stop, Spaak advises him: he can trust Schuman, who also craves a united Europe.

Of course the Italian knows beforehand that he shares affinities with Schuman and even biographical experiences. Both are frontiersmen educated in the Germanic tradition and they have a friend in common: the philosopher Jacques Maritain. Maritain's book *Integral Humanism* opened new windows of freedom and modernity to Catholics. The philosopher is controversial for traditionalists and monarchists, but he has inspired the political vision of Schuman and of De Gasperi, and has also showed how to be a Christian politician in a modern democracy. Schuman met Maritain when he was a professor in Paris, before he left to Rome as the French ambassador to the Holy See.

De Gasperi had been familiar with his work for a long time already, but had the chance to discuss with the philosopher during those days in Rome. The impact of Maritain has been so strong in Italy that it even inspired a group within the Christian Democrats.[2] Since last spring, Maritain lives in the US, where he teaches at Princeton University and is working on an ambitious project: a universal declaration of human rights that is acceptable to all countries and all cultures.

When De Gasperi arrives at the Quai d'Orsay in Paris, the introductions and the exchanges of messages from Maritain pave the way for a friendly conversation that Schuman was expecting to be tense. He feared that the prime minister would reproach his refusal to Sforza. But De Gasperi is much less aggressive and more pragmatic than his minister, and he now realises that persisting on the OEEC way is leading nowhere.

The potential misunderstanding is quickly cleared up and they start to talk, with absolute honesty, about the so-called "German problem". By

---

[2]   The most progressive fraction of the Italian Christian Democracy was led by Giuseppe Dosetti. It was called "dossetismo" and its motto was "Integral humanism".

listening to the prime minister speaking German, Schuman understands that De Gasperi does not hold any grudges against the Germans. On the contrary, he is rather fond of them, just like himself.

Upon arriving home, De Gasperi tells his wife about Schuman: "We have both lived long on the border of the national thoughts, we have both reflected on the same way and we understand current problems also in the same way."

January 1949, the Council of Europe

The project to create an assembly linked to the Brussels Pact continues, despite British reticence. In January, the five members – France, UK, Belgium, Netherlands and Luxembourg – agree to create a new body: the Council of Europe. It will be completely detached from the military organisation, and from the start it will be open to all countries.

It will consist of a Council of Ministers from member countries, an Assembly whose members are appointed by national parliaments, and a small secretariat. After tough negotiations, the British achieve for only the Council of Ministers to have any decision-making power, while the Assembly will be advisory.

Schuman proposes establishing the seat in Strasbourg, because of the symbolic value which the Alsatian capital has for peace in Europe: this region was the origin of numerous wars between France and Germany. Benelux backs the proposal. The British minister Ernest Bevin does not like it, but in the absence of any other choice, Strasbourg finally gets the seat.

And then they appoint Spaak to draft the statute. De Gasperi is happy with the choice, and he sends the Belgian a note encouraging him to be ambitious and to lay the foundations of a future European Federation: "The Council of Ministers should not be a temporary body for occasional meetings, but have the necessary power to ensure the permanent functioning of the union and to prepare its future development, in which the council may be replaced by a federal government."

Spaak takes up the job full of delight, with the idea of a federation in mind, just as De Gasperi and the European movements wish for. In February he sends an invitation to participate in a conference in Brussels to dozens of experts from all those countries who express their willingness to join the new organisation. They are ten: Belgium, Denmark, France, Ireland, Italy, Luxembourg, Norway, Netherlands, the UK and Sweden.

Germany, a defeated country, remains alien to these plans. Among the German population there is growing unrest by the strict production quotas imposed on them. Adenauer complains to the allies about the situation in which they have been left after the war, without the necessary resources to rebuild their country and to feed their people. He passes this message to Washington, where the government worries that a weak and downtrodden Germany may become a fertile ground for the anti-American messages spread by Moscow. Gradually, the American government starts to put pressure on the European states so that they improve the conditions in Germany and some American decision-makers even think that it would be wise to create some Western German Armed Forces which could stifle any Soviet attack.

When Schuman learns about the US plans he feels that the situation is already out of hand: how is it possible that France, a victim of Nazism, is increasingly isolated while London and Washington do their utmost to please the Germans? His fears come true at the meeting he holds in the US capital with the foreign ministers of the UK and the US. The three men will be in Washington DC to sign the Atlantic Pact (NATO) on 2 April and they will use the occasion to discuss the future of Germany.

The conversation between Dean Acheson, Ernest Bevin and Robert Schuman is tense. The first two want to bring the occupation status to an end and to replace it by some restrictions on Germany's sovereignty: it won't be allowed to produce weapons or to have its own armed forces. Regarding its foreign policy and the currency management, they will be monitored by the allies. The same way, the provisional authority created to manage the Ruhr region will continue to be under allied control.

For Schuman there is a red line: he cannot accept that the Ruhr is given back to Germany. This region, close to the French border, is the strongest industrial zone in Europe. Since the 19th century it has developed a flourishing production of coal and steel, which were used among other things for weapons. After the First World War, just like the small Saarland territory, the Ruhr was exploited by the victorious powers as a means to exact the payment of war reparations.[3] Then when Adolf Hitler came to power in 1933, his first act was to declare that Germany would no longer pay this price and that he would recover that German territory.

Schuman does not want to make the same mistakes, but neither can he ignore the cry of the French people who dread Ruhr military potential nor the needs of French industry for its own recovery. At the meeting, he succeeds in guaranteeing the allied control of the Ruhr, at least for

---

[3] The Treaty of Versailles established such a high sum for war reparations – 132 billion gold marks – which Germany was unable to pay and so in exchange it allowed France and Belgium to exploit its mineral resources in the Ruhr throughout military occupation in the 1920s.

the next 18 months. Then the status of the Ruhr will be reviewed and a definite solution decided.

Spring 1949, Germany

Until now, Adenauer has behaved just like the allies expected him to, but now he goes through difficult times. On 27 April the Soviets announce that they are willing to lift the Berlin blockade if the four victorious powers accept to attend a conference on the future of Germany. Adenauer suspects that it is just a ploy to delay the birth of the Federal Republic of Germany, which will definitely split from the Soviet-controlled eastern part of the country.

The Western powers accept the offer from Moscow and fix the date for 23 May in Paris. Adenauer warns them not to fall into the trap and recommends accelerating the birth of the "Free Germany". The Americans agree, so Adenauer works with the allied commissioners to adopt the Constitution before 23 May. At midnight on 8 May, the German Parliament approves the Fundamental Law.

Despite the loyalty shown by Adenauer, the Western powers still keep a direct communication line open with Adenauer's main opponent, the leader of the Social Democrats Kurt Schumacher. Adenauer is personally disturbed, but he knows that this is part of the political game and that the allied powers want to watch their backs.

Contrary to poll predictions giving a clear majority to the SPD, the CDU obtains an unexpected victory in the parliamentary elections held on 14 August. A week after the elections, Adenauer invites all leaders of the CDU and those of the Bavarian sister formation, the CSU, to his home in Rhöndorf. In an informal atmosphere, while having a snack in the living room, they discuss the government's formation and who their partners in a coalition should be. Some talk about who would be the best leader, others about the most suitable combination of parties.

At first half of the guests are in favour of an alliance with the SPD. Adenauer, however, does not think it is a good option and he does not put it to the vote. He insists on looking for alternatives. Then he starts defending a coalition with two smaller parties rather than with the SPD, not least because the CDU could keep the position of chancellor, that is to say, the head of government. Adenauer does not budge, doing everything he can to avoid a decision supported by the majority. He temporarily suspends the discussion and invites everyone to come out to the garden, where a cold buffet is served. It's his last chance: with his unwavering perseverance he approaches every single undecided guest and also those who have openly opposed his proposal. He offers them wine, and he woos them by praising their political intelligence... until he comes back to the living room and announces, without any previous voting, that the final decision is to engage in a coalition with the Liberals and with the German Party. Furthermore, if there is no objection, he will be chancellor!

Summer 1949, the Council of Europe

The centre-right also wins elections in Belgium, and in this case it implies that Paul-Henri Spaak is out of government. What appears at first to be a great disappointment for the Socialist turns into an opportunity when the European Movement asks him to chair the Council of Europe's Assembly. Of course he accepts gladly.

The opening session has to be delayed for 24 hours to allow Spaak to make the change of government in Brussels. Then on 10 August the Assembly meets in Strasbourg. It soon becomes evident that the positions of the participants are far apart. While Spinelli hands out a document calling for a European Constitution to create a federation, the British are adamantly opposed. Along with the Irish and Swedes, the British are also against the Council of Europe dealing with military matters. Spaak thinks it is a mistake, because it is precisely the question of how to defend Europe from a military threat that concerns – and also divides – the Europeans the most.

Another heated controversy starts when Winston Churchill calls on his colleagues to invite Germany to join the Council of Europe. For many that invitation is still premature.

After the meeting in Strasbourg, Robert Schuman leaves again to the US in order to keep lines of communication open on the question of the Ruhr, which has become his main headache. The long boat cruise is considerably more enjoyable than he had expected, because he bumps into Jacques Maritain and his wife, Raïsa. They were visiting friends and relatives back home in Paris and now they are returning to their current residence in New Jersey.

It takes two weeks to cross the Atlantic aboard the *De Grasse*, and the time passes amidst pleasant and stimulating conversations, especially over dinner with the captain. The minister tells Maritain he has finally met De Gasperi. Raïsa has kind words for both De Gasperi and Schuman, praising their political leadership in attempting to bring about changes in Europe. Schuman contends that Europe is also in urgent need of intellectuals like Maritain. In fact, the minister has a project in mind and he wants to engage the professor: to help him set up a European University in Saarbruecken, following the example of the new College of Europe, recently opened in Bruges, where Henri Brugmans is the first dean. Maritain likes the idea, but at this point he cannot commit himself. It is not in his near-future plans to return to Europe.

Autumn 1949, Germany

The idea of the university will have to wait. Autumn proves to be a maelstrom for the French minister. The fragile balance between the allies and Adenauer is shaken when the Soviets make their next move. On 7 October Berlin announces the creation of the German Democratic Republic (GDR). The allied powers consider that this decision is illegitimate, and Adenauer publicly agrees. In front of the Bundestag the chancellor takes responsibility for the fate of the 18 million compatriots in the East who cannot speak freely until the two Germanies can be reunited.

The panic of a direct confrontation with the Soviets takes over Western Europe. Germany has become the buffer-zone between the two blocs, and the "iron curtain" that Churchill[4] denounced in his famous speech risks moving west. Adenauer is worried about the puny support of the western powers. They may lose the support of public opinion if their constant messages proclaiming themselves the defenders of freedom are not matched by solutions for their everyday problems, and even more if Germans in the west feel that they are still outlaws under occupation.

In this context, Adenauer demands three concessions from the European partners: to return full sovereignty to Germany, to accept it as a member of the Council of Europe, and to review its plan for industrial dismantling. The allies have imposed a long list of factories to be dismantled, as punishment for Germany's role in the Second World War, but Adenauer claims that the functioning of these factories is vital to ensure economic recovery and the welfare of the Germans. Stopping the dismantling would also contribute to improving the growing negative image that Germans have of the British, the French and the Americans.

Schuman accepts Adenauer's demands reluctantly, under pressure from London and Washington, but only provided that this return of German sovereignty does not determine the result of the forthcoming negotiations on the Ruhr.

On 9 November, the Council of Europe invites Germany to join as an "associate member". The unimaginable happens when Adenauer rejects the invitation. At the request of Paris, the Council of Europe has also invited the Saar to join as an independent state and Adenauer finds this absolutely unacceptable. The Saar's final status has not yet been decided. Adenauer, like all Germans, wants it to re-join his country.

The Ruhr and the Saar have poisoned relations between France and Germany for decades. This mineral-rich region bordering Lorraine and

---

[4]   "From Stettin in the Baltic to Trieste in the Adriatic, an iron curtain has descended across the Continent." Winston Churchill at Westminster College de Fulton, Missouri (5 March, 1946).

Luxembourg was instrumental in the First World War. The League of Nations assumed control of it after the war and granted France both the administrative control and the rights to exploit the territory as war compensation. Only in 1936, 18 years later, did Germany regain full control following a referendum held in Saarland where 90% of the population voted in favour of their reintegration into Germany.

However it seems that history will repeat itself: when the Second World War ended, the United Nations took over the territory and in August 1945 its administration was ceded in trust to France, with the approval of Washington and London.

In December 1946, the French military governor decreed the incorporation of the Saar into the customs territory of France. This is how Adenauer understood that France wanted to hinder the Saar's reintegration into Germany, and to force a permanent status as an independent territory. In the worst case scenario, maybe even to annex it to France. In April 1947, the latter suspicion crystallised. France officially communicated its intentions to London and Washington: for the Saar to be economically incorporated into the French Republic.

In October 1947, Saarland held elections and chose an independent government which, in January 1948, signed a cooperation agreement with France. Thus in May 1948, the High Council in the Saarland was established, to the ire of Germany, which was occupied by foreign forces and had no government. To date, France and the other allied powers had always insisted that these were temporary measures, but the Council of Europe's invitation is the straw that breaks Adenauer's patience.

The Council of Europe is committed to seeking a comprehensive solution to the problem of the Saar and the Ruhr, so that Germany can join the Assembly. Schuman sincerely desires to overcome this pitfall. This is why in January he goes on his first official visit to Bonn. His intention is to build bridges, but the day could not have started in a worse way: when Schuman lands, he learns through German media that the French government will propose to the allies that France exploits the Saar mines for a period of 50 years.

Adenauer welcomes Schuman with a handshake and an icy expression. His angular face, marked by deep furrows and scars reflects the hardness of a natural-born negotiator, who never gives in to tension or to unexpected setbacks. He reproaches Schuman for the news, and before the Frenchman has a chance to explain, the chancellor blurts out that this loan would be unfair and unacceptable.

Schuman understands Adenauer's reaction, but he cannot promise anything. He is also in a very delicate situation: the French are convinced they have the right to German resources to ensure their own economic survival, even at the expense of the German recovery. This is the price of defeat at war. Schuman, as a minister, cannot neglect the needs of his own country. He can only give the German a warranty: "I assure you that France does not pursue the annexation of the territory of the Saar. All measures taken now, especially those that affect mining, will be reviewed with the peace treaty."

Although Adenauer trusts his sincerity, that's not enough: "Let's hold a new referendum to see what Saar citizens want," he proposes.

"France cannot forget that Germany has rights over the Saar. Germany should decide on its own mines," says Schuman. "In any case, if any modifications were to be made on the ownership of the mines, that could only be done in the form of an international control, similar to the High Authority of the Ruhr."

Adenauer's jaw clenches in anger for Schuman's refusal to hold a referendum. His lack of cooperation really upsets the chancellor and he replies: "The French attitude to Saarland makes things very difficult for me. In this context I cannot ask the German people to support the entry of Germany to the Council of Europe."

Schuman did not expect this ultimatum. What a gesture of pride! Germany should be grateful to other countries for having opened the doors of the Council to them.

"Is the Saar problem really more important than creating a United Europe?"

The chancellor does not respond. After two hours of discussion, Schuman leaves the chancellor with the feeling of having failed.

Arriving in Paris, he reads some harsh statements Adenauer has just made to the press: "The idea of the European unification is now severely compromised in Germany." The minister wanders through the halls of the Quai d'Orsay in sadness and perplexity. He goes to talk to Jean Monnet, whose modernisation plan cannot take off without the resources to revive the French industry.

"Jean, what can we do?" he asks.

"You know what I think," replies Monnet. "Peace can only be based on equality. We failed in 1919 because discrimination was introduced and a spirit of superiority. We are about to make the same mistakes."

Schuman knows this better than anyone. This conflict with Adenauer has hurt him deeply because he trusts and respects the German, but each one is caught in his national responsibility. He does not see a way out. Monnet, always optimistic and energetic, is convinced that there is an effective way to manage resources in solidarity. They just need to find the formula. And if someone is willing to risk his political career to achieve it, it's Schuman. By now this is clear to Monnet. Schuman himself is also convinced that he has a historical mission. His faith has led him to assume that providence has placed him between the German and the French, so that now from the Ministry he can sow the seeds of definitive reconciliation.

On 3 March a convention is signed in Paris between France and the Saar. It establishes the "Republic of Saarland". When asked by journalists, Adenauer's answer implies that Germany can no longer join the Council of Europe. This convention modifies, in an absolutely unacceptable way, the borders of Germany, and it abandons the spirit of the peace treaty signed at Potsdam.

"I deeply regret that France insisted on finding a unilateral solution to this issue when it would have been easy to apply a common regulation within the European framework, especially after Germany's entry into the Council of Europe," says the chancellor. "I asked Schuman insistently when he came to visit us not to resolve the issue before Germany became a member of the Council of Europe, or at least before they consulted us in the course of negotiations. The agreement they just signed [with the Saar] is a serious blow to the cause of Franco-German understanding."

Schuman responds with a statement defending the French decision: The government of Saarland is provisional, and so is the German government: "A European solution is in no way more difficult now. France is still strongly committed to the understanding between our two countries," he says.

Since the direct line of communication is now broken, Adenauer grants an interview to the International News Service in which, to the surprise of the journalist, he proposes an economic union between France and the Federal Republic of Germany as a first step towards political unity. He takes the example of Germany at the time of the Napoleonic wars: there were a large number of small German states. Each one had its own policy, its border customs, its own currency and army. A parliament was established and a customs union. The states began to exchange goods, and this was the beginning of German unity. "I think on this approach when I propose to establish a close economic union between France and Germany."

The idea is so outlandish that the interview does not even cause a ripple in Europe. But Monnet reads it and thinks that Adenauer has found his inspiration not only in German history, but also in his own proposal for the total union between France and the UK during the Second World War. Monnet smiles at the boldness of the German, who offers to give up a sovereignty which his country has not yet recovered. He sacrifices nothing, while asking France to renounce its own sovereignty. If Schuman reads the interview, he will be stunned, thinks Monnet. When de Gaulle and Monnet made their proposal in 1940, it was an attempt *in extremis* to avoid the abdication of the weak Bordeaux government to the Nazis. The pressure was tremendous. But now … where is the immediate danger? "Change will not come from within, just because people accept it easily. It can only come from outside, when the necessity compels," reflects Monnet. This is definitely not the right time for Adenauer to ask for the union.

Spring 1950, France

The following morning, as usual, Monnet gets up early, grabs his coat, his hat, and takes a long walk through the woods of Monfort l'Amaury. The fresh air and the exercise help him clear his mind. Adenauer's interview continues haunting his thoughts. The chancellor was right when it comes to identifying the problem: what to do with the Ruhr and the Saar, that is to say, how to fix the rivalry over coal and steel. From Monnet's point of view, proposing a total union as a prerequisite to eliminate a particular difficulty is unrealistic. It should be the other way around: they should use the specific difficulty as an engine of change. A concrete action on a limited but decisive point will generate a dynamic that will modify the terms of the problems as a whole, thus gradually achieving a closer union. The first stage of integration will pose new problems which, again, will only be resolved by more integration. Like a spill-over effect. Yes, that's the key to overcome the impasse in which Schuman and Adenauer are trapped!

Very soon Monnet and his team, based in the Rue de Martignac, get on with analysing the data of the coal and steel production in France, Germany, the Saar and the Ruhr. Monnet decides not to tell anyone that he is working on this project until he has come up with a finished plan. However, an unexpected event hastens the process. One day in April, Schuman passes by Monnet's office to share with him his anguish over an upcoming tough meeting: the foreign ministers of France, the US and the UK will convene in London on 10 May to decide on the future of Germany. Schuman is distressed, because he is afraid that they will not accept France's right to exploit the mineral resources of the Ruhr.

Monnet does not say anything to the minister, but accelerates his work so that Schuman can go to the London meeting with an acceptable alternative. On Thursday 13 April, the minister's chief of staff, Bernard Clappier, passes as usual by the office to say hello to Monnet and brief him on the latest news from the ministry. Schuman is anxious, and has instructed Clappier to come up with a plan, or at least a good excuse, to open a dignified way out for France from that meeting. Monnet succinctly explains that he is working on a project, but he cannot give him any more details.

The next day, Friday, a happy coincidence brings a new member to the team. It's Paul Reuter, a law professor who wants to speak with Monnet. He is an adviser to the ministry, but they have never met. Or at least Monnet has never noticed him. This time is different. He is impressed by the intelligence and enthusiasm of the young man, who talks about the problems between France and Germany with real concern. Monnet invites him to continue the conversation the following day (Saturday), because he wants to hear more about Reuter's ideas on the common management of mineral resources. But then, on Saturday time also flies, and Monnet ends up inviting the young man to join his family at Houjarray on Sunday.

Silvia is delighted to see her husband so excited again, totally enraptured by his secret plan. Monnet and Reuter lock themselves in the living room for hours along with another of Monnet's henchmen: Etienne Hirsch. This young mining engineer accompanied Monnet in London and Algeria. The three men write a first draft with the help Monnet's secretary, Mrs Miguez. The first paragraph should be shocking and clearly state the ultimate goal: "World peace can be safeguarded only by creative efforts commensurate with the dangers that threaten it. The contribution which an organised and vital Europe can make to civilisation is indispensable to the maintenance of peaceful relations."

Hirsch drafts the economic mechanisms, the production quotas, the price-fixing and the setting up of a fund for restructuring. Reuter outlines the institutional architecture: "The essential principles and undertakings defined above will be the subject of a treaty signed between the two states. The authority charged with the management of the scheme will be made on the basis of equal Franco-German representation." The principle of equality inspires the entire document.

On Monday 17 April Monnet arrives at the office, exultant. His collaborators fear his enthusiasm, for they already know that such a state can only mean endless hours in the office for them. He is a perfectionist and expects the same from others. They are not mistaken... the first draft written over the weekend becomes the first one of a total of 16 versions.

The first person to review the original proposal on Monday is Pierre Uri, an economist that Monnet fully trusts. Of course he is asked to proceed with discretion. Nobody in any ministry must know of the content. Uri accepts the condition and takes a seat in Monnet's office to read it as soon as possible. Monnet awaits the verdict. Raising his eyes, Uri says curtly: "This puts a lot of problems in their place."

"Good," responds Monnet. "That's what it is all about: putting all these problems in rational order. Then we will start solving them."

Then Uri starts structuring the project. In the third version the international authority is called "Common High Authority". In the fourth one, they refer to it as "supranational".

"Isn't there another word? I do not like it," says Monnet.

"We have to differentiate it from national institutions, but also from the international ones," Uri replies. "This will be something totally new, above the national level, but holding sovereign powers."

"Well, we will think about it. For now the important thing is that the function of this authority is clear. The text should indicate that 'higher authority decisions are enforceable in France and Germany and other member countries'."

Once Monnet is satisfied with the text, he requests an appointment with Clappier. A few days pass without any answer. Monnet is surprised by the lack of reaction, but as time is precious, he goes ahead and on 28 April he tries again with George Bidault. After all, Bidault again has taken over as head of government and is Monnet's direct superior.

Just a few seconds after giving the papers to Bidault, Clappier shows up at Monnet's office unexpectedly.

"Excuse me for not calling you before. Things have been complicated at the ministry and until now I have had no time," apologises Clappier.

"Behold the proposal I told you about, which I have just given to Bidault," replies Monnet handing him a copy of the document.

Clappier nods as his eyes slowly scroll down the pages of the secret plan. When he finishes he blurts out: "It's formidable. May I give it to Mr Schuman?"

Of course! Clappier puts on his coat, he takes the papers and rushes out. It's Friday and the minister must be on his way to the train station. Like every weekend, Schuman takes the train back to Scy-Chazelles, where he lives.

Clappier has barely arrived when the conductor blows his whistle. Looking through the window he spots Schuman, he gets on the wagon and out of breath, struggles to speak as he gives the papers to him: "Could you read this document written by Monnet? It is important."

On Monday morning, Clappier goes back to the same train station to receive Schuman returning to Paris. He is in suspense to know the minister's answer. As the old man gets off the train, he says, "I have read the project. Let's go ahead."

The next key step is to get the ministers' support. On Saturday 6 May in the afternoon, Monnet goes to Schuman's office to show him the final text with some additions that the minister had suggested. He is accompanied by René Mayer, the Minister of Justice, who has been friends with Monnet since Algiers. Monnet has told him because he knows that he would also love the project and support Schuman in the cabinet. Already back in Algiers they had discussed together how to rebuild Europe. Another ally will be René Pleven,[5] currently Minister of Overseas and another old friend of Jean and Silvia. In total, nine people know about the plan.

Schuman seeks Adenauer's views before formally proposing the plan. A member of his team will go to Bonn in secret at the time the French cabinet will discuss the decision.

The weekly ministers' cabinet meeting is on Wednesday, but the following Wednesday is already 10 May, the date of the daunting international meeting that Schuman must attend. So Pleven and Mayer manage, exceptionally and without raising any suspicion, for the ministers to meet on Tuesday.

On Monday afternoon an emissary of Robert Schuman goes to Germany. He is a magistrate from Lorraine, M. Michlich, who enjoys the trust of the minister. In Bonn Michlich is received by Herbert Blankenhorn, Adenauer's chief of staff. Upon his arrival Michlich tells Blankenhorn that he brings two letters from Schuman addressed to Adenauer. One of them is official and the other one is personal. He also explains that right now, while they speak, the French ministers are discussing the content of those letters. Also the German cabinet is meeting, and on their agenda is Germany's accession to the Council of Europe. Blankenhorn has to interrupt the meeting to talk to the chancellor.

Schuman's official letter contains the text of the draft declaration, which begins: "World peace cannot be safeguarded without the making of creative efforts which are in proportion to the dangers which threaten it. [...] The coming together of the nations of Europe requires the elimination of the age-old opposition of France and Germany. [...]" With this aim in view, he proposes that Franco-German production of coal and steel as a whole be placed under a common High Authority, within the framework of an organisation open to the participation of the other countries of Europe.

In the other letter, handwritten, Schuman explains that the purpose of his proposal is not economic but highly political. To avoid any dispute over the production of coal and steel, and the fear of a renewed arms

---

5   Pleven was director general for Europe of the American Automatic Telephone Company (1929-1939) when he first met Jean Monnet. During the Second World War Monnet appointed him his deputy in the mission of buying American planes for the French Air force.

industry, a new type of organisation between the two countries could bring calm to the spirits. Adenauer is moved when he tells Schuman's emissary his answer: "Tell him that I wholeheartedly approve his proposal."

Meanwhile, the French cabinet deliberates in the Élysée Palace. Schuman does not open his mouth all morning. He is anxiously expecting news from Bonn. Clappier is waiting in a nearby office, keeping in constant contact with Monnet by the inter-ministerial phone. Just when Bidault announces the end of the meeting, Schuman hears from Clappier. Adenauer has given his approval. Schuman requests other ministers to sit back in their chairs, because he has an important communication to make. He explains, in a very general way, that he has reached an agreement with Germany to propose an alternative plan to the governments of the United Kingdom and the United States regarding the future status of Germany.

He speaks so quickly and so low, almost in a whisper, that most of the ministers don't even grasp the magnitude of the announcement. They support the minister without being truly aware of what they have approved. Bidault does not retain the details, but understands that Schuman has a plan for the joint management of coal and steel between France and Germany and he had not been consulted in advance. He is really disappointed; because a couple of years ago he had taken the initiative to contact Adenauer and to propose to jointly seek a solution to this problem, at one of the secret meetings in Geneva.

Bidault summons Monnet in his office. He is furious. Waving a copy of the plan in his hand, Bidault says:

"Schuman has just shown me this paper and it seems that it is you who wrote it. I would have liked to have been the first to know."

"You were. I wrote to you last Friday," says Monnet.

Without saying a word, Bidault looks through the papers lying on his desk. There's the envelope with the document, which no one has opened.

Monnet leaves. It is urgent to announce the decision to the press before the document circulates around the ministries and someone tries to backtrack. They prepare a spectacular announcement. He invites French and international journalists at 6 pm to the hall of the Horloge at the Quai d'Orsay, which has been set up as a conference room. Meanwhile, and all afternoon long, Schuman's cabinet takes care of informing the European ambassadors.

More than 200 journalists await the arrival of the minister. At the back of the room, watching quietly, stand Silvia and Jean Monnet, Hirsch and Uri. Schuman takes the floor, again with that helpless and doubtful air: "France has taken the lead, and the consequences of its action can be immense. We hope they are, because France has acted essentially seeking peace. But for peace to have a chance, first we need Europe to exist."

Monnet is nervous. This is a historic moment and he wants everything to go well. This is a moment which will go down in history... and only now he realises that he has forgotten to call photographers and cameramen! He will have to ask the minister to reproduce the press conference in a few weeks, when he returns from his trip to London.

After several questions from the room, the minister tries to get out of the ministry. He is in a hurry because he must travel to London. Besides, reporters start asking for details about how the High Authority will work. Most issues have not been discussed yet. It is premature to talk about that, he explains. He feels beset by questions he cannot answer, when one journalist says: "So it's a leap into the unknown..."

"That's it – a leap into the unknown," Schuman admits. And before the astonished gaze of Monnet he concludes the press conference.

Robert Schuman

A Minister with a Tonsure

Robert Schuman (© European Commission)

Judging by Monnet's disapproving look, it is clear to Schuman that he did not like his answers to the press. Schuman was not sufficiently convincing. Jean walks up to him, with Silvia by his side, to congratulate the minister for the press conference. However, he cannot resist mentioning the obvious trap into which he fell when admitting that, indeed, the plan is nothing more than a blueprint yet to be developed. Monnet apologises for the absence of photographers and asks the minister and Clappier to find a slot in their agenda in the coming weeks to reproduce the press conference and take some photos. Schuman, who had not even noticed that there were no cameras, nods and quietly leaves the room. His mind is already focusing on the next meeting and he is relieved that the press conference is over.

The Lorraine-born man has been shy from childhood. He has never liked speaking in public or being the centre of attention. Now he has no choice but to accept it, because it goes with the job. He is a politician by accident, not by vocation. Or rather, he believes that he accidentally became a politician by divine vocation. At one point he was determined to enter a monastery, but a friend persuaded him that God expected him to remain secular and spend his life in public service. So he followed the advice, and since then he has tried not to forget that this is the meaning and the drive of his whole life, having renounced even marriage and a family.

He lives in a house in Scy-Chazelles, a little village 15 minutes away from the city of Metz , the capital of Lorraine. He has no car. Every Friday after work he goes from the ministry to the Parisian East station and takes the train to Metz; then a bus line to the village and from the bus stop he walks home. At this quiet place in Lorraine's heartland, he loves to spend his weekends reading one of the books of his invaluable collection, nourished for decades with first editions and facsimiles. During the Nazi invasion, the German Army occupied his house and destroyed some of his best specimens. In return they installed a heating system, for the brave soldiers had more difficulties than Schuman to resist low temperatures.

During weekdays he stays in an apartment in Paris close to the ministry. Every morning he walks to the Quai d'Orsay, always after attending mass in a near-by church. He leaves very early, with his missal under one arm and the rosary in his pocket. He does not hide his faith, even though it could hinder his political career and is frequently a cause for jokes and cartoons in newspapers. His baldness was recently depicted as the tonsure of a monk, and jokes circulate about the "man in the invisible cassock". By now, aged almost 64, he cares very little about what people think, let alone about his political future. When he is no longer useful he will just retire to his beloved Scy-Chazelles, where all the neighbours know him and appreciate him.

Monnet thinks he has a clerical air. He respects the faith of the minister, but he doesn't share it. They have actually never talked about it, because the two men are very discreet and not prone to air their intimate thoughts. However, Schuman has a lot in common with Monnet's younger sister, Marie-Louise. She is also celibate and her life is spent keeping the Independent Catholic Action (ICA) going; a movement that she founded in 1938. Monnet not only helped his sister financially, but during the Second World War the ICA's headquarters operated from the family home in Cognac. The difference between his sister and Schuman is that she is strong and determined, while the minister is, in his opinion, lacking in ambition and slow to act. Schuman, meanwhile, considers Monnet extremely liberal and sometimes too pushy. The minister likes to think before deciding while Monnet seems to be always in a rush.

The relationship between the two got off on the wrong foot but fortunately it improved over time: They first met in 1946, when Schuman was finance minister and Monnet reproached him for not sufficiently funding his modernisation plan. Schuman did not like Monnet's imposition of bypassing the ministerial hierarchy and working directly with the prime minister. Three years later, they came together for the project of bringing France and Germany closer. The need to stand up to Charles de Gaulle was the bond on which they came to appreciate each other.

The patriotism of the general, whose leadership and prestige permeated the French population after the war, feeds on the secular enmity with Germany. In the Assembly he swashbucklingly defends France's right to war compensation and its restitution claims to the aggressor. Schuman opposes the principle of war reparation, which can easily turn into revenge. His German accent when speaking French has cost him more than mockery in the Assembly, and he constantly has to hear comments about his being too German-friendly. Many don't understand that his DNA is incompatible with General de Gaulle's sense of patriotism. This is precisely what Monnet likes about Schuman. Although their experiences in youth were very different, both learned from childhood that borders are only artificial boundaries that separate people. But while Monnet had a cosmopolitan upbringing, Schuman grew up in a cross-border environment and suffered in his own family, without needing to travel, the effects of moving demarcations between European states in the 19th and 20th centuries.

Schuman's father, Jean-Pierre, was from Évrange, a small town in the French department of Moselle, in the Lorraine region.[1] But Robert inherited German citizenship from his father, because Jean-Pierre was forced to become German when the Alsace and part of Lorraine fell into the hands of the Prussian Army in the 1870 war. Jean Pierre, who was then 33 years old, took part in the defence of the city of Thionville

---

[1]   The region of Lorraine is composed of four departments: Mosa, Meurthe, Moselle and the Vosges.

during the months of the siege. They did not resist very long. Jean-Pierre returned to Évrange. Overnight, he and his brothers, like many others in Lorraine, became German citizens. Over the years this produced awkward situations. For instance, François Schuman, a nephew of Jean-Pierre (therefore Robert's cousin) fought in the German ranks during the First World War against other cousins who defended the French flag.

At age 47, Jean-Pierre fell in love with a girl from Bettembourg, a Luxembourg village across the border. Her name was Eugénie Duren and she was barely 20 years old. Neither their age nor the border constituted obstacles to their marriage. The couple settled in Clausen (Luxembourg), where the Duren family had some property. At home they spoke French and Luxembourgish.

In 1886 they had a son, Robert, who would be an only child. The boy inherited his father's French spirit and his mother's flexibility, matured in the Luxembourg Duchy, which for centuries had been the subject of contention between France and Germany.

At the age of six Robert began his schooling in the public school in Clausen. At that time the Grand Duke of Luxembourg belonged to the dynasty of Nassau, closely linked to Germany, so the German Empire and the Grand Duchy had established a customs union and maintained a very good relationship.

His father never inculcated resentment towards the Germans. Jean-Pierre died in 1900, when Robert was 14, and the bond between mother and son became even more intense. She relayed her life of faith and tried to make him see that the longing for a French Lorraine which his father loved so much was consistent with the admiration for Germany.

Despite the good relations between Luxembourg and Prussia, the Grand Duchy had kept the Napoleonic Code and most young people were leaving to France to study law after school. Robert wanted to become a lawyer but chose to enrol in Germany, first in Bonn, where he attended the Catholic university association Unitas. He continued his studies in Munich and Berlin, and attended graduate school in Strasbourg. After five happy years, he obtained his doctorate and decided to stay for a while in the Alsatian capital in a room he rented in No. 10 University Square.

In 1906, once his training period was completed, he settled in Metz. The town had changed a lot since the days of the siege and as a child, Robert heard from his father and other neighbours of the drama it caused and the memories of many who were exiled. After the annexation, many families of French language and culture migrated to the Republic. Living right next to the border, Jean-Pierre saw his native Lorraine change with the arrival of immigrants from Germany. While some strongly Francophone residential areas were abandoned, new areas developed for newcomers.

The city dates back to the Roman Empire, but its historical highlight is that of Charlemagne and the Holy Roman Empire. So Kaiser Wilhelm II wanted this iconic enclave as a sort of showcase for his power. He promoted an urban plan to modernise Metz. He destroyed the old walls to build wide boulevards, gardens and a large railway station, which opened in 1908.

Schuman felt at home. His Germanic upbringing allowed him to mingle easily in the workplace and to make lasting friendships both in the French and the German-speaking communities. He was living a blessed life when a fatal accident turned it upside down on 11 August 1911.

Robert and his mother, Eugénie, were invited to the wedding of a cousin in Évrange. It was the youngest daughter of his paternal uncle Ferdinand. Robert had planned to accompany his mother, already a widow, but when he started his attorney internship in the Alsatian town of Colmar in early August, he thought it would be inappropriate to leave. So he sent his apologies. Eugénie took the train to Frisange where a carriage was waiting to take her to nearby Évrange. As she stepped into the car after four other ladies, the horses suddenly bolted, out of control of the driver. Eugénie, who had just mounted, fell back and hit her head on the ground fracturing her skull. The priest at Évrange, who knew her, was passing by. He ran to her and gave her the last rites. Five minutes later Eugénie died from internal bleeding, while none of the other occupants of the carriage were injured.

For Schuman it was a very painful and unexpected loss. His mother was only 46, and the young lawyer could not stop thinking about the succession of fatalities that caused the accident. If he had been there ... if his mother had already been sitting in the carriage... if she had not fallen on her head ... Witnesses told him that the horses immediately stopped, and they were only 500 meters away from the train station.

The young man was introverted and deeply religious. He launched into prayer and reflection, trying to figure out the meaning of his life. A few days after the accident, his mother was buried in Clausen and Robert had no time to call Henri Eschbach, his best friend. Eschbach lived in Strasbourg, where Robert had met him in college. They had shared cultural and spiritual activities of Catholic students' circles. Henri wrote an endearing letter of condolence offering all his support, aware that, at the age of 25 years, Robert was suffering the great void left by his mother and had no father or siblings.

Only to Henri did Robert open his heart. He replied in a handwritten letter that he had decided to give a new direction to his life: to withdraw into silence and prayer in a monastery. On 6 September, Eschbach wrote a few lines that sought to shake his friend's conscience:

"Am I wrong in thinking that you are considering the priesthood, and you think that it is the only practicable way for you? Dare I add that I have a different opinion? In our society the lay apostolate is needed urgently, and I cannot imagine a better apostle than you, honestly... you will remain secular because that way it will be easier for you to do good, being that your only concern. I am categorical, right? I just think that I can see to the bottom of some hearts and I believe that holy saints in the future will be saints dressed in suits."

Henri's words would remain with Schuman all his life. Even today, facing the challenge of Franco-German peace as a minister, the reason why he did not enter a monastery resonates in his head: to invest all his energies in search of peace.

At first his commitment was channelled through his activities as a lawyer. He considered sitting a competition for public office but decided not to be an official of the German Empire, out of respect for the memory of his father. He preferred to be independent and start his own law firm on 5 Kaiser Wilhelm Ring – now the Avenue Foch – near the train station.

Word spread of his professionalism and honesty. His active engagement in the city made him a known character. At that time lawyers enjoyed great social prestige, and several influential people asked him to become involved in the Municipal Council. Although politics did not appeal to him, he agreed because he could be useful to the French who remained in Lorraine. Unlike him, most of them never had the privilege of growing up between two cultures and to master the German language.

As a student he was also very active in Catholic organisations, such as Caritas, and various youth initiatives for peace. In the summer of 1912 he participated with his Belgian cousin Albert Duren in an international youth conference for peace in Leuven. Through another cousin, Leon Schmit – who was a priest in Metz – he began to frequent the parish of St. Martin, where masses were held in French and German. There he found a good group of friends from both communities. Because of his growing popularity he was elected president of the Catholic Youth Association of Lorraine in 1913.

Soon events would push him towards politics. Germany declared war on France in August 1914. The border was closed and the army took over Metz. French language newspapers were banned and politicians, journalists and priests close to the French were arrested. Some acquaintances of Schuman fled to France, and others remained under house arrest in Germany. He was not in danger because he had never advocated Lorraine's independence. His cousin François Schuman was called up by the Kaiser's army. So was Robert, but he avoided any combat because in 1908 he had been declared unfit for military service. He did however wear the German uniform as he was recruited to the administrative staff of a military hospital.

Indeed, at the start of the war he was repulsed by violence but did not have a negative image of the Germans. Everything changed following a furtive visit to Messancy (Belgium) to his Duren uncle and aunt, the parents of his cousin Albert. Their son had gone to the Congo to escape the war and to take his chances in the colony. His uncle and aunt were worried about Robert, because terrible news about the Germans had come to their ears. Robert was not aware of those stories. Through the Durens he learned that summary executions had been ordered by the Prussian Army in the Ardennes and Lorraine.

Back in Metz, everyday life became a nightmare. The city was militarised, as it played a key role in providing supplies to the German troops. The situation was untenable for the French-speaking population. The authorities even banned the French language in public spaces. Then food shortages began. As the battle line approached, from February to November 1916 the thunder of the guns in Verdun reached the ears of Metz's inhabitants. Some relied on the German victory whereas others secretly wished for the arrival of the Republican troops.

Eschbach was sent to the eastern front and spent most of the war in Poland. When Schuman was asked by the authorities to assist in the administration of Boulay, a small town 25 kilometres from Metz, he accepted. He left the military hospital and combined his work at the law firm with his new tasks, which consisted of managing expropriated assets – usually to the French – and helping refugees. From time to time he would also carry out some small quartermaster tasks for population of this town in Lorraine, which was mostly German-speaking but sympathised with France. He tried to maintain mail contact with Eschbach and his cousin François, who as a lieutenant of artillery was fighting for the German Army on the western front.

By the summer of 1918 it was clear that the French would win. Over those four years, a distance from the Germany he so admired had grown in his heart. The news from Belgium made him shed his neutrality, or rather, as he himself admitted in a letter to his cousin Albert, he abandoned his frontiersman's "indifference" to outright reject this Germany which he considered unfair and brutal. He found himself placing his hopes on the arrival of the French troops.

But peace brought new problems. Things changed in the Alsace and Lorraine when the two regions returned to France. Suddenly the discrimination that many French had suffered in 1870 was back, except that now the victims were German. Most Germans left when the French authorities assumed power. Schuman tried to defend the rights of some friends who went into exile and whose properties were confiscated. Furthermore, descendants of those French Lorraine inhabitants who had emigrated in 1870 started to come back, and they tried to wipe out 50 years of German presence overnight.

Schuman was 32 and had always lived under the German Empire. His political and civic engagement was shaped more by the German culture than by the French one. In 1918, from one day to the next, he became, for the first time, a French national, something he had never experienced beyond the memories of his father.

To him, it was essential to avoid revenge and abuse, and for that he was very well positioned because he had friends on both sides. In addition to the situation of the German minority, the return to France was problematic for two regions with a peculiar history. Lorraine had been an independent Duchy for many centuries, with a particular identity which the centralist French Republic now sought to dilute. These two reasons pushed him to get involved in public affairs.

Although he did not belong to the Lorraine's Francophone elite, they managed to persuade him to actively participate in the transition and in November 1918 he joined the municipal commission whose task was to advise the new mayor of Metz, Victor Prével. "My involuntary entry into the city council is mostly an entertainment that allows me to see and hear many things and to get close to characters whose contact I appreciate," he told Eschbach in a letter. "But politics remains for me a great lady of dubious reputation, who often endangers her friends."

So finally he accepted to take part in the formation of a political party, the Republican Union of Lorraine (URL), as a way to bring together the French and the German-speaking communities. Their programme was intended to protect Lorraine's peculiarities and they also called for the separation from Alsace, for Lorraine always felt it was dependent on the neighbour.

Regarding political matters, Robert looked to two of his paternal uncles for advice: Ferdinand and Nicholas Schuman. Ferdinand had been mayor of Évrange, and then moved to Strasbourg, where they became close during Robert's days at the college. However, the most valuable political experience was that of Uncle Nicholas, who was a Member of Parliament representing firstly the Independent Party of Lorraine and then *Zentrum*, a political organisation founded in the 19th century by Ludwig Windthorst.[2]

---

[2]   Windhorst translated the German Social Catholicism taught by Father von Ketteler into a political program. After the revolutions of 1830 and 1848, von Ketteler asked Christians to tackle social problems, because that was the big challenge of the time and it was an obligation for Christians to create a society based on fairness and solidarity.

Born in Hanover, Windthorst developed his career as a lawyer. He lived at a time of political distress: the kingdom of Hanover was destroyed by Bismarck and forced to integrate into the Reich. Windthorst entered the Parliament to defend the rights of Catholics against the central power. From 1871 he had the ability to unite in one cause the rights of the Catholic minority and the defence of individual and regional freedoms.

The advice of his uncle – who had defended the regional identity of Lorraine within the German Empire – and the inspiration of Windthorst would be very useful to Robert. The problems experienced by Catholics in Rhineland against protestant Bismarck centralism in the 1840s resembled those of the Catholics in Lorraine and Alsace in the Jacobin France.

He did not need to campaign to comfortably win a seat in the Assembly. In 1919 he moved to Paris, where the rest of the members held a victorious and emotional welcome to the Assembly of the 23 deputies coming from the "recovered provinces". Schuman felt he was inexperienced and somewhat clueless in the Parisian political environment, where he had no contacts or friends. With his background, as a lawyer between two worlds, he concentrated his legislative efforts on adapting Alsace and Lorraine's Germanic laws to the Napoleonic Code.

Many in the Assembly were surprised by the attitude of the newcomers. They expected them to long for and admire French laws and the traditions of the homeland from which they had been separated for over five decades. On the contrary, the newcomers strove to maintain their identity. They were concerned about issues such as the use of language and education. Schuman also defended the retirement rights of German officials who remained in Lorraine.

After the military victory, all German property had been confiscated. In 1923 the French government centralised the management of those properties and Schuman was appointed head of the office in charge within the Ministry of Justice. He was the right person to solve potential injustices. It did not take long for Schuman to discover mismanagement and abuses. He ordered an investigation that uncovered a plot by which a group of entrepreneurs in Lorraine had only paid one-fiftieth of the value of three German factories to the French state. Some people from his region were involved and also a member of his own party, Guy de Wendel. However, despite the strong pressure he endured, he took the investigation to the end.

Another priority in those years was the teaching of religion in state schools, which was part of the Concordat signed between the Holy See and France before the French Revolution. Alsace and Lorraine were no longer part of France when the country abandoned the Concordat in 1905, so all these years they had maintained the religion classes in state schools while they belonged to the German Empire. When in May 1924 a leftist coalition won the general elections and the new government tried to impose secular education in the recovered departments, Schuman upheld a common front in Lorraine and Alsace with other members of parliament. In these two departments Conservative candidates had obtained a landslide victory (21 of the 24 seats), and felt a legitimacy to represent the majority of the population who opposed Republican secularism. Christians of different denominations and the important Jewish community in the Alsace joined the common effort. At the end they managed to save the Concordat and the religion classes with legal arguments and after many interviews with leaders of other parties.

The URL party demanded respect for the customs and traditions of their people, but other regional parties went further and called for political and administrative autonomy. Schuman did not support this movement, promoted in particular by German sectors. He advocated a "decentralisation" to respect their identity against any homogenisation, whilst maintaining the administrative structure of the Republic.

The tension between Paris and the two regions was mounting. In the 1928 elections Schuman kept his seat, but his party suffered a setback with the rise of radical positions of the left and right, both in favour of autonomy from Paris.

In addition to defending the structure of the Republic, Schuman also believed that some degree of state intervention was necessary to avoid injustices and to protect the weak. So he joined the left in defence of workers' rights, the introduction of paid holidays, and the freedom of trade unions against the monopoly of CGT (General Confederation of Labour).

During all this time, he would still go to Germany to visit friends, especially Eschbach. He stopped doing so in January 1933, when Hitler won the elections. Schuman hated the violence in the nationalistic messages. The passivity of Europeans allowed Hitler to invade neighbouring countries but many did not seem to understand the threat. In 1939 France barely noticed the effects, because war started on the eastern front. But then events escalated after the invasion of Poland. The population of Lorraine and Alsace were evacuated, and among the first to leave were many Jews. A total of 600,000 people abandoned the two regions. Schuman went with the refugees to Poitiers, a city that became the main reception centre of refugees in France. There he opened an information office for the citizens of his department, Moselle. He learned what was happening in Alsace and Lorraine through Eschbach's letters, for he had stayed in Strasbourg.

On 21 March 1940 Paul Reynaud took office and appointed Schuman undersecretary for refugees. Back in Paris, Schuman's task was getting more complicated by the week. On 10 May, the Germans invaded Belgium and the Netherlands, and Metz was shelled for the first time. The massive influx of displaced persons had to stay in shelters improvised in Paris train stations. Schuman would go to talk to them and listen to their stories and their needs.

How he craved for a return to normalcy! So when on 18 June he heard general de Gaulle's speech on the radio from London calling to resistance, he thought it was a mistake. Schuman found it necessary to exhaust all possibilities for peace, including the signing of an armistice with Germany. Nor did he consider it appropriate that the French government leave the territory of the hexagon to settle in London or North Africa, as some were proposing.

This is how, at a key moment in the history of his country, Schuman voted in favour of Marshal Pétain and of the Vichy regime in the National Assembly. Since then, his political opponents would throw it in his face, fuelling rumours about his philo-Germanism.

However, he never collaborated with the regime. The new Vichy government accepted the annexation of Alsace and Lorraine to the Reich. The Germans not only restored the province of Alsace-Lorraine as the single unit that existed before 1918, they also settled in both capital cities Strasbourg (Alsace) and Metz (Lorraine). They promised a peaceful transition and to respect all, but their true goal was to re-"Germanise" the provinces and to facilitate the return of the German-speaking population that had left some years ago. The new authorities invited Schuman to return. He thought about it for several weeks, and finally accepted in order to help the French families who decided to stay.

He arrived home on 2 September 1940 to find that they had seized his apartment in Metz. He stayed with his cousin Leon Schmidt, who was general vicar of the local diocese. Still believing in a peaceful solution, Schuman went to speak with the Nazi authorities to organise the return of French refugees from Poitiers. Instead, all the Nazis wanted from Schuman was for him to accept a position in the Nazi administration. When he categorically refused, he was jailed in the local prison.

The prison officers were amicable, in the hope that he would reconsider. They offered to bring him whatever he needed from his house. He asked for a sweater and for the 26 volumes of the History of the Popes. He thought the confinement would be long and had no intention of giving in.

Schuman's aim was to be expelled to France, but this was not part of the captor's plan. The SS lost patience and decided to send him to a concentration camp in Germany. In mid-April, the director of the prison received the order to transfer him to Dachau. But Schuman's German friends were following his case closely, and as soon as the decision came to the ears of the attorney general, Heinrich Welsch, he hurried to talk to the authorities. Welsch told the Nazi command in Metz that Schuman was loved and respected by both French and German, and sending him to a concentration camp would be highly unpopular.

Welsch's intercession was effective, and instead of the Dachau concentration camp Schuman was sentenced to an indefinite house arrest in the Palatinate. His new prison was a hostel run by the Köhler family, who did not know who their guest was. Schuman himself had to pay the expenses out of his own pocket, but at least the atmosphere was pleasant. He liked Ms Köhler's cooking and was free to go for walks and even to travel through Germany and only crossing into France was forbidden to him.

Nor was he allowed to go to Alsace or Lorraine. During his captivity he went to church every morning, as usual, and spent the day studying English, improving his knowledge of ancient Greek and reading books on history and theology. He reviewed the works of St. Thomas, thus becoming able to recite his texts in Latin. He dreamed of returning to France and becoming a teacher until his retirement, which did not seem far away since he was already 55.

He would eat with the Köhlers. Sometimes they stayed up late chatting after dinner. Schuman was convinced that things would change, that a united Europe would soon bring peace between France and Germany. Someday a generation will finally put an end to the absurd idea of the "hereditary enemy".

It took a few weeks before he seriously thought about fleeing. The freedom that his captors granted him within Germany allowed him to talk to his friend Eschbach, and together they prepared an escape plan with the help of an Alsatian banker. One autumn day, he left with nothing but the clothes he was wearing. He reached the train station in Strasbourg, where Eschbach and his wife were waiting with some extra clothes and a ticket to Poitiers. At that time the French city was occupied by the Germans, so Schuman had to hide for some time before he could cross over to French territory. He went into hiding for several weeks in an abbey on the outskirts of the Alsatian capital.

He finally managed to reach Lyon, where he immediately contacted the authorities from Lorraine who had temporarily settled down in Lyon. He offered to help other refugees. But a few days later, on 8 November 1942, the German Army invaded the whole French territory and everyone fled. Schuman hid in the Abbey of *Notre Dame de Neiges* until February 1943, leading the same life as the Trappist monks.

With the liberation of France by the Allied troops, little by little French regions were going back to normal. Schuman was eager to return home, but Metz was not released until late November 1944. The city had been destroyed by the fighting. Like many others, he found an almost empty house. He had lost numerous specimens from his bookshelves.

As soon as he could, he resettled in Scy-Chazelles. This happened in late March 1945. He had been travelling since 1939 and felt the need to stay at home quietly. He did not know what had become of his relatives, who had been scattered around Germany, Belgium and Luxembourg by the war. He dedicated his time to finding out about their fate. At the political level, he launched a campaign to help those refugees returning home and also the Germans who wanted to stay in Moselle, for they were at risk of being expelled.

Only when the war was over did Schuman find out that he was about to be sent to a concentration camp. He believed that the reason why he was spared death was because he still had a mission: to prevent the same mistakes made after the First World War being repeated. This time he has not only his experience as a bridge between French and Germans, but also the contacts and the necessary political stature in France to influence the course of history.

Despite his vote in favour of Pétain, de Gaulle restored Schuman's right to engage again in politics, and allowed him to run in the elections for the Constituent Assembly of the Fourth Republic. He ran as an independent, not representing any political party, and he won over the Gaullist candidate of his department. Once in the Assembly, he joined the parliamentary group of the Popular Republican Movement (MRP). This is a party that was founded and chaired by one of the heroes of the resistance, Georges Bidault.

The 1946 elections gave victory to MRP. The new head of government, Bidault, appointed Schuman as his finance minister. He entrusted him with one very complicated task: the post-war economy had been devastated by the destruction of buildings and factories, the stagnated industrial activity, the lack of raw materials, the food shortages and a rampant inflation.

It was under these circumstances that Schuman met Jean Monnet. De Gaulle had placed him above all ministers to modernise the economy and Bidault accepted this unusual structure. In the eyes of Schuman, the lack of coordination between Monnet's modernisation plan and the Finance Ministry was detrimental for France.

Thanks in part to the harmony between Monnet and Bernard Clappier, the relationship between Monnet and Schuman improved and evolved into a smooth collaboration. And more importantly, Schuman will always be thankful to Monnet, because his plan for the coal and steel community laid the foundations of a new relationship between France and Germany.

1950-1952

The European Coal and Steel Community

At the Council of Europe, in Strasbourg. From left to right: Robert Schuman, Alcide De Gasperi, Dirk Stikker, Paul Van Zeeland, Konrad Adenauer and Joseph Bech
(© European Commission)

"A leap into the unknown." On 10 May some newspapers' headlines feature Schuman's innocent but accurate sentence. European foreign offices awake to the shock of the news. Ernest Bevin is stunned. He requests an explanation from the French ambassador in London. On behalf of Italy, Sforza warmly welcomes the plan. The Benelux countries ask for some clarification, but their overall reaction is that of acceptance. The US government, informed by its Secretary of State Dean Acheson, holds a positive opinion.

In the afternoon the three allied ministers meet in London to discuss Germany's future. Schuman attends the meeting, much calmer than on previous occasions, as he is convinced that the "Schuman Plan" will allow him to take the initiative.

As soon as they see each other, Bevin accuses Schuman and Acheson of having concocted an "anti-British plot". The American admits that he was aware of the plan, but only a few hours before and only by chance. He had to stop over in Paris on his way to London. Out of courtesy, he requested to see the French minister. Schuman could not hide the plan that he was about to announce the following day, so he told him once he had Monnet's blessing. At first Acheson reacted with scepticism, because he imagined a cartel contrary to free competition, but within hours Uri and Monnet had prepared a technical note, and quickly dispelled his doubts.

As he reads the news on 10 May, Monnet finds out that Acheson's initial fears are shared by the majority of the British press. Some newspapers run distorted information, and this leads the Foreign Office officially requesting a clarification from the French government. All morning the telephone keeps ringing with questions to Clappier and Schuman. So finally Monnet decides to travel to London with Uri and Hirsch to clarify that his project is not a cartel.

The British are very pragmatic and want concrete facts. What is the plan exactly? How will decisions be made? What powers will the High Authority have? Monnet has to admit that none of this has been decided. To Bevin, the whole thing seems like a pipe dream and he is surprised that the governments of France and Germany are actually willing to venture into such a vague and risky project. He asks Monnet if France will move forward even if the United Kingdom steps back. "We will go ahead even if we are only two countries, but the UK may join later, when the Authority is already in place," he answers.

While Bevin and Monnet chat, Schuman is talking to the journalists in another room:

"How many countries are needed to make the plan work?," one reporter wants to know.

"We will go on with the negotiation between two countries if needed," Schuman replies.

"What role can the UK have?"

"If there is not one hundred per cent participation, there may be an association compatible with the British structures and economic perceptions," is Schuman's answer.

Schuman's words make Monnet's hackles rise. Why did he have to say that? There is no way that Monnet would accept a watered down plan.

One must maintain standards and wait for the countries to be prepared to accept. Lowering the expectations in order to bring the British on board would be a huge mistake. As soon as he sees the opportunity, he addresses Schuman privately: "Experience has shown to me that it is not a good move to grant special conditions to the British and a special status in its relations with others; not even to grant them the expectation that they will be able to benefit from it."

Schuman apologises, but he also insists that they remain flexible if they want their plan to succeed.

At the end of their meeting on 15 May the three ministers announce that Germany will gradually join the community of nations. Controls will be progressively lifted. The occupation troops will leave, except those that will remain to defend West Germany if necessary, with the agreement of the local government.

Adenauer meets with the three commissioners in Petersberg the next day. The chancellor perceives a change in attitude in the allies, who now behave more openly. The coordination between Paris and Bonn to announce the Schuman Plan has strengthened trust in Germany. And yet, also Adenauer is faced with some criticism of the plan in Bonn. Kurt Schumacher, the SPD leader, does not like the project. He says it is too vague: "The Schuman Plan is a just a frame. We'll have to see what painting they put inside it."

Monnet travels to Bonn to personally explain all the details to Adenauer. Before arriving at the Schaumburg Palace, in the shattered centre of Bonn, he passes by the Petersberg building to greet the American commissioner, John McCloy, who is a good friend of his. They met a few years ago, when McCloy worked at the War Ministry in Washington DC and the French man tried to convince the US government to build planes, so that the allies could beat the Nazis. Now Monnet wants to know McCloy's opinion on the Schuman plan. Monnet says he intends to initiate talks with Germany as an equal, even if it has not yet regained full sovereignty. The American approves.

From Petersberg Monnet goes to see the chancellor, accompanied by Bernard Clappier. In his office in Schaumburg, Adenauer awaits with Herbert Blankenhorn, his counsellor and man of confidence in the government and in the CDU. At the beginning the chancellor is very cautious and just greets his guests with a polite smile.

Monnet breaks the ice: "We want to establish the relationship between France and Germany on an entirely new basis and turn what divides us, especially the war industries, into a common benefit that will also benefit Europe. There are no winners or losers: there can be no peace without justice and no justice without equality."

Adenauer's features soften.

"The French proposal is essentially political," continues Monnet. "It even has, let's say, a moral aspect. At its core, it sets a very simple goal which our government will try to achieve without worrying, in a first phase, about the technical difficulties."

When Monnet finishes speaking, Adenauer says, full of emotion:

"I'm not a technician, and I don't speak now as a politician. I see, like you, this great enterprise in its highest aspect: the moral order. It is the moral responsibility we have towards our people, and not the technical responsibility, the one we must implement in order to realise a dream of this calibre. The reception has been enthusiastic in Germany. Nor will we dwell on the details. I have been waiting for this initiative for the last 25 years. By partnering with you, neither my government nor my country hold any ulterior motives, no hegemonic intentions. Since 1933 history has taught us how vain those concerns are. Germany knows that its fate is tied up with the fate of Western Europe."

They all vow to maintain direct and open dialogue. Clappier makes his excuses and leaves for five minutes to make a phone call. Upon his return he confirms that, after speaking with Schuman, he can confirm that Monnet will represent the French government in the upcoming negotiations. Adenauer states that he will find a "German Monnet".

"Mr Monnet," Adenauer says, "I consider that the realisation of the French proposal is the most important task ahead of me. If I can bring it to fruition, I think I will not have wasted my life."

When the chancellor begins the selection process for the German negotiator he allows Monnet to take part, under absolute confidentiality. After all, it will be Monnet's counterpart... the Frenchman disapproves of the first candidate chosen by Adenauer. During the personal interview with Monnet the candidate talked mainly on coal, steel and the mines of the Ruhr. But Monnet is looking for someone who gets excited when talking about Europe, about peace and about the future. This is not a matter of expertise. The key is to find a flexible person, open to change and imaginative. That person ends up being a university professor, Walter Hallstein, with whom Adenauer had travelled to The Hague.

Summer 1950, France

France, Germany, Italy, Belgium, the Netherlands and Luxembourg join the project from the start and their delegates arrive in Paris on 20 June for the opening of the conference. Work sessions begin the next day. When presenting the project to them, Monnet refers to the new organisation as a "European community" for the first time. He explains that it will be a *sui generis* body, one that has never existed before. Its core management institution will be the High Authority. The production of coal and steel will provide direct revenue to the community, so that it has its own resources and does not need to rely on contributions from states.

The group works in a small area labelled "European" at the ministry in Rue Martignac. They are isolated from the rest of the civil servants and subjected to a hectic work pace. Monnet hopes that these working conditions will contribute to the development of a team spirit among the participants and maybe even friendship. Although sometimes communication becomes a bit arduous, Monnet insists on rejecting the presence of interpreters. The content of the discussions is not as important as the approach: Monnet wants them to evolve from regarding the solution to a problem as a victory of one over the other, to finding a winning solution for everyone. Sometimes it's just a matter of imagination. At the dining table, sharing their personal backgrounds and family stories, it is also inevitable that they talk about the war and how they lived through it.

At home, Monnet describes to Silvia the personality of each negotiator. He is positive that together they will change the fate of Europe. He feels closest to the German, Hallstein. "It is obvious that from the start he understood that this is not an economic issue, but a union of spirits. He is a great support to me in the group." Silvia would love to meet all of them, so she suggests inviting them over the following weekend.

The negotiators spend Sunday with Jean, Silvia and the girls in Houjarray. After a nice walk through the countryside and a snack in the garden, they enjoy a simple Italian lunch washed down with French wine and accompanied by Monnet's juicy conversation, recounting youth adventures. Over coffee the animated conversation is cut short as they hear the news on the radio: war has broken out in Korea. The fragile balance of peace achieved after the second world war falters. Now it is more necessary than ever to advance towards the unity of Europe. If the US goes to war against the Soviet Union it will have fewer resources and will have to withdraw its troops from Europe. With the uncertainty of what will happen during those days, Monnet says goodbye to his fellow negotiators for a couple of weeks.

They resume work on 12 July. To the dismay of Monnet they all come back from the break with new orders. Their governments have "reprogrammed" them with their own national interests. To resume negotiations, smaller working groups based on production sectors are set up. To incorporate everyone's desires they create a new body: the Council of Ministers. It will be comprised of government representatives from the member countries. In addition to the Council and the High Authority, the institutional architecture is completed with a parliamentary Assembly and a Court of Justice.

The initial negotiating team has fulfilled its mission, and the upcoming phase of drafting the legal bases will be taken care of by jurists. As a farewell to the pioneers, Monnet invites Schuman to say a few words. The minister has avoided any interference in their discussions, but now that their work is over he willingly addresses them. As he sits at the table, he apologises for being "an outsider". And this is precisely what he wants to talk about: the need for the High Authority to be independent of economic and political interests, including national interests. Anyone who works for the High Authority must leave any nationalist sentiment at home in order to look for the common good in the most altruistic sense. Only by doing so will they give birth to a real community.

Despite the success of the negotiations, the fear of a third world war grips spirits and throws uncertainty on Europe's future. Schuman and Monnet are determined to continue, while the ups and downs of that hot summer end up favouring their interests: a governmental crisis brings down Bidault and he is replaced by René Pleven. Monnet is thrilled. He met the new prime minister a long time ago, even before he met Silvia. Actually, a young and successful Pleven was invited to that memorable business dinner where Jean fell in love with Silvia. Since then Pleven and the Monnets have become friends. Moreover, Pleven usually likes to hear Monnet's advice on the economy and foreign policy. On top of that, the new government will be happy to use Monnet's international contacts and friends.

Following guidelines set out from Washington, commissioner McCloy starts to say – first in private and then in public – that Germany must be able to defend itself. In late July, he tells journalists that Germany should have at least 50,000 troops. His statement is like a bucket of cold water on the French public opinion, which turns against Germany.

Adenauer reacts quickly, taking some distance. In no way would he want Schuman to interpret the American's position as a German betrayal. "Even if the allies asked me to, I would oppose any rearmament," the chancellor says in an interview, intended to be a signal to his French friends. "I would only accept a German Army within a European Army."

Monnet speaks in confidence with McCloy to understand the ultimate reasons for the American proposal. McCloy explains that the US is worried about the capacity of the Europeans to repel a potential Soviet attack on their own.

The Assembly of the Council of Europe meets in Strasbourg in August. As planned, Schuman speaks on 10 August to present the progress in the project for coal and steel. However the urgency is now far from the coal and steel mines: it is the potential breakout of another world conflict. At the opening, Spaak, as Chairman of the Assembly, adds to the agenda a discussion on the Korean war.

The next day, on 11 August, Churchill takes the floor:

"We are invited to approve the action of the United Nations in Korea and to proclaim our 'complete solidarity' with the resistance to aggression, the burden of which is now being borne by the United States, but which involves us all. No one can doubt what our answer will be or that the European Assembly will do its utmost to sustain the cause of freedom and the rule of law in the face of a most grievous and violent challenge. But what is our position here in these smiling lands and war-scarred cities, their peoples so rich in tradition, virtue and glory, striving to rise again from the consequences of the tragedies of the past? [...]".

"I am very glad that the Germans, amidst their own problems, have come here to share our perils and augment our strength. They ought to have been here a year ago. A year has been wasted, but still it is not too late. There is no revival of Europe, no safety of freedom for any of us, except in standing together, united and unflinching. I ask this Assembly to assure our German friends that, if they throw in their lot with us, we shall hold their safety and freedom as sacred as our own."

Members applaud. He goes further: it would be "futile and absurd" to discuss the future of Europe's role in the world without including the military dimension. And then he launches a proposal that has already crossed the minds of Monnet and Spinelli, but nobody expected to hear from Churchill's lips: the immediate creation of a common army subject to proper European democratic control. The Assembly approves the motion by an overwhelming majority.

The federalists see an opportunity: How can there be a European Army without a government? That same day Spaak introduces a petition for a federal union pact. When doing so, he highlights the political implications of a European Army.

Once again, however, Churchill raises high expectations among the federalists but his words are not followed by action. Neither he nor the Scandinavians are willing to let the Council of Europe's Assembly draft a Constitution for the alleged Federation. De Gasperi is truly disillusioned. He realises that this Assembly is not quite taking shape because it lacks courage.

However, some see things differently. Harold Macmillan, a Conservative MP, loses patience when he attends the endless discussions about institutions and federations. He thinks it is a waste of time to debate for hours on unfeasible projects. A federation is light-years away, and it would be best to discuss urgent, real and concrete problems.

During these days Adenauer is resting in Switzerland with his two daughters, Lotte and Ria. He suffers from pneumonia, and his doctor has advised him to get fresh air and steam treatments. Every morning he takes his breakfast on the terrace of his hotel in Burgenstock, overlooking the mountains, drinking a hot coffee and reading the newspaper. That's how he learns about the risky proposal made by Churchill in Strasbourg. His first reaction is one of anger. Despite his daughters, pleas to stay calm he remains agitated and can no longer enjoy his breakfast. He needs to speak to his cabinet and goes back to his room.

Churchill puts him in a difficult situation. Why is everyone talking on behalf of Germany? But as he considers the proposal carefully, he sees that it can be an advantage: the words of the British leader and the favourable vote by the Assembly actually put pressure on the allied powers: if a third world war broke out, German steel production would be determinant for victory on European land. The integration of mining production should be fast, he thinks. As soon as he arrives back in Bonn, he speaks with the three commissioners. He asks them to commit themselves to defending Germany in case of a Soviet attack and to let him create an equivalent force to the "people's police" in East Germany: 150,000 officers and same type of weapons.

September 1950, United States

In early September, the Schuman Plan conference resumes in Paris, but the attention of the French minister and of Monnet is elsewhere. They are thinking about the meeting that the allied powers will hold in New York at the same time as the United Nations General Assembly. Monnet fears that the UK and the US will insist on giving weapons to the Germans. Monnet wants to speak with Schuman in private to come up with a strategy. Definitely, the rearmament of Germany would spoil the coal and steel plan.

"It should not find us unprepared," warns Monnet. He doesn't question Adenauer's good will, but if Germany regained full sovereignty ahead of schedule, the incentive of the European Coal and Steel Community would disappear: The Schuman plan is based on France's magnanimity, agreeing to share resources with Germany while it is still controlled by external forces, as well as waiving its own right to claim war reparations.

"I am persuaded," says Schuman, "but the position of this government is simple: we will not talk about the rearmament of Germany, whatever the conditions. I prefer to think that the problem will not come up."

Despite the warning, Schuman gets caught off guard in New York on 12 September. Dean Acheson raises the issue:

"The United States is ready to take a step never before taken in history and send 'substantial forces' to Europe." However, they want the American combat force to be part of a collective defence capable of defending Western Europe on the ground. But the Americans will only take that step if the European allies do what is necessary to "make this defence of Europe a success". And it would not succeed without a German military contribution.

He asks the UK foreign secretary and the French foreign minister to accept the idea of German rearmament because the US urgently needs an answer.

"This force would consist of 60 armoured divisions, out of which ten should be German," Acheson adds.

Schuman looks pale. Until now, the Americans had only spoken of an economic or industrial contribution by Germany to Europe's defence. What he now hears involves armed Germans. This is absolutely unacceptable for the French and, as Monnet had wisely said; German rearmament would mean the failure of his peace plan.

Aware of Schuman's fearful reaction, Acheson states: "It is not about remaking the Wehrmacht, but including these units in NATO under a unified command with an overall supreme commander, who would most likely be General Eisenhower."

"But why precipitate events like this?" Schuman complains. "You can first make your unified command by integrating what already exists, and there will be time to add the Germans. Meanwhile, their contribution should be material."

The ministers negotiate for several days on the 37th floor of the Waldorf Astoria hotel. The positions do not change. The American insists on having Germany from the beginning. Schuman looks at his British counterpart, hoping that he will be on his side. But Bevin backs Acheson.

On 17 September Adenauer receives a call from New York. The allied ministers want to know how he feels about German participation in Europe's defence. "You ministers know that it is up to the Bundestag to decide on this issue. Only the Parliament can take a stand if a formal request is made to the government by the allies."

For Adenauer, things are going too fast. He wanted Germany to recover its sovereignty, but never imagined that he would decide on a German Army so soon. To show that the allies will not leave Germany alone in case of a Soviet attack, the three ministers announce on 19 September that there is only one legitimate Germany: the Federal Republic. Any attack against West Berlin or West Germany will be considered an attack on the allies. In addition, to demonstrate their willingness to return sovereignty to Germany, they will allow the country to handle its own diplomatic relations. They accept the creation of a federal police, but for the time being there will be no German contribution to European defence.

However, Adenauer is showered with criticism from across the German political spectrum. He had already expected criticism from Socialists and Communists – who oppose any kind of army –, but he faces as well harsh opposition within his own ranks. An influential Protestant group leads the friendly fire. Dr Martin Niemöller, the president of the Protestant Churches in Germany, already criticised the coal and steel community last year. He said it was "a baby conceived in the Vatican and born in Washington". Now he firmly fights rearmament. In his opinion, its promoters have not learnt the Second World War lesson and they contravene the pacifist desire of the German people.

On 4 October, Adenauer receives a very strong letter from Niemöller saying: "the German Evangelical Church informs you that it does not want to hear of any rearmament, be it in the East or the West". He reserves his right to advise his parishioners not to obey government decisions. Gustav Heinemann, Minister of the Interior, takes Niemöller's side so Adenauer dismisses him, much to his dismay. The chancellor strives to explain why Germany must show the Soviets that they can defend themselves. But most Germans think otherwise.

It is crucial for Adenauer to maintain the collaboration with France and makes it clear to McCloy: "We are willing to participate with a contingent to a European Army. Likewise, I formally state that I refuse the re-militarisation of Germany by creating its own national military force." The chancellor wants to talk about this issue directly with Schuman.

Autumn 1950, France

For his part, Schuman seeks the advice of Monnet, who sees only one way out: another surprise plan previously agreed with Adenauer. This time, the project will propose the creation of the European Armed Forces Monnet is clear:

"We only have a few days to invent such an army, for which there is no precedent or model. We cannot wait, as we had imagined, for a political Europe to be at the helm of an ongoing construction because a common defence can only be conceived under a common political authority."

Although the French government's official position is to reject any German rearmament, Schuman tells Monnet to go ahead. Hirsch, Uri, Reuter and Clappier start work on this new plan during breaks in the Schuman Plan conference. A new member joins the team, Hervé Alphand, a lawyer who served in the French Embassy in Washington during the Second World War.

The project must remain secret. It is important that the military doesn't find out, or they will be outraged. The experts will join later, because Monnet fears that technicalities may complicate things before a political agreement can be reached. This is the only way to prevent that on 28 October – when the next meeting of the three ministers is scheduled –, France finds itself isolated again. Monnet speaks on a daily basis with Pleven, who demands strong arguments to defend their proposal.

Above all things, Monnet wants France to keep the political initiative. Pleven recommends the following steps: before 28 October, the French government should reiterate its unwavering opposition, in the interest of Europe and of peace, to the reconstitution of a German Army. Then it will propose a military solution with the spirit and methods of the Schuman plan. There should be a common military command and a common budget, and ensuring that this solution will be implemented only once the European Coal and Steel Community (ECSC) is signed.

When the team finishes the first draft, Monnet and Schuman present it to Pleven:

"The setting up of a European Army cannot result from a mere grouping together of national military units, which would in reality only mask as a coalition of the old sort. An army of a united Europe, composed of men from different European countries, must, so far as is possible, achieve a complete fusion of the human and material elements that make it up under a single European political and military authority."

The overall idea seems good, but Pleven warns Monnet that he has gone too far by proposing that all military wear the same uniform, regardless of their country of origin. Monnet agrees to withdraw this paragraph in order not to offend patriots like de Gaulle.

On 24 October 1950, the French National Assembly listens for the first time to Pleven's Declaration for the creation of a European Defence Community (EDC), which would consist of a European minister accountable to a Council of Ministers and an Assembly. The new Defence community and the ECSC would share the same Council and the Assembly.

Faced with such a crazy plan, many MPs think that this is just a delaying tactic to derail the American plan to rearm Germany. It is not only in France that the plan is received with scepticism, the US also dislikes the idea and it doesn't even take it seriously.

Monnet understands that they urgently need to have a high-level private meeting with their partners to clarify things. In a more relaxed atmosphere, perhaps at home with Silvia and the girls, his plan will be better understood. So he invites McCloy, Pleven and Schuman for lunch at Houjarray. Monnet passionately defends the project and, from now on, McCloy also becomes a defender of the EDC. He assures his host that he will forward their message to Adenauer.

January 1951, Germany

The chancellor trusts his partners and favours a European approach to a defence system, but he does not like the Pleven plan as it has been conceived. It would assign some specific tasks that could be considered secondary and humiliating to the German contingent.

Adenauer accepts an invitation to attend the conference on the European army in January 1951, but he warns beforehand that he dislikes the solutions proposed by France. He asks Hallstein, who participated in the coal and steel negotiations in Paris, to inform his counterparts that "the Federal government does not approve of the Pleven plan, but accepts it as a basis for discussion."

Adenauer is willing to allow for his country's rearmament only on an equal footing with the others. He accepts for his country's sovereignty to not be fully restored as long as other states also accept to give up part of their own sovereignty to the Community.

Again he receives lots of criticism at home. Schumacher describes the Pleven plan as the "French Foreign Legion" and the right-wing politicians say that Germany should refuse to become "a nation of mercenaries".

In addition, animosity against the "westerners" grows among the German population because they perceive the ECSC as a French attempt to weaken German industry. And now more than ever, in the aftermath of the war, the Federal Republic requires a strong industry.

"We don't understand why the Allies insist on decartelising the industries of the Ruhr," Ludwig Erhard, the German Finance Minister, tells Monnet. "It is as if you were deliberately trying to put German industry in an inferior competitive position vis-à-vis its partners. But above all, in the spirit of the Schuman plan, it is unacceptable to continue to legislate for us as if there were no German government."

Monnet says that his goal is not to slow down Germany's recovery but just to avoid excessive concentrations of steel and coal mines of the Ruhr, where the former Konzerns – trusts which had embodied the Third Reich's military power –, were being reconstituted. In the end the text of the ECSC treaty is finished with a few clarifications and minor last minute changes. Now the task ahead is for Schuman and Monnet to explain the defence project to their ECSC partners, so that they also get involved.

February 1951, Italy

Alcide De Gasperi follows with dismay the vagaries of European integration. He and Sforza convey to Paris their disappointment in the new defence plan. They both expected that any integration plan would have emerged from the Council of Europe, the institution born after the Congress of The Hague. In their opinion, the Council of Europe should have already drafted a constitution for a federation.

To undo any misinterpretation, the Italian government invites French representatives to a bilateral summit in February. On the French side, René Pleven and Robert Schuman, his foreign minister, will attend and on the Italian side, De Gasperi and Sforza. The chosen location is Santa Margherita Ligure, in the Genoese Riviera.

Over the long hours at the Grand Hotel Miramare, De Gasperi and Sforza become persuaded that the Council of Europe, which faces strong opposition from the British and the Scandinavians, does not represent the best way forward towards a federation. Pleven proposes the functionalist method defended by Monnet: to expand the ECSC experiment to other sectors of the economy such as trade, transport and energy. The idea is to progressively extend the scope of the community despite the absence of a constitutional process. De Gasperi disagrees, for he prefers a European democratic entity with a Parliament where the sovereignty would lie.

Pleven and De Gasperi get locked in their debate as their views on how to build a united Europe are very different. Luckily, the amity between Schuman and De Gasperi facilitates a way out. The waterfront seems like a more suitable environment than the meeting room to continue chatting, and so they go out into the sun and the breeze.

Their lives have run along parallel paths as frontiersmen growing up in minority communities within larger empires, one in the Trentino region and the other one in Lorraine. For both, Europe is the only solution for stable peace. The issue that separates them is how to build it. De Gasperi wants a democratic structure, which would find its legitimacy in an assembly directly elected by universal suffrage. Schuman can envision such an organisation in the long-term. However the cold war and recent events put pressure to accelerate the process and they must therefore be pragmatic. After the long walk, De Gasperi promises to support the European Defence Community plan, while Schuman says he will do his utmost to persuade other partners that the EDC treaty should express the need for a political union to manage a common army.

Spring 1951, Paris

When the European Coal and Steel Community treaty is ready to be signed, the chancellor is invited in his capacity of foreign minister, which he assumed in March. The signing ceremony will take place in Paris on 18 April but the ministers should meet beforehand for a week to tie up the loose ends. For Adenauer, the journey is full of emotions. This is the first visit of a German ruler to the French capital since the war.

On 11 April in the morning, Adenauer gets on the private plane of André François Poncet, the French High Commissioner. During the flight, the chancellor often looks at his watch: it takes 20 minutes to cross Belgium, seven for Luxembourg, and half an hour later they arrive in Paris. "When you take a plane you realise to what extent our countries are linked," he tells Poncet shortly before landing.

No official welcome awaits him. To avoid any public protest, the French authorities decided to give a low profile to the visit. Schuman already agreed with the chancellor that he would not go to the Orly airfield. Instead, Jean Monnet is waiting at the steps of the plane.

"It is not without some emotion that I step onto French soil," Adenauer confesses to Monnet. "This the first official trip abroad that I make as chancellor and foreign minister, and I wanted the French capital to be the first place I visit."

Through the window of his room at the Crillon hotel, Adenauer gazes at the facade of the National Assembly. Many wrong decisions and mistakes against Germany were made there in the past. This time he and Schuman will try to act differently.

Things are already changing. That same day his visit to the president of the Republic, Vincent Auriol, fills him with optimism. In front of the Élysée Palace, the Republican guard honours him and the chancellor feels his historical responsibility.

The following day Adenauer begins the first working session at the Quai d'Orsay. Schuman chairs the meeting and the other ministers present are Count Sforza (Italy), Paul-Henri Spaak (Belgium), Dirk Stikker (the Netherlands) and Joseph Bech (Luxembourg).

The experts left some unresolved issues: where the seat of the High Authority should be, its composition, its staff and its powers. Regarding the Council of Ministers and the Common Assembly, the number of votes given to each member state, the voting method, the working language and the rights of the High Authority's chairman remain to be decided. And yet, despite that long list… the most difficult obstacle to an agreement is not on the agenda: the Saar question. Its integration into the coal and steel pool will solve some economic problems, but only France and Germany can decide on the final political status of the territory.

Schuman and Adenauer take a chance during a break in the meeting to discuss the issue privately in one of the empty lounges. Schuman reassures him that "France will respect the interests of Saarland within the pool in the same way it has always respected the Principality of Monaco."

"That's not enough," replies Adenauer. The SPD insists that the Schuman plan involves the tacit recognition of the final separation and the political independence of the Saar. Adenauer wants an explicit statement from the French government denying such claims.

Schuman proposes that they together find an acceptable solution for both the French Assembly and the German Parliament. Even though they do not reach an agreement on a specific solution, this gentlemen's agreement is sufficient guarantee to tie up the remaining loose ends of the ECSC and for both of them to sign the treaty with a clear conscience. They have already overcome other tense situations and by now they know they can trust each other because they share the vision of the relations between their countries and of Europe as a whole.

One day later the chancellor has the opportunity to explain to the European press how he sees the future of Germany. At the Parisian correspondents' club, Adenauer expresses with conviction that he and his ECSC partners will do everything within their power to "overcome pure rhetoric and truly implement the plans that we are proposing."

The process has already begun, and although in its infancy, the ECSC lays the foundation for a new era:

"Now a war between France and Germany has become not only unthinkable but materially impossible. The conclusion of the treaty establishing the coal and steel pool marks the solemn and irrevocable end of a past in which these two great peoples only ever found themselves facing each other with a gun in hand."

The unifying engine will be France and Germany, but it is open to all:

"The solution we have found is not only for us France and Germany, but it should benefit all of Europe, I would even say the whole world. The coal and steel pool has not been set up to separate Europe from the rest of the world, nor to extend the national egoism to continental limits."

He insists that the economy is just a tool; it is the cement to solidify the unit:

"It seems now that the day is not far off when the European peoples, full of freedom and rights, can come together under the same roof carrying the highly revered name of Europe. Such a truly new Europe, this paternal and common house of all Europeans should be the citadel of western and Christian tradition, a source of spiritual strength and a place of peaceful work."

Upon returning to the Crillon hotel that evening, he finds that someone has left an envelope for him at the front desk. His name is handwritten on it, with elegant calligraphy. He runs upstairs, but starts opening the envelope as he goes. He discovers a French First World War cross. In his room, he sits in an armchair to read the letter accompanying the medal. It was sent by Simone Patouilles, a Parisian student whose father died in that war. She wants Adenauer to keep the posthumous medal awarded to her father as a sign of the hope she places in reconciliation.

Adenauer, moved, answers immediately: "Dear mademoiselle, I have received with deep emotion your letter with your father's war cross. I want to see in this gift a symbol of the friendship which must now unite the youth of our two countries."

In an exultant mood Adenauer returns the next day to the last phase of the ECSC negotiations. Anything is possible with determination and he hopes that he and his colleagues will find a way not to disappoint so many millions of Europeans, people just like Simone Patouilles. They still need to agree on some points, and those last details take four days. Finally, on 17 April they close all the chapters, except for the seat of the High Authority.

Each participant defends his own turf: Van Zeeland proposes Liège; Stikker, The Hague; Sforza, Turin and Bech goes for Luxembourg... Schuman surprises them with the option of Sarrebrück. He believes that the Saarland could be granted a "special political status", the American-style federal capital advocated by Monnet, assuming that the local population will support the idea. Adenauer rejects it upfront, because in Germany it will look like a French stratagem to wrest the Saar, and therefore the Bundestag would reject outright the whole ECSC treaty. Schuman quietly gives up, and calls them to a meal break in order to continue the discussions in a more relaxed mood.

The afternoon and the evening go by and they cannot agree. At midnight there is still no decision... and they are not even close to an agreement. At 4 am the chancellor is already bored with all the comings and goings through the map of Europe. Aware that no German city will host the High Authority he goes to sleep. An hour later and out of exhaustion, they accept the partial solution proposed by Bech: Luxembourg will be the temporary seat until they agree on the permanent one.

And so, 18 April arrives, the date of signing of the ECSC where all loose ends are tied up except for the Saar. As Adenauer and Schuman don't want to paralyse the integration process of the six partners due to this standing issue, they commit themselves to finding a solution through a gentleman's agreement. At the request of Germany, it will be put in writing in the form of an exchange of letters from both governments:

"The definitive settlement of the status of the Saar can only be made by the Treaty of Peace or a similar Treaty. In signing the Treaty the government does not in any way express its recognition of the present status of the Saar."

Then the six ministers sign the text of the Schuman Plan in the same room where almost a year before it was presented to the international press. One of the Monnet staff, André Lamy, has prepared a surprise for signatories: a copy of the treaty issued by the French National Printing House on paper from Holland with German ink, with the binding taken care of by Belgium and Luxembourg, including Italian silk stitches.

Schuman has achieved his goal of signing the ECSC before negotiating German rearmament. The destinies of France and Germany are bound together. Changing the course of the two countries lies in his hands and those of Adenauer.

In late August, about to finish his summer break and to resume a busy schedule, the chancellor writes a letter to Schuman stressing the importance of the upcoming few weeks. He confesses that he considers "a providential sign and one particularly propitious that this difficult task" of completing the peace project lies with him, Schuman and De Gasperi, who have developed the same indomitable will to construct a new Europe built on Christian fraternity.

In his letter, Adenauer shares his views on De Gasperi, with whom he had a chance to get better acquainted during his first official visit to Italy in mid-June.[1] Also the Italian understands his political vocation on a peace-building mission, aimed at overcoming aggressive nationalisms. "In De Gasperi I found the true spirit of European policy," writes the German chancellor. Adenauer even claims to have lived the most beautiful moment of his life when walking and chatting with De Gasperi around the *Piazza del Popolo* in Rome.

He also speaks about an interview with Pope Pius XII, who received him in his private library and encouraged him to engage in the construction of Europe: a united, free and peaceful Europe. The Pope is concerned about the freedom of the individual against the fascist and communist totalitarianism, and the chancellor agrees with him on the need to establish new links and new elements of international solidarity. The Pope regards federalism in a positive light as a form of global political organisation, because it can guarantee peace.

Autumn 1951, West Germany

Despite the good omens, the chancellor feels once again let down on 24 September when he goes to see the French commissioner François

---

[1]   De Gasperi and Adenauer met for the first time in 1921, when the Italian accompanied D. Luigi Sturzo in a trip to Germany.

Poncet at his residence and is presented with a disappointing proposal for the recovery of German political autonomy. Adenauer cannot see the principle of equal rights he had discussed with Schuman. He cannot accept it. He wants to speak with the minister, because this new French attitude will inevitably affect the defence project: "There can be no 'community' where there is no trust," argues Adenauer.

Schuman invites Adenauer, as an equal, to the next meeting of the three administrative powers to be held in Paris. On 22 November the four men get together. Germany will regain its sovereignty and in return it will contribute financially to the defence of the West. The details of the contribution and the status of allied troops remaining in Germany will be settled in additional protocols to the agreement.

The country's image has deteriorated so badly that is hard to convince Europeans to trust Germany. Adenauer experiences this mistrust during his visit to London in early December. He is received with full honours at the airport, but on his arrival at Downing Street he finds the unpleasant surprise of a citizens' protest. About 300 people are waiting outside the residence of Winston Churchill, who is back in office. Some shout "Heil Hitler" and others "No weapons for the Nazis!"

The chancellor looks puzzled and concerned as he passes through the crowd. It is the most hostile reaction that he has encountered so far. Fortunately Churchill greets him warmly. The prime minister entertains him with a lunch attended by leading British personalities. As soon as the guests have left, Adenauer addresses what for him is an essential problem: the position of the United Kingdom with regard to European integration. During a visit to Germany, a British high official stated that the UK wants to be a 'good neighbour' to Europeans.

"I am always surprised to hear that the English consider Europeans only as good neighbours," says Adenauer sharply. Churchill, far from being annoyed by the comment, confirms that his vision of Europe does not include joining the common project. "It is not possible to completely eliminate national feelings. Germany and France should be friends and follow the same path," states Churchill. "Britain will do everything possible to help that Franco-German friendship."

The chancellor leaves London with the assurance of British military support, whatever the future of the EDC, although disillusioned by the blunt refusal of the British to engage in any kind of political union.

During the autumn, Schuman, Adenauer and De Gasperi coordinate a strategy. Italy and Germany would prefer the French to take the lead. In principle Schuman agrees, but De Gasperi's positions are much more ambitious than his. Also the French public opinion is far removed from the Italian one. Whilst in Italy federalist ideas and their main promoter Altiero Spinelli are quite popular, in France there are many doubts.

De Gasperi wants to use the European Defence Community as leverage to convene a Constituent Assembly and set the grounds for a federation. As it is a very sensitive issue, Schuman suggests waiting to discuss it in person in Strasbourg rather than speaking on the phone or by mail.

December 1951, Strasbourg

The Council of Europe Assembly meets on 10 December, and many expressions of frustration are heard in the room from those who believed there would be a move towards a federation.

Schuman is cautious:

"We have never doubted the need for such political integration. Our declaration of 9 May 1950, even then proposing the establishment of a European Coal and Steel Community, looked forward confidently to the ultimate constitution of a European Federation, without necessarily giving this word 'federation' its strict juridical meaning. The urgent need for a European policy made itself felt even more imperatively when the plan for a European Army came under consideration."

He points out the problem of creating an army for a non-existent political community: a de-nationalised army would no longer owe allegiance to a national authority. The only valid orders must come from an authority recognised by all participating states.

"What form will this supranational authority take? Who would be the Commander in Chief? He should be subject to the orders of a political authority. If the two powers, political and military, were united in one person the result would be a dictatorship."

He continues: "In the event of its formation, the European Army would be placed under the combined authority of six governments. How would this authority be exercised when it came to deciding whether or not the army should come into operation or be involved in war?"

The logic of national sovereignty suggests that states would use the right to veto, with the consequent inefficiency. The minister ends with a string of questions on who would form the college to decide any military action, who would appoint the members, and whether they would be responsible to a European Parliament or to national governments. He ends by admitting: "I am asking the questions, but I don't have the answers yet."

When Adenauer takes the floor he praises the achievements of the Council of Europe. When the pro-Europeans met in The Hague three years earlier, they wanted to have a permanent organisation and it now exists. And it will slowly advance towards a federation, "although we cannot yet provide an accurate picture of what kind of federation".

"The pursuing of the technical military plan itself has therefore compelled us to make a decisive contribution to the political integration of Europe, in the true sense of the term. A similar problem is posed when questions of the European Defence Budget are discussed. In both these cases, the question of European parliamentary control of the executive inevitably arises. So we see that in this manner we penetrate into the sphere of political integration immediately and very quickly. As similar necessities urge themselves upon us, also in the case of the other plans, it can easily be seen how urgent the need for these European political competences will be."

However, not everyone is ready to go that far, and the chancellor understands that there should be two ways: one for those willing just to cooperate, and a more in-depth organisation with a view on a political union:

"I believe that the participation of all European countries in the permanent political organisation of Europe, which is to be all-comprehensive as far as possible, should be the supreme and ultimate goal of our efforts. But I believe, too, that this aim is quite compatible with the existence of certain closer connections, of smaller circles within a Greater Europe. There will be certain communities, I imagine, that will combine in a particularly intensive and compact manner, namely those states which now already are prepared to surrender part of their sovereignty to a Community formed between them."

The chair of the Assembly, Paul-Henri Spaak, tries to remain neutral and to facilitate discussion, but he cannot hide his displeasure at the attitude of the British delegation, which openly opposes a federation. He realises that the Council of Europe works on a confederate vision and he wants something else. So he steps down. "Here the chances have become almost zero, it is time to look beyond these walls," he says as a farewell. Already in the corridors, he tells his friends: "Of all international organisations I know, I have never found one so timid, so helpless." He decides to join Spinelli's European Movement and to expend his energy in supporting the ECSC and the future project of the EDC.

Since they are all in Strasbourg for the Council of Europe Assembly, the six ECSC foreign ministers organise a parallel meeting. On the 11th, De Gasperi presents a revolutionary proposal, which he had mentioned in advance to Adenauer and Schuman: giving a constitutional mandate to the EDC Assembly.[1] This would answer Schuman's questions, because the Constitution would establish a federation with its governing body and its democratically elected parliament. The executive power should take the form of a college responsible to the Parliament. The Belgian and Dutch representatives do not like it. De Gasperi acknowledges that the parliamentary system may cause concern to countries with a small population, but he indicates that the Council of Ministers – in which all countries would have equal representation – would balance out the distribution of power.

Schuman does not wish to contradict his friend in front of others, so he says that he agrees in principle with De Gasperi but is concerned about the details. De Gasperi, who is already familiar with Schuman's personality, reassures him by saying that he is not proposing anything impossible. "I'm realistic, but the EDC has to offer more than NATO, and we must explain from the beginning what is the ultimate goal of this defence community that we want to create."

The Benelux participants express reserves, and Schuman mediates saying that the problem of definitive political institutions could be addressed later. But De Gasperi affirms the opposite: "We need to decide as soon as possible what the definitive representation organs will be. Only once they have been established, can we proceed to study the interim period."

Adenauer is silent, and it is clear that the Italian's insistence begins to unnerve the Benelux ministers. But De Gasperi does not give up. The Dutchman Stikker is really annoyed and complains about the Italian monopolising the discussion. So De Gasperi apparently concedes his defeat and lets the other ministers continue with other issues. However, in the afternoon, during one of the breaks, he approaches Schuman and invites him to go outside and speak in confidence. He explains the problems that he would encounter in the Italian Parliament if he were not able to clarify which political authority would control the new army. It was René Pleven, the French Prime Minister, who launched the proposal. Now the French cannot ignore the fundamental political decisions involved in their proposal. In addition, De Gasperi reminds Schuman of the overall aim of the project: brotherhood among peoples. And that fraternity requires an assembly where European citizens can elect their representatives.

While De Gasperi fails to dissipate Schuman's doubts, his passionate defence softens the French minister, who changes his attitude as he returns to the negotiating table. He proposes a new wording of Article

---

[1]   Since 26 July 1951, De Gasperi acts as foreign minister while Carlo Sforza becomes secretary of State for European Affairs.

7H, so that a transitional parliamentary assembly would set up another permanent assembly linked to the EDC whose members would be elected by universal suffrage. The transitional assembly would also study which powers the permanent parliament would enjoy.

Despite the discontent of Stikker and Van Zeeland, the ministers eventually accept Schuman's proposal. As he leaves the table, Schuman avoids De Gasperi's complicit look. Adenauer, on the contrary, goes up to De Gasperi with a sly smile. In the course of his long political career the chancellor has not often met a man with perseverance like his. Adenauer's resilience is legendary, but in De Gasperi he has found his match.

January 1952, West Germany

Back home, the chancellor will need all his energy to get the Bundestag to ratify the ECSC treaty. So far, Schumacher remains opposed.

On 9 January the debates begin and they last for three days. In the first two ballots, Adenauer fails to gain enough support. He tries to convey to the MPs what's at stake for the country:

"Our people, Europe and the world await our decision. You have to say whether you are for or against Europe. The Federal Government asks everyone, regardless of their political party, to speak out in favour of Europe as the French Assembly and the Dutch have done. The unity of Europe depends on your assent. I ask you, ladies and gentlemen, to make a decision which is in keeping with the task ahead of us."

The Schuman plan would allow Germany to come out of isolation for the first time since the war:

"We have been feared opponents. Then we became a people under occupation. Tomorrow we will be partners. Above all, it is important to convey with conviction the message that the Germans are a peaceful nation, a nation which desires the community of peoples and intends to live with all the other free peoples of the world in peace, friendship and freedom."

He cannot persuade them all. The Bundestag ratifies the Treaty of the ECSC on 11 January 1952 without the support of the Social Democrats, the Communists and some independent members. The chancellor regrets their decision because he thinks the vote is a landmark opportunity for all groups to unite. But the important thing is that he has achieved his goal: ratification.

The Old Chancellor, Konrad Adenauer

Konrad Adenauer in Rhöndorf, Germany (© European Parliament)

The sullen countenance, the hard features, the deep furrows and the scars left on his face by a car accident are the traces of a life filled with suffering. Konrad Adenauer became tough in the face of adversity, and that turned him into a virtually unassailable fortress to his opponents. Despite his age, his physical and emotional resilience are unbeatable. His grey-blue eyes, with their penetrating gaze, rarely disclose his feelings; except when he is angry.

He has inherited an irascible temper that he tries to tame; a temper his family and colleagues know only too well. When his parents argued, his father would leave home to avoid confrontation and to get some air, returning after a few hours having calmed down. Adenauer himself has learned to imitate him and also seeks solitude whenever he is upset. If he is at home, he goes out to the terrace to take care of his rosebush. In fact, his best childhood memories are from the garden, where the task bestowed by his parents consisting in taking care of the plum tree and the pots became the best therapy to release tension and soothe his spirit.

At home they did not speak a lot, and affection was expressed through quiet sacrifice. Misfortune had beset his father, and the premature death of Konrad's younger sister had changed the mother's character. Helene was by nature optimistic and full of vitality. Konrad remembered her singing in the kitchen while she cooked and the children hovered around her. Helene was happy when the first girl was born after three boys. But the little baby fell ill shortly after birth. For weeks Konrad, who was then six years old, heard his mother and his sister crying at night. Helene was constantly praying for her daughter's recovery, but as the days went by, the illness worsened and doctors no longer gave them any hope. Then Konrad and his father prayed for God to take her away soon. When the baby died, the mother gave herself into a continuous mourning. But she never lost her faith. Konrad was deeply affected by the loss of his sister and the void she left in his mother. It felt as if someone had turned off the lights in the house.

The father, who was 16 years older than his wife, was sober and taciturn. Even though he was a hard worker, he could not provide his family with the comforts he would have liked. Konrad's paternal grandfather worked as a baker in Bonn and never sent his son to school, not even to primary education. Konrad's father worked in a farm first and then enlisted in the army with the hope that it would help him get a job in the civil service. But in the battle of Sadowa[2] he was badly wounded and became crippled. When he returned, all he found was a modest job as a clerk in the court of Cologne.

---

[2]   The Austrian Empire and Prussia fought a battle in Sadowa, which was at the time part of Bohemia (today Czech Republic) in July 1866.

Konrad and his family lived in only a quarter of a two-story house in the Balduinstrasse. Hardship led them to sublet the second floor and half of the first one. In such a small space for five people, the three boys slept in the same room, and then some years later another sister was born. Konrad was the youngest boy, after August and Hans. The father used to give his entire salary to Helene, who managed the domestic finances and worked wonders to make ends meet.

The children were diligent and easily passed their exams. Konrad had good grades, but he did not stand out in any particular course. He was somehow solitary and his favourite activity was reading, especially Jules Verne novels and *David Copperfield*, by Charles Dickens, which he read four times.

When the boys were a little older they began to give private lessons to help at home. They gave all the money to the mother, and they would not allow themselves to indulge any whim. Despite their efforts it was a very hard existence. So to increase their revenue, the mother would clean the tenants' apartments and do some needlework. In the evening she sewed with the dim light of a kerosene lamp, and Konrad sometimes helped her after school.

The tenant upstairs, called Tonger, became like one of the family. He was single and enjoyed spending time with the Adenauers. Tonger was Konrad's godfather and Helene looked after him when he fell ill with severe pneumonia. When he died, he left everything he had to the Adenauers: 30,000 marks. And to his godson a gold watch that the chancellor always kept with affection.

Tonger's money was a relief for the everyday life and brought hope to the boys. Konrad's father invested the money in shares in the industry sector, expecting that it would gain interest and cover the college expenses of the three. However, when Konrad finished high school and wanted to study law in 1893, there was almost no money left. A portion had been spent on Hans' and August's studies, and another part had been lost in the financial ups and downs of a volatile financial period of speculation.

The parents, who had not touched any of the money themselves, would have liked to give the same chances to their youngest son. His father encouraged Konrad to work in banking. He praised his commercial skills, his good sense for the administration, and told him that he would do very well in that field without studying. Konrad was well aware of his father's sadness and sense of guilt for not being able to pay for his school. The boy did not want to cause him any more pain, so he did not insist and accepted the job at the bank, pretending to like it.

In 1894 he began an internship at the Segimann bank in Cologne. It turned out to be a horrible experience. He had to get up very early to be the first one there, because the main task was opening the door, taking out the accounting books from the safe and placing them on the desks. Later in the day, he served coffee to employees and, whenever necessary, he took the telegrams to the Post Office. He said nothing, he did not complain. But he arrived home every evening dejected. After two weeks, his father asked him to sit down with him and have an honest chat. He and his mother had been discussing it. They would reduce their expenses whatever the cost and pay the little they could for his university studies. He also recommended him to look for a grant to complement the income.

With his parents' support Adenauer quit the job and enrolled in the Faculty of Law at the University of Freiburg, close to the Alsace. He had no fixed monthly allowance but his parents sent him as much as they could, usually around 90 marks. It was not much, but he was not out of place amidst his classmates. Most of the students were also sons of low civil servants or small traders. As soon as he arrived Adenauer signed up for the local Catholic student association called Breisgau, where he met most of his friends. He never felt ashamed of his insolvency as he was accustomed from childhood to living with little, and did not suffer in Freiburg.

The Breisgau boys made excursions to the Black Forest. Adenauer enjoyed the outdoor activities because of the beautiful nature and the physical challenge. In the mountains he discovered his extraordinary strength. One Saturday they went hiking to the highest peak of the Black Forest, the Feldberg. The trip got out of hand. After a long day's march they reached the mountain after nightfall. After just two hours sleep the young men descended the mountain and arrived back at their residence at dawn. When they left the previous day there were 13 boys in the group, but many decided to stay in little villages along the way when they saw that it was getting dark because they were already exhausted: Titisee, Menzenschwand, Himmelreich... those who finished the round trip had walked 85 km, but only three of them made it home on time on Sunday afternoon. And out of those three, only Adenauer showed up in class the following morning at 8 am.

In the first semester Konrad met Raimund Schlüter, who would become his best friend; in fact, his only true friend. Like him, Raimund was a very quiet boy who came from a poor family hit by tragedy. The son of a farmer in Westphalia, he had moved to Cologne with his father to start a new life. The mother and brothers had died of tuberculosis within a short time of each other. The father sold the farm, took the money and went south, seeking the best for the child.

With Raimund, Konrad could speak with full sincerity about his childhood experiences. When Konrad decided to leave for a semester to

Munich, Raimund followed. They spent a very happy six months in the Bavarian city. They would walk through the majestic avenues and along the Isar River, under the shade of the chestnut trees. They visited all the museums and in the afternoon they would go to the theatre and to the opera whenever they found affordable standing room tickets. Back then, Konrad was still passionate for Richard Wagner, a composer he would distance himself from over the years.

During the holidays, Konrad and Raimund travelled together to Switzerland, Italy and Bohemia. Sometimes they went on foot, sometimes by train. They would stay over at farms or in shelters, enjoying the adventures of travelling. Upon their return, the two decided to continue law in Bonn. They studied a lot, and Konrad graduated in the shortest possible time: three years.

After they both passed the final examination, it was time to say goodbye. Adenauer found a job in Bonn, while Raimund moved to the town of Schwäbisch Gmünd, near Stuttgart. They often wrote to each other, sharing the latest news of their life. Only a few months after they separated, Raimund had great news: he was in love and wanted to marry. He was anxious to introduce his girlfriend to Konrad.

Two weeks before the wedding Raimund was found dead in his bed, with a prayer book on the nightstand. Konrad was told that he had suffered a stroke. Adenauer never spoke about his friend again, and went through a difficult process of maturing in his faith. The death of his sister had marked him as a child, and this new misfortune forced him to face his doubts.

Although he felt the nearness of a God he had been speaking to since childhood, he could not grasp the meaning of death and suffering. He had received religious education from his parents, but this was not enough as an adult. He needed his own answers. He found them by reading Christian writers, in particular two works by the Protestant Swiss philosopher Carl Hilty: *Happiness* and *What is faith?* They explore the ultimate sense of the inevitable tragedies and violence in all lives. "Only those who have experienced firsthand the suffering of winter can enjoy the fruits of spring," wrote Hilty.

With the impression of having been forced to mature in just three years, Adenauer returned to Cologne to his family. He got a job in the prosecutor's office and gained prestige as a lawyer. In parallel, he began to acquire political influence through a Catholic group in the city council, and lost no time in becoming its president.

It was around that time when he met Emma Weyer, his future wife. They both frequented a tennis club very popular among university students and girls of the local bourgeoisie. Emma belonged to a well-known and prosperous family in Cologne. Adenauer, although coming from a much more humble background, had already proved that he was a responsible man and capable of sustaining a family. Emma's mother appreciated the fact that the young lawyer seriously fulfilled his religious duties.

They became engaged in 1902, and she started writing love poems almost daily. Konrad, who was very discreet and uncommunicative, felt moved by Emma's poetry. He also liked to go with her to social gatherings where he could meet the interesting and influential characters of the city.

They married in January 1904 and settled in a small apartment in Cologne-Lindenthal. She was always supportive and encouraged him to take up a political career, because she saw that he had a talent and truly enjoyed discussing projects to improve the city.

In 1905 Konrad joined the *Zentrum* party, and a year later he was a candidate for city council. He won easily, but the joy of victory did not last long: three days after the elections his father died of a heart attack.

A few months later, in autumn, his first son was born. They named him after his father and grandfather, Konrad, but soon everyone was calling him Coco. The baby's arrival opened a period of personal and professional happiness for Adenauer. In 1909, at age 35, he was elected deputy mayor of Cologne. The new responsibilities also meant a bigger wage, allowing him to afford a more comfortable life-style. Two years later he built a house at number 6 in the Max-Bruchstrasse, as the family kept growing.

In 1910 his son Max was born, bringing both joy and sorrow to the couple. Emma's first delivery had been complicated and had caused a curvature of her spine that damaged her kidneys. With each new birth her health worsened to the point that she lost mobility with the arrival of their third child, a girl they named Ria. Thereafter, she could only go from the bed to the sofa and vice versa.

Konrad tenderly took care of her and the children with help from his mother, Helene. He was strict and demanding as a father. He educated his children in the Spartan austerity he had grown up with. At home there was no drinking, no smoking, and he almost never bought clothes. As long as mending could fix any holes and the cloth was clean, all clothes and shoes were re-used.

Family happiness was tarnished by Emma's illness and the outbreak of the First World War. Adenauer was given the responsibility of guaranteeing supplies to the city of Cologne. In order to feed and keep warm up to 600,000 people he signed several agreements with farmers in neighbouring regions. He would spend his time between the office and his wife's bed. Sunday was devoted entirely to the children. He would take them to Siebengebirge, and would take the opportunity to take long walks in the mountain to chat with them, tell them stories and share laughs.

Although Emma tried to encourage the children and her husband, in the last months of illness she became unable to hide her distress. In December 1915, when they were all gathered around the Christmas tree, Konrad noticed that she had crept out of the room. He found her sobbing in the hallway. She did not want the children to see her crying, so little by little she enclosed herself in her room without letting anyone enter except Konrad. Despite all the troubles at the city hall, he went home for lunch every day to see Emma and returned to his office in the afternoon. He finished as soon as possible in the evening to go back home and sit at the foot of her bed, take her hand and keep her company.

Emma died on 16 October 1916. For months Adenauer couldn't find the strength to look after the children. His mother Helene took care of them while he took refuge in his office and always arrived home very late.

He was still mired in depression over the loss of his wife when he suffered a spectacular car accident that shattered his face. The neighbours, the Zinssers, felt pity for Emma's illness and subsequent death, for the misfortune of Adenauer and the sadness of the whole family. They invited the children over and the daughters of Professor Zinsser played music for them. The three Zinsser sisters played the piano, violin and cello. While Adenauer was in the hospital, his children became very close to the neighbours as they waited for their father to come back, without knowing how his health would be.

At first the doctors thought he would stay blind, but after some months he regained sight and went back to work. The children were eager to see him, because they feared that they would lose both their mother and father within a few months of each other. Adenauer understood his children's needs and gradually regained the habit of going home for lunch, talking to them and going hiking together.

In 1917, Konrad became mayor and threw himself into an ambitious plan to modernise Cologne. He tore down the walls around the city to make it a green belt; he expanded the river port and built a second bridge. He developed the skills of a superb negotiator, becoming a master in exhausting the opponent. He called meetings and prolonged them infinitely, aware that the others would just get tired and give up. "Whoever resists, wins," was his motto. That's how he managed to impose his view to build the Molheim Bridge, even though the project he liked was rejected by a majority vote in the council. He went around the issue so many times, asking again and again without accepting defeat, that in the end the rest of the council members yielded to his wishes.

As the youngest mayor in Germany he gained a reputation at state level. He was very active in national politics and became chairman of the Prussian Upper House, where regions were represented. In the debate over how to pay compensation to France for the first world war, some in Berlin proposed giving a piece of German territory to France: the west bank of the Rhine, the so called Rhineland. Adenauer opposed the split of Germany and put forward a counter proposal: the autonomy of the Rhineland. He would rather have a government independent from France and linked to Prussia. He feared that the Berlin government would sacrifice the Rhineland's citizens to avoid the payment of high fees as war compensations and he rejected annexation of his region to France. So in his eyes autonomy was the best compromise.

His political career was taking hold and the house, little by little, was joyful again. Adenauer's children had become regular guests at Zinssers' and he occasionally accompanied them. One of the neighbour's daughters, Auguste, felt a profound admiration for the mayor and often went over to his house to chat and to exchange tips on gardening. When the girl's parents learned that Konrad was formally courting Gussie – which is how they called their daughter –, they were not happy. She was only 19, almost the same age as Adenauer's children – the oldest was 13 years old – and on top of the age difference, the Zinssers were Protestants.

Gussie was willing to do anything to marry Adenauer, and agreed to convert to Catholicism, which was a prerequisite for him. Despite their initial fears, the family finally granted Gussie's hand in September 1919, and the couple got married in a ceremony officiated by Hans (Konrad's brother), who had been ordained a priest. The honeymoon was not very exciting, for the mayor could only take a few days off so they just went to a nearby village.

They had their first son, Ferdinand, in June 1920. But again misfortune pursued Adenauer: Gussie suffered from a kidney disease during her pregnancy and the baby died four days after birth. Adenauer was devastated thinking that she would also die with the same condition as poor Emma. Fortunately, he was wrong. She recovered fully and a healthy child was born soon after in 1923. He was called Paul, and was followed by three siblings: Lotte (1925), Libeth (1928) and Georg (1931).

Germany was going through troubled times amidst financial problems, rampant inflation, the heavy compensation burden of the First World War and growing social instability. However Adenauer at last enjoyed a few years of relative happiness and a brilliant professional career began to thrive. His name circulated as the potential *Zentrum* candidate to lead the government.

But problems erupted for him in 1933. Adolph Hitler's populist message had convinced many and in the July 1932 elections the Nazis won a major victory with 37.3% of the votes. On 30 January 1933 President Paul von Hindenburg agreed to appoint Hitler as chancellor.

A few weeks later Hitler announced that he would attend a party congress in Cologne. The National-Socialist Party asked the mayor to deploy the swastika flag on the facade of the city hall to welcome the new chancellor. Adenauer refused to do so. He disliked the Nazi party's authoritarianism. He responded that the city was a neutral institution and therefore it never deployed flags of a particular political party.

When on 17 February the *Führer* came to Cologne, Adenauer did not go to the airport to greet him. Although he had clearly stated his refusal to deploy the national-socialist symbols, several Nazi activists hung their huge swastika over the Cologne-Deutz Bridge. As soon as Adenauer found out, he ordered a city official to go with the police and remove it, and to tell the Nazi activists that the flags would be placed in the room where their meeting was to be held.

From then on, the National Socialists did all they could to make the mayor's life unbearable. They spread rumours accusing him of lacking patriotism. They purposely distorted his proposal for an autonomous Rhineland – which he once proposed as a way to avoid the region's annexation to France – portraying him as a traitor who sought independence. Once the false accusations had penetrated into the public opinion, the Nazis offered protection to Adenauer against potential attacks from angry citizens or groups. The mayor obviously refused.

Adenauer felt increasingly threatened, to the point where one day a trustworthy person told him that the Nazis were planning a terrorist attack against him. The following Monday someone would go up with him to his office and push him out of the window, pretending a fatal accident or a suicide. This was too much. Full of anger and fed up with living in constant anguish he travelled to Berlin to complain directly to Hermann Goering, the founder of the Gestapo and Hitler's interior minister. Adenauer told Gussie that he would be back in a few days. Little did he imagine how things would get complicated.

On 13 March the newspapers announced that the mayor had fled Cologne and he was therefore dismissed. Of course Adenauer was unaware of the news from his home town, as he was waiting in Berlin to be received by Goering. It took three days for the minister to meet him. And then all he said was that they had nothing to talk about because there was an ongoing investigation: "Mr Adenauer, why did you order the flags to be removed from the bridge during the visit of the *Führer*?"

"I did it because I had the impression that most people did not want those flags displayed there. They were put up at night without the consent of the local authority," replies Adenauer.

"I have asked the former secretary of state, Schmidt, to open an investigation on you. He will study whether the accusations against you in Cologne are true." is Goering's retort.

He never heard from Goering again. He learned that a Nazi official had replaced him in the city hall and was pursuing those who had collaborated with Adenauer. He decided to write a letter to the new mayor, Günter Riesen, asking him to leave his assistants and colleagues in peace and to give him the opportunity to defend himself publicly. He appealed to his sense of justice and institutional loyalty.

Riesen's answer, dated 21 March in Cologne, was blunt: He did not even want to listen to the former mayor. "The charges against you made public so far are just the beginning," he said in a written response. "You are a criminal, Mr Adenauer. You are a criminal to the people who had put their trust in you and whom you brought to a state of extreme poverty. You are a criminal against the city you have ruined, to officials dependent on you and to those from whom you have taken away all human dignity. Many of them would have been perfectly honest without your influence, and instead are now facing serious charges. You are a criminal, guilty of crimes against your family and your wife, for whom, in her blissful ignorance, I can only feel sorry. You are guilty of crimes against our Lord God and against all those who have come into contact with you. You are the accused; I am your accuser; the people are your judge. That is the position between us."

He was without a job, without money, far from his family and trying to defend himself from the accusations of mismanagement. But the National-Socialists made every effort to discredit him. One of the most bizarre situations occurred during a popular fair in Rhöndorf in 1935. A municipal band enlivened the festivities and in deference to the former mayor, the director asked if Adenauer had any special request for a song. Konrad liked a military piece called the *Deutschmeister Marsch*. As the band was not familiar with that particular march they offered instead to play a similar one, the *Badenweiler Marsch*, which happened to be Hitler's favourite piece.

When the Nazis heard about it they thought that Adenauer intended to make fun of the *Führer*. They considered it a grave insult and in retaliation he was forbidden to enter the city of Cologne. He was forced to stay on the other side of the Rhine, isolated from his family. His wife and children crossed over every day to keep him company and bring food. The punishment lasted several months. Once he was free, the whole family left Cologne and moved into the house that Adenauer had built in Rhöndorf, on the slopes of a mountain near Bonn, in an area of vineyards overlooking the Rhine. When he was building it he thought it would be his holiday house, where they could go on weekends and in the summer. But now it became their permanent residence.

Unable to clear his reputation or to continue in politics, he withdrew from any public activity. He found himself again in economic hardship and with no short-term solution on the horizon. Overnight, at the age of 60, he had become a virtually anonymous old man in his retreat. He would help Gussie at home, plant trees and flowers in his garden and entertained himself and the boys by designing inventions and original devices. Things improved thanks to the mayor who took over from the despotic Riesen, as he pitied Adenauer and granted him a modest pension.

The two elder sons, Max and Konrad, were forced to enlist in the army when the Third Reich began its military campaigns. The father stayed home with Gussie, his daughter Ria – whose husband was an engineer and was also obliged to join the army –, the sons' wives, Adenauer's younger children and grandchildren.

Although someone would show up in Rhöndorf occasionally to talk about conspiracies and subversive plans, he preferred not to know about such issues. However, in 1944 two men came to inform him about an operation that had been cooked up in the greatest secrecy, aimed at overthrowing the regime by killing Hitler. Only a few people were aware of it. One of them was Carl Friedrich Goerdeler,[3] a Conservative politician. The mayor had little hope in their success and found their methods immoral, so he refused any involvement.

The bomb attack against the Führer was undertaken on 20 July that year, but the coup was unsuccessful. Hitler survived and the Nazis spitefully retaliated: 200 men were automatically put to death accused of conspiracy and 5,000 others would pay with their lives in the following months.

One day in August, very early in the morning, Konrad and Gussie woke up to the sound of someone banging on their door. Adenauer himself went down to open. Two policemen came to take him with them. They would not elaborate on the reason. He obeyed, leaving his wife and children with the uncertainty of when he would return.

He spent the first days of captivity in the Kreuzbergweg police headquarters in Bonn, where Nazis were "storing" prisoners before

---

[3]   Goerdeler was a member of the German National People's Party (DNVP).

sending them to concentration camps. After a few days he was sent to a labour camp near Bonn.

The most distressing for Adenauer were the barrack bunks, where they were piled in to sleep without any privacy. He was on the brink of a depression when an unexpected friendship with a communist activist brought a new light. It was Eugen Zander, who had already served nine years for his alleged "subversive activities" when Adenauer arrived. In recognition of his seniority, the Nazis had appointed Zander the concentration camp's *kapo*. His mission was to welcome the newcomers and to help them adjust. He enjoyed the privilege of a room to himself.

He immediately recognised Adenauer from the photos he had seen in the newspaper. So he introduced himself to the old man with great respect, addressing him as "mayor" from the outset. A few days later Zander noticed that the mayor was ill. He was thinner and his face had visibly deteriorated: his cheeks were red and swollen. Adenauer explained that the noise of his cellmates and the bed bugs prevented him from sleeping. So Zander asked permission to invite the former mayor to settle in his room with him. It was granted.

Adenauer improved daily, but he was still in very low spirits. Once, Zander saw him coming back sorrowful from the patio. He had seen his wife and daughter Ria in the distance. They were trying to get closer and speak with him, and when they had almost succeeded a sentry ordered them to go. A few days later Gussie returned. The last time she came she had seen where her husband lived, so this time she directly went to his building bringing some food with her. From that day on, she would periodically bring him food and warm clothing, which he shared with his fellow prisoners. Zander valued his generosity, but complained about the flow of 'friends' who would come to his room looking for Adenauer's gifts.

At the camp, the former mayor missed the musical evenings back home, so he organised performances in the camp. He managed to find some instruments and several prisoners who could play. Zander himself could play the guitar, Adenauer the violin and two other inmates accompanied them on the mandolin. One evening the little group gave a recital of two of Adenauer's favourite composers: Mendelssohn and Meyerbeer. Both Jews! Suddenly, in the middle of the recital, the door opened. The chief commander of the camp came in with his dog, and all the prisoners had lumps in their throats. They thought it was the end... and then they realised that the top official did not know the composers and was there only to enjoy the music, just like them.

Although they tried to lead as normal a life as possible, distress was permanent. Every day a convoy would leave the camp with people who were being taken to extermination camps. At night they heard the patrols taking people from the barracks. The following morning, the names of those missing were published under the heading: "Escape attempts".

One day Zander heard that Adenauer would be on the list the next day and would be transferred to the extermination camp at Buchenwald. He told his friend and together they devised a plan. Zander trusted the prison's doctor and shared his concern about Adenauer with him. The doctor came into the room to examine the patient and told the security chief that Adenauer was suffering from a serious heart condition and had to be taken to hospital. The commander was very upset by this unexpected setback, but agreed to take him to St. Elizabeth Hospital in Cologne. Zander went with him in the ambulance. As he held his hand, sitting next to the stretcher, Adenauer assured him: "I will never forget what you are doing for me, Eugen."

The medical director of the hospital, professor Uhlenbruch, was an old acquaintance of Adenauer's. He allowed his family to see him, and all together came up with a plan to escape. At first they thought about just disappearing at night, but that would have put Uhlenbruch in an indefensible situation, so they decided instead to include him in the plan, and he accepted. So did a friend of Adenauer's, Hans Schliebusch, who at the time was a commander of the Nazi Air Force, the Luftwaffe.

One morning commander Schliebusch arrived at the hospital in an official car. He went straight to the administrator's office and gave an order: he had to take Adenauer to Berlin for interrogation. It was a false order, and Gussie was waiting in the back seat of the car. The head of the hospital could thus easily obey the official without risking his own career or even his life. The commander fled with the couple to Bonn, where they took shelter in a friend's house. Upon arrival they found that the hosts were petrified and only allowed them to stay overnight.

The next day, the three drifted apart to lower the risk of travelling together. Gussie returned to Röhndorf as if nothing had happened. The following day she would go to the hospital, as usual, and would pretend to be shocked at not finding her husband. Then after two or three days she would report his disappearance.

Adenauer was given the contact details of the Roedigs, a family living in a mill located in a tiny village about 70 kilometres southeast of Cologne called Nistermühle. When he arrived he introduced himself as Dr Weber. The couple knew that this was not his true identity, but it was safer for them not to know who their guest was. Adenauer could not complain about life there, as he spent his time reading and walking in the countryside. Meanwhile, the allied troops advanced and the shelling over Germany was more frequent. Also the Gestapo had intensified its search for opponents.

On the morning of 24 September two agents arrived in Rhöndorf looking for Mrs Adenauer. They had learned that her husband had fled the hospital and wanted to question her. She was alone with Libeth, the youngest daughter, who could not prevent her mother from being taken away. She was only allowed to take a toilet bag.

She was transferred to the Gestapo headquarters in Cologne where she underwent a gruelling interrogation. She ended up unveiling her husband's hideout faced with the threat that they would retaliate against her two daughters who were left home alone. Then she was interned in the Brauweiler prison, where she attempted to commit suicide with an overdose of sleeping pills and by cutting her wrist. She was distraught for having betrayed Konrad. They found her in time to save her life, but she would bear the physical and psychological scars for the rest of her life.

The morning after Gussie's confession, the Gestapo showed up at the mill. Adenauer had been hiding there for only two weeks and that precise day was his and Gussie's silver wedding anniversary. The officers found Adenauer in his pyjamas, huddled in the attic of the mill. When he was discovered, he stood up with utmost dignity and asked to be allowed to dress.

He invited them to breakfast to celebrate his anniversary and then they drove to the Brauweiler prison, unaware that his wife was only a few metres away in the same building. He was locked in a tiny cell, unheated, dark and with only a small barred window. They barely fed him. He asked for a blanket, a book, a pen and some paper to write. But they denied him all of these, as well as his request to see a priest.

After five days of confinement he was weak enough to be interrogated. As soon as he was in front of the prisoner, inspector Bethge went up to him and told him right away – with a mischievous smile – that it was his wife who had tipped off the Gestapo about his hiding place. "She did well," Adenauer replied, leaving no room for further interrogation along those lines. The inspector wanted to know why he rejected the Nazi Party and about his involvement in the bomb plot against Hitler. Adenauer did not answer, because he had nothing to say. So after a while he was left alone. However after the interrogation the doctor found that the health of the former mayor had seriously deteriorated and recommended that he be transferred to an ordinary cell and to have better food. The guardian who was in charge of his new cell treated him better and allowed him to read and write.

When her mother was taken, Libeth ran to tell her siblings. She sent a telegram to Max, who was serving at the front as an officer, and she also sent another telegram to the General Consul of Switzerland in Cologne, a good friend of the family. The Consul had left Cologne, but returned as soon as he received the news from Adenauer's daughter.

Max received the telegram from his sister on 4 October 1944 but had to wait 20 days to receive the permit to go and see his father. On 26 October, he finally arrived at the prison. He was shocked when he saw to what extent his father had aged in such a short time. He thought he would only be able to see him for a few minutes, but they were allowed to spend three hours together. The old man did not complain, except for the cries he frequently heard from other prisoners while they were being tortured, as his cell was directly above the interrogation room. He was not mistreated, even though he was questioned repeatedly until they realised that he really had nothing to do with the attack on Hitler.

The son was outraged when he said goodbye, and determined to free his father. He travelled straight to Berlin and it did not take much effort to convince the authorities to free Konrad and Gussie. "What do you think the reaction of a soldier at the front is when he learns that his parents have been arrested without cause and are locked in prison?" he told the head of the police. A few days later Mr and Mrs Adenauer were united with their daughters and daughters-in-laws in Rhöndorf.

The family went through the throes of war together. With almost no food, no water, no heating, they longed for the arrival of the Americans. They spent the last week before the liberation like most other families: in the basement of the house to protect themselves from the shelling.

On 6 March the US troops entered Cologne. A delegation went to Rhöndorf to ask Adenauer, in perfect German, to resume his duties as mayor. He wanted to accept but urged them to wait until the final victory and suggested that, in the meantime, he could be an advisor. The reason behind this request was that the war was not yet over – it would last two more months – and he had two sons fighting in the front against which the Nazis could retaliate. The Americans agreed and asked him to accompany them in a tour around the city centre.

Cologne was destroyed. Only 300 houses remained intact. Also the council was in ruins. The first thing that Adenauer advised the Americans to do was to rebuild the bridges so that help could arrive. People lacked everything: food, fuel, medicines… and Adenauer also missed the team he used to work with. The few officials who had stayed in the city had joined the Nazi party and were therefore excluded from any public service. This was a decision taken by the occupying powers.

Adenauer focused on the most basic needs of the population: hunger and cold. He organised teams of volunteers and he temporarily requisitioned vehicles so that the volunteers could go to the countryside and bring food: mainly potatoes, cereals and pulses. The accommodation was more complicated, as each day between 6,000 and 7,000 people returned, mostly on foot, from all parts of Germany.

That spring the US forces liberated the Buchenwald concentration camp, where Adenauer could have ended his days and where the Nazis had locked Zander, Adenauer's comrade in the concentration camp. The first morning after the liberation, an official car arrived at the entrance of Buchenwald. Two city hall officials went around asking if there was anyone from Cologne. When Zander identified himself the driver said: "Greetings from our new mayor, Mr Adenauer". And they took him home.

Adenauer did not last long in office. A few months after his official appointment, when the British took over the administration of the Rhineland, they removed Adenauer. He never knew why. However, there was one event which the English considered an unacceptable lack of obedience from the mayor: the British military governor in Cologne ordered the trees in the parks and public gardens to be chopped down to use as fuel for warmth, but Adenauer refused to execute the order. He argued that this would ruin the beauty of the city and would not solve the problem. Instead of cutting down trees, he publicly called on the British to let the population use the coal reserves seized by the British Army. To put pressure on the governor he gave an interview to several foreign media criticising the *modus operandi* of the British.

Anyhow, the fact of the matter was that he was banned again from politics and seemed again doomed to an unsustainable situation, with no income and a large family, this time at age 69. Moreover, Gussie fell ill again. Actually, she never recovered full health after she was released from prison. She was admitted to a hospital in Cologne, but the British did not allow Adenauer to go to the city centre, so he could not visit her. He complained about their cruelty and was finally granted a permit to visit her twice a week for a maximum of one hour.

Once again he raised his spirits in face of the difficulty and threw himself into a frenzy of activity. He invested his energies in rebuilding a team of aides in Cologne and in weaving a national network between people in different cities who were willing to revive the country using Christian values.

Since 1922 he had been a member of the catholic *Zentrum* party, but after the war it seemed more evident than ever that Protestants and Catholics ought to unite. Before the conflict the religious question was irrelevant in the political environment, with the exception of the Catholic minority. But the traumatic experience of nazism had put Christian humanism in the centre of the political thinking of many citizens and leaders who had opposed nazism. Adenauer hoped that these spiritual values would guide the moral regeneration as well as the economic and social progress of Germany.

He discreetly engaged in founding the new party until December 1945, when the British lifted the ban. It happened following the visit of a British official to Rhöndorf. He was interested in the opinion of the former mayor on the political situation. Adenauer refused to talk to him on the grounds that he was forbidden by the British to talk politics in his country. He suggested, sarcastically, that they meet on French territory, where he would be free to talk. A few days later the ban was lifted.

As his brother-in-law Willi Suth had succeeded him as mayor and Adenauer had ambitions at national level, he did not claim back his position in the city hall. Instead he asked Suth to lend him an official car and a driver. He began a tour of cities and towns in Germany looking for contacts to create the Christian Democratic Union (CDU), always returning to see Gussie and the children.

The CDU was born out of thousands of local organisations that emerged after the war in many German cities and towns as a result of citizens' assemblies. The leaders of the Rhineland and Berlin brought together many small local organizations and invited them to unite around some values, which they defined as "Christian, democratic and federal".

At one of the first meetings of the future CDU Adenauer spoke in a firm tone to claim leadership. He cut short any dispute with the clear objective of becoming chancellor: "I was born in 1876, so I am probably the oldest person here. If no-one objects, I will regard myself as president by seniority." There was no further discussion.

On 6 March 1946, the opening session of the Zonal Advisory Council was held in Hamburg. The aim was to address the government of the area of Germany that fell under UK control. The British commander in chief, Sir Sholto Douglas, was there, as well as the Social-Democrat leader Kurt Schumacher and Adenauer on behalf of the CDU. However the former mayor of Cologne felt despised by Sir Douglas. In the air was the conviction that the SPD was much more powerful than the CDU and that the Social Democrats would win the first free elections in Germany. Adenauer had the impression that Sir Douglas already wanted to side with the winner.

There had never been chemistry between Adenauer and Schumacher, but their aides thought it would be good that the two German leaders hold a bilateral meeting, without the Englishman, to try to reach a common position *vis-à-vis* the foreign authority. They agreed to meet in the afternoon, at the meeting room of Hamburg's mayor.

Schumacher, like Adenauer, had a strong character.[1] He was in his heyday with the support of the British. When he saw Adenauer he addressed the problem of supplies for the population right away, as well as the obligation imposed by the allies to dismantle the German factories. He said that democracy could not be established with that imposing attitude. Adenauer fully agreed with Schumacher and reminded him that this was also the position of the CDU, which had been officially adopted in several resolutions of the party.

Schumacher then offered him a partnership agreement between the SPD and the CDU, with one condition: "That you and your young party, Mr Adenauer, admit the right of the SPD to leadership. I do not think this is an exorbitant request. Every objective observer will admit that the SPD is the largest party with the greatest future and will remain so."

Adenauer replied coldly: "Personally, I am of another opinion. I do not think that the SPD will be the first party. Let the polls decide."

The farewell was icy, and witnesses had the impression that an irreparable rupture had just taken place, that a duel between the two men would last a lifetime. The polls proved Adenauer right: The CDU won the elections held on 20 October 1946 by a large majority, opening a long period of several governments to Konrad Adenauer.

---

[1]   Kurt Schumacher served in the First World War, where he lost his right arm. He was a Member of Parliament between 1924 and 1933. When the Nazis came to power they arrested him and imprisoned him for ten years in concentration camps.

1952-1954

The European Army fiasco

Jean Monnet and Paul-Henri Spaak (© European Parliament)

As usual, the chancellor arrives very early at his office and reads the press sitting in his leather armchair. It is early January, he is just back from the Christmas holidays and his diary is full. His secretary suddenly appears round the door with a note that has just arrived from the Foreign Office in London. From her body language, Adenauer knows it is bad news. The letter warns him of a looming diplomatic crisis: a controversial book by a German general, praising German military power, will soon be published in the UK.

The author is Heinz Guderian, head of the German armoured divisions in Poland, France and Russia until December 1941 and promoter of tanks and other technological developments in the battlefield. Under the title of *Panzer Leader* he defends Germany's inborn military leadership and blames its Second World War defeat on Hitler's childishness and insanity.

Adenauer winces in his armchair and goes screaming into the corridors. Who in his right mind could write such a book? He asks for information about the publication and orders a damage limitation effort by the diplomatic service. Criticism will rain down in the UK, and a wave of panic attack and indignation will probably strike France if ever it is translated into French.

This book comes at the most inconvenient time, right before a NATO conference to discuss the role of Germany in the different European defence projects. In Germany, it will add fuel to the national debate on whether Germany should forever abandon all thought of having an army.

That is the sad paradox, thinks Adenauer, that the French and the Germans agree on the fact that Germany should not have an army; the first from fear and the latter from guilt. Yet the threats from the USSR and US pressure have put Schuman and Adenauer in a Catch-22 situation. They would both prefer a European solution to the security question, but for now the only organisation that ensures Europe's defence is NATO, in which Washington and London are the leading voices.

A few days later the chancellor has the opportunity to speak privately with the allies. Adenauer knows that French, British and American ministers will meet informally in London to discuss military issues. He is not invited, but the death of Britain's King George VI provides an excuse to turn up. He politely attends the funeral, and when Schuman, Eden and Acheson learn that the chancellor is in the British capital they invite him to join them.

The ministers talk for two days from dawn to sunset. The trust already established between them facilitates open dialogue on all the outstanding issues: financial contributions to Europe's defence, its arms production and security measures. Germany is asked for a statement that its intentions in joining a military organisation are peaceful and of an exclusively defensive nature. Adenauer does not question the personal respect that his partners have for him, but he has the impression that Germany as a country is still under suspicion.

"I think you are going too far," he complains. "Is it normal that a partner in a community has to repeat three times that his intentions are good? I recently saw Churchill and he told me: 'Broadmindedness creates trust'. Gentlemen, bear that in mind. Everything that you want from the

Federal Government is already enshrined in the Treaty of the European Defence Community."

Although Schuman tries hard to be conciliatory, his sense of responsibility as French minister makes him call for guarantees. "What will be the model for the German police? There has been talk of a *gendarmerie* or *carabineri*, but these two kinds of force are linked to the army."

"I don't know why you are so worried about the German police, for it doesn't have any weapons," the chancellor retorts angrily.

Even though Germany is not allowed to produce weapons, it seems necessary to draft a list of the types of arms and number of police battalions that the country would need to protect itself. Adenauer recommends letting the military experts gathered in Paris to negotiate the EDC discuss the list. But Eden and Schuman want to deal with it now.

The Frenchman states: "It is well known that foreign ministers are usually readier to understand one another than military leaders are."

Adenauer impatiently contradicts him: "On the contrary, I believe that it takes less for the military to reach agreement than for ministers."

Schuman is worried that a future German chancellor will renege on whatever they decide today if it is not put down on paper.

"For God's sake, have a little trust," snaps Adenauer, about to lose his temper.

In February, NATO holds a big summit in Lisbon on the need for a European Army. The United States fully supports the EDC, including Article 38 calling for political union, and it promises financial support for the project. Dean Acheson announces that France will contribute 14 divisions to that European Army, while Germany and Italy will contribute 12 each, with five from each of the Benelux countries.

Twelve German divisions! That figure makes Schuman shiver. He spends the next two days trying to convince others to limit the impact of the US decision to begin recruiting German forces. He wins a commitment that no German contingent will be recruited either for the EDC or NATO until the member countries of the EDC have signed and ratified the Treaty. That gives Schuman some breathing space at home because the French would never agree to Germany building its new army before it had officially given its approval.

Schuman must be cautious. In the parliamentary elections of June 1951, the MRP – a pro-European party – lost ground to Communists and Gaullists, both opposed to the common army. The Assembly debate on ratification of the ECSC Treaty made it clear that there is growing animosity to the integration project. It passed by only 377 votes to 233.

Schuman fears a popular reaction against the EDC if Adenauer looks too impatient and puts too much pressure on Paris.

The chancellor for his part, understands Schuman's position, but thinks it would be a waste of time to wait for ratification of the EDC when they can already start thinking about the shape of the European Army and establish a Constituent Assembly to design a political authority for the EDC, as provided in Article 38 of the Treaty. De Gasperi and Spaak, both convinced federalists, are enthusiastic about the German's approach. For several months now, Spaak has been working with the Italian Altiero Spinelli on an Action Committee for a European Constituent Assembly. Now at last, he sees an opportunity to translate theories into action.

The United Kingdom does not like the turn of events. This is why on 19 March in Strasbourg Anthony Eden proposes that the Assembly of the Council of Europe be consulted on the EDC. Spaak, Monnet and Spinelli will in no way play the British game. The three of them agree that Eden's plan would strengthen cooperation between national governments, so putting an end to political union. Spaak, Monnet and Spinelli count on De Gasperi's firm support. Spaak promises to talk to his Benelux colleagues so that they all stand together against Eden. Their goal, as proposed by Pleven, is to grant full control of the European Army to the ECSC, completely independently from the narrow-minded Council of Europe.

Surprisingly, the battle in the Consultative Assembly in Strasbourg is less fierce than they feared, for the MPs are unable to choose between the Eden plan and the Pleven plan. Members request that the six governments of the European Defence Community appoint the Assembly that will draft the statute of a supra-national Political Community open to all member states of the Council of Europe. For ECSC ministers this is a sure sign that they must go ahead instead of waiting for the UK.

May 1952, Bonn

So the six ECSC members come together on 27 May to sign the EDC treaty. They are all aware that this is a giant step towards Europe's political integration and Germany's return to the European family. Everything goes smoothly until an unexpected event threatens to blow everything up: on the eve of the signing, a last-minute demand by the French government puts the draft agreement on hold.

The crisis broke on Friday 23 May in Bonn, where the three allied ministers were to sign the end of the occupation and the return of sovereignty to Germany. It was a pre-condition for Adenauer's signing of the EDC agreement on 27 May for he could not sign an international agreement without his country having full sovereignty.

The chancellor had prepared a great reception for Acheson, Eden and Schuman, who would be arriving in the West Germany capital on Friday morning. Once the ministers were installed at the residences of their respective high commissioners, Schuman learned that the French government had decided after five hours of talks against submitting the new German statute to the National Assembly if there are not further guarantees. When Clappier communicates the news to Schuman, the minister pales. How will he tell Adenauer? The entire peace project is teetering.

Schuman runs up to his British and American colleagues. After expressing his heartfelt apologies, he explains his government's new demand: the commitment of Anglo-American protection in case a re-armed Germany one day abandons the EDC. Paris also wants the US to support French policy in Northern Africa.

Acheson, Eden and Schuman spend all Saturday arguing amongst themselves and calling their capitals for approval and recommendations. On Sunday the 25th at noon they agree at last on the final text of the two treaties: the German statute and the EDC. Schuman is nervous. He is still not sure if the French government will accept the new drafts, which are expected to be signed on Monday and Tuesday respectively. It takes a new meeting of the French cabinet to get the final approval, on Sunday afternoon. Schuman can finally breathe – and look Adenauer in the eyes.

On Monday at 10 am, the three allied ministers sign the repeal of the statute of occupation in the Bundestag. The allied troops are no longer occupying forces, but represent NATO and their task is the protection of the German Federal Republic. The occupying taxes imposed on Germany are ended. In return, Bonn will contribute 850 million marks a month to cover its own defence, which is to be shared between the EDC and NATO.

Only West Berlin will remain under the protection of the Western powers. In addition, London, Paris and Washington retain the right to suspend the German government if it loses control of the situation through war or revolution. The SPD party does not agree with these conditions. This is why it calls for a "day of mourning" on the occasion of the signature.

In the afternoon, the three ministers and the chancellor fly to Paris for the signature of the EDC Treaty the next day. The ceremony will take place in the Quai d'Orsay, in the same room where two years earlier Schuman read his 9 May declaration to the world.

The foreign ministers of Belgium, Germany, France, the Netherlands, Italy and Luxembourg state that any aggression against a signatory country shall be considered an attack on all. The US secretary of State and the UK foreign minister attend as observers. Schuman is deeply grateful because without them France would have rejected the agreement at the last minute. As host, he feels compelled to say a few words to sum up: "We do not make peace against anyone. We hope we can do it with everyone."

Despite his success in overcoming a new hurdle in his peace plan, the French minister doubts that the EDC will succeed. Everyone in Paris knows about growing criticism of it and even René Pleven, who sponsored the project, is worried about how difficult it will be to take it forward. On top of that, some people in Washington believe that the EDC is just a smokescreen successfully used by the French government to delay German rearmament, because rearmament is now linked to a political union that will never happen.

To Schuman it is important to keep the 9 May spirit alive, and he will not stubbornly push for one sectoral project or the other. His partners avoid asking Schuman and Pleven openly how far they are committed to the EDC, because it would get them nowhere to highlight their weakness and expose them to the Eurosceptics. However, behind closed doors, Germany, Belgium, the Netherlands and Italy wonder which direction the French government will take.

The Christian Democrat leaders believe it is the right time to revive their secret meetings. With the approval of their founder, Georges Bidault, the French MP Pierre-Henri Teitgen convenes a meeting on 16 June at the usual place, Victor Koutzine's apartment in Geneva. Teitgen, who is a federalist and attended the conference in The Hague, assumed the presidency of the centre-right party, the MRP, last month and he feels a responsibility to convince his own ranks of the need for the EDC.

This time Adenauer and De Gasperi send trusted emissaries. After the introduction of each participant, Teitgen explains that he would like to use the structure of the New International Teams (NEI) to mobilise Catholic opinion in favour of the EDC. There is potential to expand popular support among the faithful, since Pope Pius XII has publicly spoken in favour of a European federation. None of the participants opposes the initiative.

Teitgen wants to be pragmatic and proposes a different model of integration: maintaining the long-term aim of a federation, but setting short-term goals for different stages along the way. "A project, in my opinion, more realistic than that of the European Movement," he says, without explicitly mentioning Spaak and Spinelli. His idea is to sign a new federal pact between the six ESCS countries. This pact would set up a common political authority with limited powers, overseen by a bicameral parliament.

The German delegate Heinrich von Brentano, a man who enjoys the chancellor's absolute trust, supports Teitgen and asks him to draft a memorandum that he can show to Adenauer. The Italian Enrico Tosi thinks that De Gasperi will be concerned. He is sure that his boss will back the substance of the proposal but will probably insist on having a constituent assembly to draft a Constitution.

De Gasperi is currently in Rome with Spaak. The latter was invited to take part in the events of the Federalist Youth Movement as chairman of the Action Committee for the European Constituent. At all times, the Italian prime minister has accompanied and supported his Belgian friend, to the point that he has told the press: "We are two proponents of the same idea and we have discussed the best way to speed up the process for the European Constitution [...] We agree on everything." How could De Gasperi now let Spaak down? Teitgen frowns and promises to write a memorandum and consult both Adenauer and De Gasperi.

June 1952, Italy

The head of the Italian government would have liked to be in Geneva but could not leave Rome for two reasons: first, because neither the government nor the Christian Democrats have yet recovered from the internal crisis caused by the progressive branch in *Democrazia Cristiana* (DC), represented by Giuseppe Dossetti; and second, because at the same time as the leaders were meeting in Geneva, his daughter Lucia was taking perpetual vows as a cloistered nun.

The father was filled with delight when, in the autumn of 1947, his little Luciola shared with him her intention of becoming a nun and asked for his blessing to enter a convent as a novice. She was 22, and two years later she took temporary vows in a ceremony celebrated by Monsignor Montini, a good friend of the family.[2] Then on 15 June 1952, the ceremony for her final vows was to be held in the large chapel of Viale Romania.

All the family is there for the happy occasion: Alcide, Francesca and their four daughters: Maria Romana with her husband, Lucia and the two younger girls Paola and Cecilia. The parents are also celebrating their 30th wedding anniversary. Religion was an important part both of their relationship and of the upbringing of their children. However, faith forged a special bond between the father and the second daughter. He can confide in Lucia his troubles and concerns, including disappointments with friends who betrayed him out of envy or fear. The leader finds consolation and peace in the advice of his daughter, particularly in the religious texts she recommended. The life of a politician has proved to be hard, especially when he fights to be honest. There is nothing unexpected in these setbacks. Back when De Gasperi and Francesca were engaged,

---

[2] Monsignor Giovanni Battista Montini was elected Pope in 1963 and took the name Paul VI.

he warned her that, if she agreed to marry him, they would live a humble life full of sacrifices. But the fact that it could be foreseen did not make it less painful.

Silence fills the chapel when Lucia and another novice, lying facedown on the floor in front of the altar, promise poverty, obedience and chastity. De Gasperi knows the priest celebrating this ceremony. They met when De Gasperi was working at the Vatican Library, where he took refuge during the time that Mussolini banned him from politics and no one had dared to employ him. The memories of that hard time now merge in De Gasperi's mind with new sufferings, perhaps as intense as the old ones. The difference is that now they go unnoticed, for few know that the source of his misfortune is the incomprehension of the Pope.

When De Gasperi founded *Democrazia Cristiana* (Christian Democracy) after the fall of fascism, he received explicit support from the Holy See that proved quite useful in winning the elections. He also received full papal encouragement in his eagerness to build a new Europe based on fraternity among peoples. Now, however, Pius XII is upset because he would like to see stronger opposition to the Communists. This is the message that the Pontiff's emissary, Monsignor Pietro Pavan, gave De Gasperi last December. The Pope did not like De Gasperi's reluctance to marginalise the Communist Party.

Last spring, ahead of the municipal elections in May, some members of Catholic Action and other lobbyists representing conservative Catholic groups openly criticised the prime minister for his "excessive tolerance" towards the Communists. They thought that this tolerance threatened not just democracy in Italy but also the freedom and survival of the Vatican State.

Despite strong pressure, De Gasperi did not give in, and he refused to create a common centre-right front in Rome to stop the left, as he was asked to do. The promoter of the idea was Luigi Gedda, president of Catholic Action. The leader of DC refused, even when he was told that the head of the hypothetical electoral list would be Don Luigi Sturzo, an Italian priest who was the founder of the People's Party.

Even today, De Gasperi cannot believe that Sturzo was part of that plot. He feels respect and admiration for his old friend. In any case it was out of question for De Gasperi to join Catholic Action and, much worse, the post-Fascist candidates. And regardless of the potential partners, there is a matter of principle for him: he is willing to base his political vision on Christian values, but not to accept the interference of the "long arm" of the bishops in his political decisions.

De Gasperi shared the underground opposition to Mussolini with communists, socialists and anyone willing to oppose fascism. So his conscience would not allow him to associate with those who imposed dictatorship in Italy. He is convinced that his duty is to win the elections with his own programme and then to include representatives of all parties in his government, as a way of finding consensus. That is his recipe for dealing with the current political crisis. And despite the split in the progressive sector of DC, he would like his party to remain in the centre of the political spectrum, and not to turn right. He deeply regrets that the Pope does not see it that way.

In an attempt to build bridges, De Gasperi explained to the Secretary of State of the Holy See, Monsignor Montini, why he decided to run alone, with his own programme and principles. In his opinion, creating a right-wing front to counterbalance the leftist bloc created by Communists and Socialists would only lead to greater confrontation and perhaps even to civil war, as had happened in Spain. Montini understood and promised to pass the message to the Pontiff.

Apparently it did not work, because there was another attempt to convince him right before election day. This time the emissary was Father Lombardi, a priest working for Vatican Radio whose nickname was "God's microphone". He tried a new tactic and called Francesca. She agreed to see him, out of courtesy, but once face to face she again explained her husband's reasoning. De Gasperi does not understand the short-sightedness of certain Catholics, who cannot understand that a Catholic politician must govern for all, not just for Catholics. This is the only way to build a peaceful society.

Fortunately facts proved him right, and the DC won the elections in Rome together with the Social Democrats (PSDI) and the Liberals (PLI). However, in other areas of Italy the extreme left and extreme right grew. So even after the polls, political tension and clerical pressure on the head of government continue.

It has been one month since the election and Pius XII is still upset with De Gasperi. So much so that he refused to grant him the private audience that the prime minister had repeatedly requested on the occasion his daughter's vows and his own 30th wedding anniversary. Francesca and he were excited because they had never had a private audience with His Holiness. Their friend Montini's mediation was in vain.

The effect of the failed "Sturzo Operation" will not easily fade away. Little could Alcide and Francesca imagine that the Pope would keep up the pressure during the summer holidays when the De Gasperi family enjoys a few weeks at Francesca's childhood home in Sella Valsugana. Despite the unwelcome surprise, the De Gasperis politely greet Monsignor Pavan and offer him a drink when he shows up.

Around 6.30 pm, the two men go to a private room to discuss this sensitive issue which has given De Gasperi sleepless nights for months already. He explains that the goal of DC is to represent Catholics from any walk of life. He considers his to be a centre-left party open to the right, and in no way does he want it to move to the right. Pavan suggests that it would be positive for DC to form a coalition with the monarchists. De Gasperi disagrees: it would divide the followers of DC and it could have a counter-productive effect and push the die-hard Republicans towards the Socialists or the Communist Party.

"The Christian Democrats alone cannot govern Italy. They need the support of other minority political groups," insists De Gasperi.

"Why don't you meet the Holy Father in person and set your views directly? That would avoid any misunderstandings," suggests Pavan.

"A meeting with the Holy Father would be nice, really nice. But I cannot forget that I am the leader of a political party and the head of a government. So I cannot afford to seek a meeting that might not be granted," replies De Gasperi.

Monsignor Pavan then offers to prepare the ground for the meeting. De Gasperi wants to make sure that they agree on the terms:

"I will present my approach quite frankly and if the Holy Father wants to take it into consideration, so much the better. If, however, for his own reasons, the Holy Father does not find it convincing but leaves me freedom of choice, then being deeply convinced of the appropriateness of my ideas at this moment in history, I will act accordingly, with the certainty that I will be doing the right thing, both for Italy and for the Church.

"If the Holy Father decides otherwise, I will retire from political life. I am a Christian, I am at the end of my days and I will not act against the express wishes of the Holy Father," says De Gasperi in a broken voice. "I will retire from politics, for I would be unable to take a political course that in all conscience I saw as detrimental to the country and to the Church. In that eventuality, someone will replace me"

It was the last time he heard from Pavan

Summer 1952, Luxembourg

At about that time in August, Luxembourg is celebrating. Its provincial capital, usually quiet, is in the international spotlight. Journalists from around the world are here to cover the premiere of this political experiment, dubbed ECSC. Under the presidency of Robert Schuman, Jean Monnet takes up his post as chairman of the High Authority. Aside from being the godfather of the project, the French minister has a special bond with the Grand Duchy, where he and his mother were born.

The host, Joseph Bech, offers a reception at the city hall attended by leading personalities, including Prince Felix. In recognition of the new institution representing more than the citizens of just one state, Bech established a new order of importance for participants and gives priority to Monnet over the national ambassadors.

The new chairman emphasises that the High Authority shall be independent of any national government and any private interest. For Monnet it is fundamental to surround himself with an open-minded team. He needs people who can feel part of a community and who are not just government emissaries, so he carefully oversees the selection process. He wants to leave his imprint from the beginning. So he takes Pierre Uri with him. At the end of the day he and Uri invented the institutions, and their mission is not over: they must now put their dreams into effect in their everyday work.

As in Paris, Monnet makes his employees work long hours. He intends to reproduce his old working method and draw the newcomers together. The locals in Luxembourg soon begin to call the building "the mad house" because the pace of activity is frantic and the lights are always on late at night.

Jean and Silvia Monnet stay with their daughters in a hotel at first and then in a house next to a golf course, where Jean plays with his guests from time to time. On the green he can socialise with political and civil-society leaders, which is part of his consultation strategy for managing the High Authority. Apart from the Community Assembly and the Council of Ministers, Monnet attaches great importance to the advisory committee to the High Authority. It has representatives of economic and social actors in all member countries. It is clear to him that Europe cannot be built without trade unions, business and manufacturers.

Over the summer, ECSC leaders, including Monnet, coordinate their efforts to make sure that the European Community will also be independent of the Council of Europe, even if the assemblies of both institutions will share a seat in Strasbourg. The quarrel is mainly symbolic, more than a dispute over competences, since the Assembly of the ECSC will have little effective power. The truly powerful institution in the new European Community is the Court of Justice, whose task is to ensure that the law is observed in the interpretation and application of the Treaties. And this is what matters most to Monnet. Since his disappointing experience at the League of Nations, he wants at all costs to avoid another fiasco such as the OEEC or the Council of Europe, a mere talking shop, a place in which to make grand declarations. At the ECSC there will be obligations once the Treaty has been signed and ratified.

The Council of Ministers meets for the first time in Luxembourg between 8 and 10 September. Adenauer holds the rotating presidency as representative of the first country in the (French) alphabetical order of member states. He opens the session by recalling the main role of the High Authority: to promote common interest.

Without much preamble, De Gasperi goes on the offensive, insisting again on his federalist plans. He wants the ECSC Assembly to draft a treaty setting up a European Political Community (EPC) and he would like it to be ready within six months. His colleagues back the motion. The proposal is presented to the ECSC Assembly in the evening, right after the Council of Ministers.

The session continues on the morning of 11 September. It is the first session and the Common Assembly must elect its chairman. In the close race between Paul-Henri Spaak and Heinrich von Brentano, the Belgian wins. While respecting his opponent, Spaak thinks that von Brentano is poorly equipped for the post. "He does not have a very strong personality, but working for Adenauer, who could?" he thinks, as they shake hands after the vote.

The chamber accepts the task of drafting a text for a political union by unanimity of its 78 members. However, the future Defence Community Assembly will be larger than that of the ECSC, so they decide to establish a temporary assembly of ECSC members along with Council of Europe members from France, Germany, Italy, Belgium, the Netherlands and Luxembourg and some observers from other European member states. They call it the *ad hoc* Assembly. At the same meeting, and as compensation for losing the presidency of the Common Assembly, Von Brentano is appointed chairman of a constitutional committee within the *ad hoc* Assembly in charge of drafting the first proposal for political union.

The following week, De Gasperi travels to Bonn. It is the first official post-war visit to Germany by an Italian leader. However for De Gasperi and his wife this meeting with Adenauer is much more than a diplomatic formality. Francesca, like De Gasperi, was born and raised in Trentino, speaks German fluently and is familiar with Germanic culture. So the conversation with the chancellor is friendly and flows naturally.

The official meeting takes place in the Schaumburg palace, but the meaningful exchange of personal stories happens at the dining table and during long walks outdoors. They both resisted totalitarianism, and for both it came at a high price. For De Gasperi, the highlight of the visit is the trip to Aachen to receive the Charlemagne award in the third edition of this prize for the work carried out in the service of European unification.

During the ceremony, he confides in Francesca that this is the most valued award he has ever received.

In his Austrian accent he delivers a speech outlining his vision for Europe and calling for patience: "The future will not be built by force, nor through a desire to conquer, but by the patient application of the democratic method, the constructive spirit of agreement, and by respect for freedom."

He defends the need to develop a European mentality:

"Supranational institutions will not be enough on their own and they might even turn out to be no more than a place for competition between particular interests if the people in charge do not feel they must honour a mandate to promote higher European interests. Without training in this vocation, our shared dream might remain no more than a legal abstraction."

Despite the sincere commitment and mutual understanding between the promoters of a united Europe, the autumn confirms that goodwill is not enough. Animosity to Germany stirs again in France as does rejection of a common army. In early October, a statement by a Radical Party MP makes front-page news: "My children will never fight alongside anyone who in an earlier life would have been his father's mortal enemy."

German media also report the sentence. Adenauer understands such a visceral reaction by French politicians who lived through the hell of the concentration camps. So he does not respond, but in private tells his daughter: "If only men could understand that we cannot have a new beginning in Europe if we do not forgive one another."

When everyone seems to be running out of steam, a new development brings fresh impetus to the European project: the arrival of Johan Willem Beyen at the Dutch Foreign Ministry, replacing Stikker. His election was not the outcome of a deliberate strategy, but it would prove critical to the advancement of the union. The close election results in the Netherlands required a consensus between Social Democrats and Christian Democrats, but they could not agree on who should be foreign minister. Apparently Beyen was acceptable to everyone, because he is not member of any party and has international experience, gained in the creation of the World Bank and the International Monetary Fund.

December 1952, Benelux

Unlike Stikker, Johan W. Beyen is certain of the need for a political union. It is a priority for him and he is backed by Dutch civil society and the Crown. Beyen knows Spaak, Bech and Van Zeeland from the exile of the three governments (the Netherlands, Belgium and Luxembourg) in

London during the Second World War. Beyen was a very young government advisor on economic matters. Although they belong to different political families – Van Zeeland and Bech are conservative, Beyen is a liberal and Spaak is a socialist –, all of them understand that protectionism creates tensions and nationalist struggles for energy and raw materials. Together they designed a plan to unite their economies in the Benelux.

The most experienced in the group is Joseph Bech. He was prime minister when Luxembourg had to face the technical problems of the Belgo-Luxembourg Economic Union established in 1921. Under that agreement, the two countries abolished customs barriers and established parity between their currencies.

Negotiations to include the Netherlands and to deepen their integration were difficult and public opinion was at first unfavourable when they signed the Benelux Treaty in 1944. But they refused to give up. It took time to overcome old grudges, especially between the Dutch and the Belgians. A decade later, the project is solid: since 1944 their economic union has progressed and in 1952 they set up a tripartite committee to coordinate foreign policy.

They think that the six-member European community could evolve in the same direction: from the elimination of trade barriers to a union in different policy areas. Given the apparent exhaustion of France and Germany, the Benelux countries take up the leadership of the integration process and create a new dynamic with a surprise proposal.

On 11 December they propose the economic integration of the ECSC countries. The original idea comes from Beyen, who defends a customs union between the six, as already exists in the Benelux, leading to a move together towards a common market instead of looking for the vertical integration of specific economic sectors such as coal and steel.

At first, Schuman is worried. While other partners are willing to endorse the plan, Euroscepticism gains ground in France. In late December, Pinay dissolved his cabinet and René Mayer, the new prime minister, begins to give in to pressure from the Gaullists.

Schuman is replaced at the Foreign Office by Georges Bidault. Despite also being pro-European, he arouses less suspicion than Schuman, who is occasionally accused in the Parliament of being a *bosche*, a derogatory French word referring to the Germans.

Adenauer, De Gasperi and the three Benelux leaders regret Schuman's departure. But Bidault quickly lets them know that he will stick to the same policy line. Thus, in the ministerial meeting in Italy in February 1953, Bidault supports the Beyen proposal for a common market and gives assurances that France will continue to support political union.

Bidault stays in Rome for a couple of days after the summit to talk informally with the prime minister. He knows that De Gasperi has become a good friend of Schuman and intends to gain his trust. Bidault considers that France and Italy should strengthen their bilateral relations. De Gasperi agrees, but perceives that the new French minister is hesitant about the pace of integration. He stresses the urgency of making decisions while Adenauer is in power. With this chancellor there is a chance to put an end to German nationalism. "We don't know if there will be one like him afterwards," he warns.

Within the six-month deadline, the committee chaired by Von Brentano finishes its work. It envisages a bicameral parliament with a Lower House elected by direct universal suffrage and a Senate chosen by national parliaments. It also advocates a government elected by the European Parliament and assisted by a Council of national ministers. A Court of Justice and an Economic and Social Council complete the institutions. The ECSC and the EDC would be merged into the Political Community, which would have new competences in order to create an economic union and to coordinate the member states' foreign policy. That economic area would progressively establish a common market with free movement of goods, services, people and capital.

The text recommends that, with the possible exception of the Court, all institutions of the European Community and of the Council of Europe be located permanently in the same town. Despite the single seat shared by both institutions, Von Brentano clarifies the independence of the European Political Community from the Council of Europe. Relations between the two institutions are to be studied further.

March 1953, Strasbourg

Between 6 and 9 March, Assembly members discuss and adopt political union with only five abstentions and no vote against. On 9 March, at a session in the newly built "House of Europe" in Strasbourg, the Assembly officially hands over the draft Treaty establishing the political community to the ECSC foreign ministers.

Spaak reads the first article: "The present Treaty sets up a European Community of a supranational character. The Community is founded upon a union of peoples and States, upon a respect for their personality and upon equal rights and duties for all. It shall be indissoluble."

Bidault as chairman of the ECSC Council thanks the Assembly: "On behalf of the governments, I convey our gratitude and our warm appreciation to the architects of this great work and to you, gentlemen, for the important effort you have made." And he says: "I am delighted to bestow upon you with admiration and not without envy the homage that

Queen Elizabeth the First of England paid to the founders of the empire: "I salute you, adventure seekers." He concludes by sharing his hope that, very soon, "it will be possible for any of us to say, Germany, Belgium, Netherlands, Italy, Luxembourg and France, my fatherland; Europe, my destiny."

Once the Assembly adopts the proposal, the six ECSC foreign ministers gather to determine the next steps. Bech, De Gasperi, Adenauer and Van Zeeland attentively listen to Bidault and Spaak who explain the roadmap towards a stronger Europe, to which there must be transfers of sovereignty. De Gasperi is eager to start working on the political community right away, even before the ratification of the EDC. He sees no need to wait for the European Army to be in place before drafting the political, economic and trade strategy. He calls on the other leaders to take a stand within two months.

Bidault urges patience and tells the Italian that experts ought to analyse the different issues before the politicians decide on anything. After heated discussions, they agree that ECSC experts and national governments will study the draft Treaty for a European Political Community and that the ministers will meet on 12 May.

However, when De Gasperi reads the draft press statement about the meeting he says that there must have been a misunderstanding, because it does not explain why the ministers will meet. In the evening, during a reception at the Prefecture of Strasbourg, the Italian makes a comment which highlights discrepancies in the interpretation of the leaders' decision early in the day. While De Gasperi and Adenauer understood that they had already agreed on 12 May as the date for an intergovernmental conference to take decisions, Bidault insists that 12 May is in the diary simply for discussion of the experts' recommendations.

De Gasperi is exasperated and raises his voice. The French minister, as host, feels uncomfortable and tries to avoid an argument by changing the conversation to less important matters. But the result is that De Gasperi gets even angrier and publicly challenges Bidault, to the stupefaction of the French prefect. Adenauer jumps in to ease the tension. To avoid making a scene, the chancellor suggests that the ministers move to a room upstairs and find a compromise on new wording. The new one is as vague as the original: "The six ministers decided to meet again on 12 May. Meanwhile, the secretariat of the Council of Ministers shall do the preparatory work to facilitate their task."

Things do not get back on track even by the time the ministers return home. Bidault makes every effort to delay political union until the EDC Treaty has been ratified. The three Benelux leaders, without going so far, justify Bidault's reservations because it is understandable that he does not want to commit himself to further integration until the French people have spoken about the first new step, the EDC. Only De Gasperi and Adenauer seem to be in a hurry. They fear that the window of opportunity may soon close. The death of the Soviet leader Jozef Stalin on 5 March is giving some people hope that tension between Eastern and Western Europe will ease. Particularly in France, some sectors of society and across the political spectrum hope that the United States will abandon its plan to rearm Germany. If there is no imminent threat from the Soviets, there may be no need of the EDC either, they think.

Finally on 12 May the six ministers meet at the Quai d'Orsay under the presidency of Bidault. They accept Von Brentano's proposal to merge the ECSC and the EDC into the political community. They discuss the future Parliament and how proportional representation can ensure that smaller countries are sufficiently influential despite their small populations. De Gasperi is pleased that the French government supports direct universal suffrage. Ministers will continue their discussions in Rome, under Italian presidency, from 12 June to 1 July.

This is the last summit that De Gasperi hosts. Even though Democrazia Cristiana wins the elections in August, he does not have enough parliamentary support to lead a coalition, so he is out of office. The new government, supported by the monarchists, gives international politics less importance than solving the problem of Trieste.[3] So the EDC is no longer a priority.

Now De Gasperi follows Schuman's example and fully engages with civil society, talking to young people and to journalists. In October, the European Movement organises a big new conference in The Hague, at the same Knights' room where everything began in 1948, and again with the presence of Queen Juliana. This time De Gasperi can attend, as well as Schuman, Von Brentano and Spinelli. Spaak chairs the meeting as president of the European Movement.

Robert Schuman summarises progress over the last five years. Their main goal was to influence public opinion in Europe, particularly the younger generations. "Without their long-term and enthusiastic engagement nothing durable can be achieved," he says. He and Von Brentano stress joint efforts to avoid any conflict between their two countries, France and Germany.

When he takes the floor, De Gasperi introduces himself as an "old activist" who until now fought "in the trenches of statesmen". He thanks

---

[3]   When Italy signed an armistice with the allies during the Second World War, there was a battle between the German and the Yugoslav armies for Trieste. Communist Army won over the Germans and it occupied the city, which only returned to Italy on 4 November 1954.

the French and German delegates for their commitment, stressing that only through solidarity can Europe overcome obstacles.

Summer 1953, West Germany

Now with Schuman and De Gasperi out of power, Monnet and Spaak are concerned that Adenauer could lose the next German elections on 6 September. The chancellor tries hard to win over public opinion during the summer, asking the Germans to let him complete his work on regeneration.

A week before election day, he receives a blow when the SPD speaks out against the EDC and in favour of German neutrality regarding the Soviet and Western blocs. They demand a system of mutual guarantees between the four powers (Britain, France, the United States and the USSR). The Social Democrats accuse Adenauer of not caring about the eastern part of the country – and incidentally some accuse him of anti-Protestant discrimination. They claim he does not care about Berlin because it is a "pagan city" and sees the territories east of the Elbe river as no more than "colonies".

The attacks do not affect the old chancellor, who keeps calm until election day. On that fair Sunday 6 September, Adenauer wakes up early. He slept well and is in a good mood. He goes to church with his daughter Lotte, and then to the polling station. Adenauer is again running for the Bonn constituency. His visit to the polling station is short. After greeting delegates and colleagues, he casts his vote and goes home, where a family meal is waiting for him, just like any other Sunday.

He likes to spend important days away from party headquarters, which is full of stress. At home, his children and grandchildren know they should not talk about politics. Grandpa doesn't like anyone to talk about work at the table. They are not even allowed to turn on the radio.

In the afternoon, when everyone except Lotte has gone, he goes out to the garden and sits next to the rose bush to watch the sunset over the Rhine and the vineyards. He trusts that the Germans will make the right choice. After a cold, light dinner he goes to sleep, giving orders to not to be disturbed. But as soon as he is in bed, his daughter runs to the radio to hear the latest news.

Around 3 am it seems clear that the CDU has won. Although the housekeeper knows that the chancellor usually gets up at 6.30 am she has no choice but to wake him at 5 am after a phone call. It is the head of the chancellor's cabinet, Otto Lenz, who wants to give him the happy news: "The first results give you the victory!" announces Lenz.

"Thank you, Mr Lenz," he replies laconically.

Adenauer goes back to bed, but the phone soon rings again. This time it is his press officer, Von Eckardt: "We now have the final result: You have won."

The response is the same, with the same impassive tone: "Thank you Mr Eckard."

On 20 October, Adenauer presents his new cabinet backed by a strong majority: the gap between the CDU and the SPD has risen from 8 to 94 seats; a major success. He announces the government's priorities: to reinforce German sovereignty and to work for reunification and the inclusion of a united Germany in Europe.

Reunification is a complicated task and Adenauer is often accused of sacrificing it by giving priority to friendship with France. Then the new Russian leadership seems to open up, creating expectations that it could work with Western countries.

In late November, Moscow proposes a meeting with the allied powers in Berlin on 25 January. The Russians want to speak not only about Germany – as has been requested by Paris, London and Washington for months – but also about NATO and the rearmament of the continent. Adenauer is suspicious of the Russians' intentions. Since the signature of the armistice in Korea last summer, the temperature of east-west psychological warfare has cooled down and the possibility of opening a dialogue with the Soviet Union encourages critics of the EDC: the German Social Democrats advocate a pacifist approach so as not to provoke the Soviets, while the French would be relieved if they did not have to accept German rearmament. Adenauer warns his Western partners against falling into the Soviet trap, which would endanger both the military and the political union.

Meanwhile, De Gasperi's health worsens. In 1953 he was diagnosed kidney sclerosis and in late January 1954 he takes the floor in the Parliament for the last time. Despite his evident weakness, he attends European gatherings whenever he can. On 21 April he takes part in the European Parliamentary Conference,[4] where he argues that all countries of the European Movement should be members of the Political Community that is under construction.

He speaks about the common European heritage, based on Christian ethics, liberal democracy and social justice:

"None of these tendencies which prevail in one or another area of our civilisation can pretend to become the only and dominant idea for the architecture and the life of the new Europe. Rather, these three tendencies

---

[4]   The Parliamentary Council was born in 1952 through the merging of the European Parliamentary Union and the Parliamentary Group of the European Movement, both being fora to discuss between MPs.

must together contribute to building on this idea and to nourishing its free and progressive development."

He follows closely the fate of the EDC in France. At first he is optimistic because he receives news from reliable sources that ratification would take place in June. Adenauer was also assured that ratification in France would happen before July. But as May progresses, a shadow hangs over the EDC. On 13 May, the fall of Dien Bien Phu, a key French stronghold in Indochina, shakes France, fuelling nationalist discourses and militaristic patriotism embodied by General de Gaulle.

In this adverse climate, the National Assembly's Foreign Affairs Committee debates the EDC on 9 June. Three days later, the government steps down. The military defeat in Indochina and opposition to the EDC are the mortal blow to Joseph Laniel, the Prime Minister, who is replaced by Pierre Mendès France. In his first statement, the new prime minister sets out his priorities: first, to end the war in Indochina; second, to reorganise the economy; and third, to ratify the EDC.

Monnet, Schuman, Adenauer and Spaak all interpret this announcement as a dangerous setback to the EDC. De Gasperi even suggests a postponement of the vote by the National Assembly. Mendès France, at the age of 47, has a long political career as well as the experience of prison during the resistance to nazism, and then as finance minister in de Gaulle's government-in-exile. He is not afraid to take tough decisions.

Spaak, who like Mendès France is a socialist and speaks French as his mother tongue, takes the initiative and travels to Paris to talk in person with the new prime minister. Very recently he has again been appointed as foreign minister and wants to use his new influence to defend the EDC. Spaak thinks that Mendès France is giving in to pressure from de Gaulle. On 30 June, in a meeting at the Hotel Matignon, the French leader tells Spaak that he will propose a new text for the EDC Treaty. Spaak leaves, disgusted.

Aware of the intentions of the new French government, Adenauer publicly confirms his willingness to collaborate with Mendès France. For him it is essential to safeguard trust between Paris and Bonn. He also thinks that they must speed up the process. Unlike De Gasperi, who advocates postponement in France, Adenauer wants a quick decision. It has already been two years since they signed the EDC Treaty and the allied commissioners have still not left because France linked the return of sovereignty to Germany to its ECSC and EDC membership. France cannot keep the Germans waiting. Many begin to distrust Western partners.

On 1 July 1954, Adenauer grants a radio interview in which he urges Mendès France to submit the two treaties – the end of German occupation and the common army – to the National Assembly

"I do not consider the possibility of the EDC not being ratified. I believe it is the only practical option. We could obviously envisage other scenarios, but none of them seems satisfactory. If the defence community is not accepted, there will be no other option than to form a German national army, even though the German people do not want that. We also know that the national army would raise new suspicions and new fears in France. It would be a strange paradox if, by its own rejection, France forced us to establish this German national army that it fears so much."

The interview unleashes a diplomatic clash with Mendès France, but Adenauer is backed by the United States and the United Kingdom. On 3 July, the US Secretary of State John F. Dulles shares his concerns with Spaak: "My dear friend, I follow with great attention your efforts on behalf of EDC. Our conversations with Sir Winston Churchill and Anthony Eden stress the confusion and chaos into which Europe would fall if this creative and constructive project were to be abandoned."

However, in France there is growing indignation over Adenauer: a German cannot speak to France in that tone. The chancellor sends another message through the press to calm down his neighbours. He promises to "implement the clauses of the treaty instituting the EDC so that France is satisfied and can see its worries disappear".

The explanations come too late for Mendès France. As the weeks go by, he is more and more convinced that the National Assembly will not adopt the treaty texts as signed. So he begins to draft a memorandum including new amendments that France will put to its partners.

The memorandum has 60 articles. Its content destroys the spirit with which the EDC was originally written. It is a deadly blow to political integration. France demands the right to exit the EDC if ever Germany is reunited and British and American troops leave the European continent. Mendès France intends to give this new text to the other five partners at a conference in Brussels scheduled for 19 August.

Alcide De Gasperi

Husband, Father and Leader

De Gasperi and his wife with a group of Christian Democrat members
from Lombardia, at their house in Sella Valsugana
(© Fondazione Trentina Alcide De Gasperi)

As August progresses the outlook for the EDC seems doomed. At home in Sella Valsugana with his energy depleted, De Gasperi speaks on the phone with his European partners and with his party. Although his illness has left the leadership of Italian Christian Democracy to his friend Amintore Fanfani, De Gasperi seeks to maintain his influence in the party and feels frustrated by its apathy. The lack of a strong defence of the EDC against French nationalists and conservatives appears to him as a "truly devastating scene and a sad omen for the future". This is his message to Fanfani in a letter on 14 August. "You can hardly imagine my grief, aggravated by the fact that I have neither the strength nor the possibility to speak out."

He would like to use his remaining energy in the political union of Europe. He doesn't listen to Francesca and Maria Romana's pleas to rest. Alcide is determined to go to Brussels for the ECSC ministerial meeting on 19 August. He writes to his colleagues in Rome asking them to arrange a plane to take him from Verona to Brussels. He intends to personally persuade Mendès France to delay the vote in the Assembly. But his DC mates, including his loyal friend and now President of the Council Mario Scelba, discourage him, for Scelba knows that De Gasperi's health is extremely delicate. In a phone call full of affection and respect, Scelba deters him with the promise that Italy will stand firm in the defence of both the European Army and its political dimension.

When Alcide hangs up the phone with Scelba, he tells his daughter Maria Romana: "I have done everything I could, and my conscience is at peace".

On 18 August the ministers arrive in Brussels with the faint hope of changing the French position. With undisguised anger Adenauer requests an urgent meeting with Mendès France. He wants to hear from his lips what changes he wants to introduce to the Treaty.

In the afternoon De Gasperi receives a call. His aides update him on the new position of Mendès France. When he hangs up the phone he can't avoid the feeling of having left the work half finished. He is exhausted and the conversation has left him so disheartened that he goes to bed early.

At night he feels sick and Francesca calls the doctor, who confirms their worst fears. The couple requests the presence of a priest and of their daughters, Maria Romana, Cecilia and Paola. Francesca sits serenely on the bed, helping her husband recite the prayer for a peaceful death. Time passes by, while they both hold hands and look through the window to the mountains of their beloved valley. At 2 am he draws his last breath. In the room, only the silent presence of the doctor and the priest breaks the privacy of the farewell. Maria Romana phones the Arcinazzo convent to inform her sister Lucia.

The following morning the news spreads from the Trentino town to Rome and the whole of Italy is shaken by the death of this good, honest man. He was not always understood but today, faced with his loss, politicians of all persuasions mourn a father of the homeland.

All day on 19 August in the house of Valsugana, relatives and friends hold a wake over Alcide's body. At 11 pm Sister Lucia arrives by train. The following morning they accompany the body first to the city of Borgo Valsugana and then to Trento for the first funeral. As De Gasperi would have liked, Francesca asked for the Charlemagne award to be put in the coffin.

Francesca thinks of all the happy moments they shared in this house in Valsugana: the summer holidays with their daughters, the long walks on the mountain when they were dating and later on as a family. Here the young Alcide noticed Francesca for the first time. They had been acquainted before because he studied with her brother Pietro Romano in Trento. However he did not really notice her until Easter 1915, as before he had only seen her as a child, 13 years younger than him. That summer, when the war had already broken out, Pietro invited Alcide to the house of the Romano's, a family of the industrial high bourgeoisie in the Trentino region. And there he saw Francesca. She was 21 and had just come back from her studies in Switzerland and London. Her cosmopolitan education had not erased her simplicity, the hearty mountain air in her lungs and her passion for sports.

Alcide, who was already 34, fell in love with her friendliness, her pleasant conversation and also knowing that Francesca had become a Red Cross volunteer. It was hard for him to say goodbye after his visit, but he had to go back to Vienna, where he was a member of the Austro-Hungarian Parliament. From then on, however, he would try to visit Pietro more often.

With the excuse of learning English he asked Francesca to teach him from a distance. He wrote letters in his broken English and she replied in her more elegant style. Through this epistolary relationship they got to know each other better and developed a friendship that would lead to a love, and then to their wedding in 1922.

What they had in common were the Trentino and a Catholic education. There was a considerable age gap and also a social one: their family stories were diametrically opposed. She grew up wrapped in cotton wool and studied at the most prestigious institutions, while he barely managed to go to college on a grant and ate in soup kitchens. Alcide was upfront with her from the start. In the same letter in which he declared his love in 1921, he warned that he could not offer the easy and comfortable life to which she was accustomed. He asked her to be his companion in the pursuit of an ideal: to dedicate their lives to building a more just and fraternal society. In exchange for giving up all luxury he offered a passion for worthwhile convictions. A life of politics, lived cleanly, does not provide much money. She understood immediately and always shared with him his endeavours, supporting and admiring a man who had struggled his way out of poverty without ever giving up on his principles.

Alcide was born in 1881 in Pieve Tesino, a small village in the Trentino. Back then this region was still part of the Austro-Hungarian Empire and was called South Tyrol.[1] Trento and its surroundings enjoyed a certain

---

[1] South Tyrol (*Südtirol*) region would later become part of Italy. The Italian name of this province is Trentino-Alto Adige.

degree of autonomy, as it was ruled by a bishop-prince for centuries, following a system of political and religious organisation inherited from the 11th century.

He was the son of a local policeman who moved every two or three years around the South Tyrol villages. It was a poor area of the empire, with an economy based on subsistence farming and marked by difficult communication between alpine villages. Many young people migrated and a high percentage of men from Pieve Tesino would be away for years travelling the world from Mexico to Moscow to sell prints, a local speciality that had gained international renown. This local business helped to improve the shortage for many families.

Despite material scarcity, the empire made education available to all its subjects. Moreover, the Empress Maria Theresa created a network of public schools and grants and imposed prison penalties to parents who did not send their children to class. Thus, illiteracy had disappeared in South Tyrol at a time when it amounted to 74% of the population in Italy.

At the age of ten Alcide entered the Bishops' College of Trento, where children from the least affluent families followed the German educational system. Thanks to his good grades at the end of secondary school he was awarded a grant to go to college in Vienna in 1900. He enrolled in philology and at 19 he moved to the capital, leaving behind his parents and three younger siblings: Luigi Mario, Marcelina and little Augusto, who was only seven.

He was impressed by the huge avenues, the palaces, the museums, the opera house and the intellectual and artistic turmoil of a bustling city in which the elites sought evasion cultivating the transgressive and the irrational. In the cafes everyone talked about a book just published by Sigmund Freud about the interpretation of dreams; and also about the pictorial and architectural revolution of Gustav Klimt and his Secession friends. They were the designers of a still unfinished avant-garde building that had already unleashed controversy.

De Gasperi could not afford to have much of a social life, or even to pay for a coffee, but the college experience with peers from Bohemia, Moravia, Galicia, Hungary, Bosnia and neighbouring Croatia opened his eyes to a previously unknown cultural and linguistic wealth.

At first it was very hard for him, away from his family and in such a different environment compared to his rural Trentino. He found support in other Italian students and also in migrant workers from his region. De Gasperi recounted his hardships only to his brother Luigi Mario, two years his junior. He confided in a letter and on condition that their parents would not know, that he had to queue with the poor for hot food and that his coat was not thick enough for the cold and wet weather of Vienna.

Since the grant did not cover all the expenses, he sought to give some tutorials to other students. He found strength in his faith, he went to church every day, and that is how he met other young Catholics, some of whom were involved in politics. They were dazzled by the figure of the mayor of Vienna, Karl Lueger. He was the founder and leader of the Christian Social Party and had modernised the city in a few years, bringing gas and electricity and building parks and hospitals. He had also challenged Emperor Franz Joseph by demanding equal rights for all nationalities and languages of the empire.

During all that time Alcide's heart remained anchored in Trento. Every summer he returned home and enrolled in Catholic associations of students and workers with whom he would keep in touch when he was back in Vienna. Pope Leo XIII's encyclical *Rerum Novarum*, published in 1891 to expose the social doctrine of the Catholic Church, gave rise to many initiatives in Trento, just like in Austria and Germany. The Trentino Catholic movement started a cooperative network for agricultural production and sales, and they also eased access to credit through the Trentino Catholic Bank.

De Gasperi enrolled in philology thinking about teaching, but his experience in Vienna gave him a new view of the world and a desire to engage in politics to contribute to the progress of his region. He found support and inspiration in his teachers, particularly in his theology professor Ernst Commer. With him he travelled to Rome for the first time in 1902, to attend a papal audience on the occasion of the 25th anniversary of the pontificate of Leo XIII. He encountered members of the Church and Catholic secular leaders, and the experience definitely made up his mind to become a politician.

Some in Trento criticised the administrative organisation and the connivance of the prince-bishop with an invader empire. There were growing voices calling for the independence of the Italian Trentino and Alto Adige (the two territories forming the Austrian region of South Tyrol). Secessionist groups existed also amongst Italian students in Vienna, but Alcide never joined. He aspired for his region to gain greater rights within the empire, as he believed that a multiple inclusive identity was possible. He felt at ease being a *Trentine*, an Italian and a subject of the Emperor.

His respect for the authority did not prevent him from being involved in conflicts. In 1904 he was arrested with 136 other Italian students who protested at the University of Innsbruck. This was the nearest Law School to the Trentino, and the Italian students went there to express their frustration for not having an Italian university close to home.

When the first students asked for an Italian-language university in the late 19th century, it seemed that the government was willing to accept and even suggested opening it in Trieste. In the end they found a halfway solution: in 1899 it created two chairs of Italian language in Innsbruck, but it was not enough for the Italians and from then on they protested and there would be occasional clashes between students. After a few years a Law School for the Italians opened. Not in Trieste, though, but in Wilten – a city near Innsbruck –, for fear that an Italian university in Trieste would feed the "Irredentism" political movement for independence.

In November 1904, Italian students from all parts of the empire went to Wilten to the opening of the faculty, and De Gasperi was one of them. German-language students went to oppose the Italians and a major riot erupted. De Gasperi ended up in prison with many of his classmates, including Pietro Romano. In that prison they sealed their lifelong friendship. When they were released, after 20 days, he learned that the government had decided to close the school.

In 1905, after five years in Vienna, he finally earned his degree in modern languages and in late July he returned home. He found out that Luigi Mario was ill. He had been ordained a priest the previous year and was taking care of the sick, but he caught an infection and died a few months later at the age of 23.

Through his commitment to Catholic organisations De Gasperi met the new prince-bishop, Monsignor Celestino Endrici, who asked De Gasperi to become editor in chief of *La Voce Cattolica*. He agreed and changed the name of the newspaper to *Il Trentino*. Both these moves, removing the word "Catholic" from the name and placing a lay person as head of the paper were revolutionary. But Endrici was an unusual character. He had come back to Trento, his homeland, after studying and teaching theology in Rome. He returned as a bishop at the age of 38, eager to modernise his principality. He wanted to progressively give more space to lay people in political and public life.

Endrici also entrusted De Gasperi with the task of separating the political organisation that could represent Catholics from the Catholic Church institution. He wanted to move towards the separation of Church and State that already existed in other parts of Europe but not in Trento, as this city still linked to the medieval tradition of the Holy Roman Empire. He encouraged De Gasperi and others to found a political party. They did so, and called it People's Party of Trento.

De Gasperi's PPT little by little worked its way between Socialists and Liberals, the two major parties. It spread its message at meetings and through the pages of *Il Trentino*. Also from the pulpit the clergy tried to mobilise the faithful to support the political party they considered theirs.

In contrast with the "irredentists", De Gasperi advocated a "positive national awareness", which could include multiple layers of identity. On this point he collided with another charismatic leader, the Socialist Cesare Battisti, for whom there was no other political option than independence and his region joining Italy.

In 1909 De Gasperi was elected to the municipal council of Trento. He tried to give voice to the peasants and workers, and collaborated with the Social-Christian unions. In particular he was concerned about the defence of the "woodcutters", workers exploited by loggers' monopolies.

With the motto "Catholics, Italians, Democrats" in the campaign, De Gasperi obtained a seat for the PPT in the Parliament. So in 1911 he returned to the capital, this time as one of the best connoisseurs of Vienna out of the Trento dispatch, which was composed of nine members: seven PTT, one Liberal and the Socialist Battisti.

An official of the Parliament made a mistake when he enrolled De Gasperi that would change his surname forever: Instead of typing "Degasperi" as all the ancestors had, the clerk wrote "De Gasperi", perhaps thinking that he came from a noble lineage. This would provide an occasion for his enemies to accuse him of being elitist, and also for Battisti to coin the nickname "Von Gasperi" for supposedly being pro-Austrian and a traitor to Italy.

In this chamber there were representatives of Austria, Bohemia, Hungary, the Czech Republic to a total of eleven nationalities, and each member could speak his own language. As in the Parliament that De Gasperi would dream of many years later for his revered Europe, the members were seated according to their political orientation from left to right, and not by their geographical origin.

From his seat De Gasperi called for social and economic improvements for workers and for the linguistic rights of the "Italian nation". He stressed the need for an Italian university and spoke out against the centralist attempts at Germanisation.

He never claimed independence, but in 1914 the assassination of Archduke Franz Ferdinand precipitated events. The Austro-Hungarian government declared war on Serbia and the Parliament of Vienna closed down. When Rome announced its neutrality, De Gasperi's efforts were aimed at preventing Trentino becoming a battleground between Italy and Austria. He was exempted from military service due to his weak health and joined the "Relief Committee for the Southern refugees".

Despite his distrust of the Italian minority, Emperor Franz Joseph issued a mobilisation order by which some 60,000 soldiers from the Trentino went to fight with the Austrians and other soldiers from the empire. Out of them 10,000 never returned from the eastern front, where they fought against the troops of the Russian Tsar. Among the fallen was Giuseppe, a brother of Pietro and Francesca, who died in 1916 at the age of 24 in the prison camp at Taskin (Russia). The Romano family then moved to Italy, while Alcide decided to stay in the Trentino and deal with the refugees.

The Italian-speaking inhabitants of South Tyrol were divided. Some 700 soldiers deserted and joined the Italian troops after crossing over the mountains. To Battisti and other Trentini, the First World War presented the chance to realise their irredentist dream of joining Italy.

Tensions between the Italian-speaking population and the neighbouring German-speaking Bolzano province were mounting and the Italians felt growing animosity and suspicion from the authorities. On 22 May 1915, *Il Trentino* was closed and a new official newspaper less "Italian" was started: *Il Risveglio austriaco* (The Austrian awakening).

Two days later, on the 24th, Italy declared war on Austria and Germany, despite the efforts of De Gasperi, who had gone to Rome several times the previous year to try to avoid this move. Austrians and Trentini, who until then were brothers, clashed at Austria's southern front, where soldiers from both sides were stationed in shelters on alpine summits for more than three years in what was later called the "White war".

Austria evacuated 70,000 Trentini. The official message was that they were taking civilians away from the battlefield, but people thought that it was rather due to the Emperor's mistrust. To the dismay and disappointment of De Gasperi, those citizens were taken to detention centres for civilians in other parts of the empire.

In 1917 the Parliament in Vienna reopened. De Gasperi intervened to denounce the violent arrests and deportations of his countrymen. Were they not subjects of the Emperor? Did not they have the same rights and dignity as other provinces? Others, like Battisti, refused to recognise the authority of the Emperor and paid their treason with their lives. Along with some of his men Battisti was executed in the courtyard of the Bishop's palace.

The First World War ended on 4 November 1918 with the signing of an armistice. At the peace conference in Paris, Italy was among the victorious powers and as such it won the territories of Trentino, Alto Adige and Venezia Giulia. The joy of the irredentists was not complete, though, since they continued to claim the territories of Istria and Dalmatia.

De Gasperi immediately accepted the peace agreement and adopted as his main goal the avoidance of a clash between the Italian population and the German-speakers in the province for if in Trento it was the Italian-speakers who had felt oppressed by the empire, now it would be the German-speaking population of Bolzano – the capital of Alto Adige – who would feel abandoned by Vienna and discriminated against by the rule of Rome.

The Trentini were received in the Parliament in Rome as heroes. Irredentism had created a flood of literature and inspired poets, painters, romantic composers who dreamed of unity. So many Italians were disappointed when their northern brothers made it clear from the start that they hoped to maintain their particularities and autonomy, at least to the same degree which they had enjoyed under the Emperor's authority. Many did not appreciate one of the first speeches of De Gasperi, when he said: "Trentini, let's not divide ourselves. Now we come to Rome to defend our autonomy as we did before in Vienna."

The rest of the PPT program coincided with the Christian view that the priest Don Luigi Sturzo wanted for Italy, so together they founded the Italian People's Party in 1919. In Italy the Catholics had not participated in politics since 1870, when the Pope Pius IX forbade their engagement in Italian politics because of his dispute with the government over the lost Papal States.[2] The situation changed in 1919, when Pope Benedict XV revoked the prohibition so that the PPI could run for elections. In that context, De Gasperi was one of the few in the new party who had a long political experience.

In 1921 he went to the polls as a candidate of the PPI in Trentino, teaming up with his friend Pietro. It was an eventful year: Francesca accepted his proposal to marry, and the PPI chose him as leader in the Parliament. Even after accepting a PPI national position he kept praising certain standards of the Austrian Empire – such as education and administrative efficiency – from which Italy could learn, and also demanding rights for the population of Bolzano.

That summer, once the Trentino issues were already on track, he truly became a leader in Italian politics. He travelled with Sturzo to Germany to meet with representatives of *Zentrum* and try to coordinate European parties of Christian inspiration. At the time *Zentrum* was collaborating with the Social Democratic Party to improve labour rights in Germany. This example, coupled with his experience with the unions in Trento, prompted him to defend the collaboration between the PPI and the Italian Socialists.

---

[2]   On 20 September 1870 Italian troops occupied Rome. In October a referendum decided to incorporate the city of Rome to the kingdom of Italy. Pope Pius IX said he was "prisoner" in the Vatican and cut any relations with the Italian government.

Apart from the social issues, the People's Party and the Socialists had another common goal: to stop the advance of fascism. However, not everyone in the Socialists or the PPI accepted this collaboration. Neither did the Holy See. The pragmatic ways of De Gasperi, focusing on solving problems, did not fit in with the inflamed rhetoric of other Catholic leaders.

Amid these turbulent times he married Francesca. It was their first taste of life together, as they had barely been able to see each other in the previous months and he had not been able to take care of the wedding plans. Even though they exchanged letters almost daily, she prepared the ceremony and also the apartment where they would live, right over the newsroom of *Il Nuovo Trentino*. The social upheaval was so that De Gasperi did not even know if they could go on honeymoon. They married on 14 June 1922 in Sella Valsugana. They went hiking for a few days to the south of Italy. Then Alcide received an urgent telegram from his party alerting of the outbreak of Fascist violence and he returned to Rome.

That is how he would spend his life in the following years, commuting between Rome and Trento. The situation did not improve when their first daughter Maria Romana was born, in March 1923.

That summer the Fascist pressure on the government provoked a serious crisis. People's Party members and Socialists were unable to present a united front: PPI senators rebelled against any agreement with the left wing. Not even the King seemed to have the ability to influence a strategy to stand up for democracy. De Gasperi wrote in *Il Nuovo Trentino*:

"Except for the great fundamental principles on which the political programmes of the various parties are based, everything is relative in politics, and it would be absurd to reject in advance the collaboration with a particular party if doing so could somehow serve the supreme interests of the country, which are the first objectives of politics."

A gap opened within the PPI. Some of its members accepted to take part in the first government of Mussolini. Having weighed up the complicated decision, De Gasperi decided to accept collaboration and remained at the head of the political group in the Parliament. He thought that a coalition government would force fascism to moderate itself. Don Sturzo thought otherwise, and advised De Gasperi not to negotiate with the Fascists. De Gasperi realised his mistake when Mussolini, in one of his first decisions, annulled the autonomy of Trentino.

Sturzo intended to take the opportunity of the upcoming PPI party congress in Turin in April 1923 to end the "collaboration". There was no need, because right before the party event Mussolini himself threw the PPI out of his government.

But that did not end the internal PPI problems. Another controversial front remained open by the difficult triangle between the PPI, the Fascists and the Holy See. Pope Pius XI wanted to maintain direct relations with Mussolini, who since coming to government had lowered the tone of his angry criticism of the Church. The Pope was worried about the legal status of the Papal States in Italy and feared Mussolini's reprisals against the little territory that was left to the Holy See in Rome. The Fascist leader asked the Pope to compel Sturzo to leave the country because he was bothered by the constant criticism of the priest.

After a tough campaign against Sturzo by the fascist press, the Holy See asked Sturzo to resign as PPI general secretary. So on 10 July 1923 he did, and one year later he departed for exile in London. Within the PPI the division between supporters and opponents of Mussolini deepened. Catholics were also split between those who accepted the government and the defenders of democracy.

In the elections of April 1924 the Fascists won 60% of the votes. The press denounced abuses and a wave of violence was unleashed. The assassination of the Socialist MP Giacomo Matteotti, after publicly denouncing irregularities in the polls, caused a shake up in people's minds. From exile in Paris, Socialist Filippo Turati proposed an anti-Fascist alliance to De Gasperi, who accepted. Beyond left and right there was the moral legitimacy of democracy, he thought. Most PPI followers supported De Gasperi, although there were also detractors, and the unofficial newspaper of the Holy See, *La Civiltà Cattolica*, stated that such an alliance would not be "appropriate, timely or fair".

De Gasperi sought the support of the monarch to ensure social stability and asked him to dissolve Parliament on 11 June 1925. However King Victor Emmanuel III felt that there was nothing he could do. Meanwhile, the Fascists began their campaign against the PPI, chasing and attacking militants.

The politicians and journalists in the opposition felt harassed, and publications were confiscated. More and more Italians chose exile. The official press was critical of De Gasperi and exposed the alleged dirty laundry of the "Austrian". De Gasperi ended up resigning as PPI secretary. On the one hand, he admitted his mistake in trying to collaborate with Mussolini. He also thought that perhaps his resignation would save his friends and colleagues from harassment. It was not the case. Several PPI members who attempted to enter the Parliament were attacked by the Fascists. He also resigned as director of *Il Nuovo Trentino*. Furthermore, he wanted to disassociate himself from the Trentino Catholics so that they would not suffer more attacks.

De Gasperi shared his hardships in a letter to Sturzo. Being barred from politics and journalism, he became a pariah who could be dangerous for any institution or company trying to thrive in the new Fascist state. He did not see any future in his country and considered going into exile with his wife and two daughters Maria Romana and Lucia. He confided his intentions to Sturzo as well as his disappointment over some comrades who had adapted to the new situation, renouncing their principles.

While he made up his mind about his future he left Rome and returned to his region with his family. He settled in Sella Valsugana and through the mediation of Sturzo began writing for some international newspapers using a pseudonym. But the regime did not stop pursuing him. On the night of 1 to 2 November 1926, fascist squads vandalised the newsroom of *Il Nuovo Trentino* even though De Gasperi had already resigned.

On 5 November, Alcide was with his brother Augusto when a lieutenant *carabiniere* and two policemen forced them to get into a car, saying they intended to protect them. They were taken to the Fascist office in Vicenza to face a trial for treason. De Gasperi refused to accept the principles of fascism. They feared torture or execution right there which most certainly would have happened had it not been for Luciano Marzotto, a moderate Fascist MP. Marzotto protected the brothers and took them to his home overnight. They left safely the following day by train from Verona.

Fate seemed hopelessly clouded. On 9 November the Parliament expelled all anti-Fascists MPs in response to two terrorist attacks perpetrated against Mussolini in September and October. That same day an order decreed the dissolution of the PPI for their "anti-national activities against the State". Police watched over the party leaders, so it seemed to De Gasperi that his family could be at risk and so he decided to leave Francesca and the girls and go underground. He used a fake identity to move around, first to Milan and then to Rome.

He and Francesca were looking for ways to escape and reunite elsewhere. On 11 March 1927 the Florence police arrested Alcide and Francesca on a train on their way to Trieste, in north-eastern Italy. He was accused of "illegal expatriation" and sentenced to four years in prison. On 12 March, by express order of Mussolini, Alcide was taken to the Regina Coeli prison and his wife was locked in the Delle Mantellate women's prison, a former convent near Regina Coeli.

She was soon released and returned to Valsugana to her daughters. She would write letters of encouragement to her husband with photos of the girls. From his prison he reflected on his life and career. At the age of 46 he saw a bleak picture before him. He was far from his family, without a job and abandoned by almost everyone he had considered his friend. He was left with his loneliness and a bitter sense of failure.

His health was delicate, and in July that year he had to be taken to hospital. This is where he would spend the rest of his captivity while his lawyers tried to have the sentence reduced. Only because he gained the friendship and trust of his captors was he allowed to receive his wife's letters. He suffered for her and for his aging father, who was not even told that his son was in prison.

He wondered if he had acted righteously in sacrificing his own family to politics. But he could not have done otherwise. "It was my conscience that imposed it, my convictions, dignity, self respect and loyalty to my flag and to my life," he wrote to Francesca. In addition to the letters he wrote, he read the Bible, prayed and helped the prison officers to write letters to their wives and relatives.

His 16 months of anguish and loneliness ended in August 1928, thanks to the appeal introduced by his lawyers and also to the mediation of Endrici, who was still bishop of Trento. When he was free, Lucia was three and a half and did not recognise her father when he arrived home.

Upon release he would remain under vigilance and was unable to resume his career. The condition for his freedom was for him to stay in Rome and away from his constituency. Besides, he did not want to put his loved ones in danger begging for work at one of the cooperatives or companies in Trento. At least he was granted special permission to spend the month of August with his family in Valsugana.

In September he was back in Rome feeling completely lost, trying to restart. He survived financially with the help of some friends and the income from translations. Despite the solitude and uncertainty, or perhaps because of them, he took refuge in his spiritual life. A few weeks before Christmas 1929 he went up to the dome of St. Peter's Church. Staring out at Rome, he was comforted to think that he was at the epicentre of Christianity and of a universal community.

But soon he would be disappointed when on 11 February 1929 the Lateran Pacts between the Fascist government and the Holy See were signed to establish the Vatican State. On the one hand, De Gasperi understood the Pope's need to ensure independence of the Vatican from the Italian State, and especially from the Fascist regime. But he feared that the temporal and political power would be confused with the spiritual mission of the Church and that it could be interpreted by Italians as papal support for Fascism.

When the president of Catholic Action, Luigi Colombo, publicly called on Catholics to vote for the Fascist Party in elections to the new Parliament De Gasperi could not believe it. How could he forget so quickly the insults and violations of the most fundamental rights!

Bishop Endrici again intervened to get him a job, and in April the Vatican Library offered him a position. It was a relief for De Gasperi, a haven of peace. When Mussolini asked the Holy See to fire De Gasperi from the Vatican library, the answer was given by Pope Pius XI himself: "The Holy Father does not and will not regret having given an honest man and a father some of the bread that you have taken away from him."

The whole family moved with him into a small apartment, the only thing he could afford with his minimum wage. He felt he was going through a long "dark night". He prayed and developed a very humane and spiritual concept of religion. He also took the opportunity to review the biographies of Christian characters from different countries who over centuries had built a social doctrine and fought for freedom. Although he wrote under a pseudonym, the regime was trying to trip him up.

In 1939 he was promoted to secretary of the Vatican Library and his salary rose, making life a bit easier. In the meantime he had two more daughters: Cecilia (who they called Lia) and Paola. The family moved to a larger apartment in Via Bonifacio VIII, where they could see St. Peter's dome from their roof.

On 10 June 1940 at the Roman Piazza Venezia, Benito Mussolini came out to balcony and gave a heated speech in which he declared war on France and Britain in the name of honour and of the fatherland. The crowds cheered him to cries of "*Duce, duce, duce*" (Leader).

De Gasperi was horrified. In the evening he invited some friends to his apartment to evaluate the situation. He could already envision Italy being defeated by an allied bloc of which the US would be part. He began to seek contacts with opponents, such as the Socialist Reformist Ivanoe Bonomi.

In the spring of 1942 he suffered an episode of nervous exhaustion and went with his family to Trentino for a few weeks to rest. In Borgo Valsugana he took long walks, he saw friends... and also met some leading anti-Fascists from Trentino.

The Catholic opposition to fascism wanted to revitalise the PPI and in 1942 decided to create a new party, that they called *Democrazia Cristiana*. De Gasperi was the natural leader and immediately became its president.

In spite of being vetoed from politics, his work in Rome allowed him to be in contact with other opponents. He attended secret meetings held at friends' homes. This is how the National Liberation Committee (NLC) was born, launched by members of different political groups including the DC, Communists, Socialists and Liberals.

In the summer of 1943 the political instability made him fear an outbreak of violence, so Francesca returned to Trentino with the four girls. The King, Victor Emmanuel III, fled the country on 8 September, and then the Germans occupied Rome and other parts of Italy. Underground meetings were organised at the apartment of Archbishop Pietro Barbieri where some Jews and other persecuted individuals took refuge. When it got too late, they would stay over.

The Germans threatened to deport opponents of Fascism and De Gasperi was forced to take refuge. He first hid with Pietro Nenni and Ivanoe Bonomi in Laterano, a church in Rome but considered to have a diplomatic status. However when the SS violated the extraterritoriality right of several basilicas, De Gasperi changed hiding place and moved in with Monsignor Celso Constantini. His daughters did not see him again until the liberation by the Americans in June 1944, although Francesca travelled to Rome now and then to meet with him in secret.

Once democracy was back in place Ivanoe Bonomi formed a government supported by the six parties of the NLC. De Gasperi became minister without portfolio. Some exiled Italians started coming back. *Democrazia Cristiana* was legalised as a political party and held a congress where De Gasperi was unanimously acclaimed as political secretary. In his acceptance speech he claimed for the moral reconstruction of the country and recalled that his was to be a secular party, capable of overcoming the extreme left and right, a great national party in the centre which would stop the spread of communism by bringing real solutions to the problems of workers and the less privileged in society.

A few months later, in December 1945, he won the national elections and became head of government. He tried to avoid the outbreak of several conflicts: a civil war between monarchists and republicans, between German-speaking and Italians in his own region, between communists and anti-communists. The first thing he did was to hold a referendum in June 1946 to choose between the continuity of the monarchy with House of Savoy or the Republic. The left called for the republic and the right for monarchy. He just wanted peace and said he would accept any decision. The republic won and De Gasperi promised to lead a peaceful and orderly transition.

Another difficult issue was the peace agreement with Austria and the future of Trentino-Alto Adige: Austria claimed the German-speaking area, but the peace agreement stated that the former Austrian region of South Tyrol, including Bolzano, would remain in Italy. In September 1946 he signed the final peace agreement with Austrian minister Karl Gruber. De Gasperi ensured the administrative autonomy of the region and the right of the minority to use its language. He was convinced, though, that the minorities' issue would only be solved in a broader European context.

He formed a tripartite government with Christian Democrats, Socialists and Communists, resisting the pressure from the Holy See to not work with the Communists. One third of the Italians had voted for the Communist Party and De Gasperi had to listen. The clerical right-wing resented his independence. It was the first time that a Catholic was in office in Italy and certain sectors expected him to implement the religious doctrine.

On 12 November 1946 De Gasperi had a conversation with a high level Vatican official who threatened to withdraw support for the DC if he continued working with parties who were critical of the Church. But De Gasperi wanted broad political support to address the real problems. His main concerns were to contain the post-war violence threat posed by armed groups, to tackle unemployment and to boost the economy after so much destruction. He favoured reconstruction loans and increased minimum wages. He devoted all his energy to the pursuit of social peace.

Over the years, he got used to criticism. After he retired to Valsugana he told a friend in a letter: "I lived deadly dangerous hours. I felt alone, abandoned by many friends, and what kept me going was to know that I was working for peace."

What many did not see during his lifetime, they commended after his death. His funeral in Rome, in the church of San Lorenzo, was attended by thousands of people. The Via Nazionale was filled with crowds who wanted to see Francesca and her daughters, all dressed in black, following the coffin draped in an Italian flag. Behind them followed many Christian Democrat colleagues, some who were faithful and some who had betrayed him, and beside them, fellow Liberals, Socialists and Communists, a proof that he had achieved the goal of peace and reconciliation. Only the dream of a united Europe had escaped his grasp.

1954-1957

Benelux Breathes New Life into Europe

Joseph Bech, Johan W. Beyen and Paul-Henri Spaak at the Hotel
San Domenico, in Taormina (Italy) (© Council of Europe)

The ministerial meeting to solve the crisis of the EDC could not start
with worse news: De Gasperi's death. His loss weighs heavily on the
minds of the ministers, who learn about it early in the morning. Spaak
cries like a child next to Bech, who tries in vain to comfort him.

In the morning of 19 August, while the rest of the participants are attending a reception with King Baudouin, Adenauer has a bilateral meeting with the French premier. Without beating around the bush he accuses Mendès France of placing him in an untenable situation. And only because he trusted the French promises: two years after the signing of the Bonn and Paris agreements, his country is still officially under occupation. The high commissioners have not yet been replaced by ambassadors and the German people are impatient with the lack of progress. Adenauer cannot keep relying on the patience of the Germans.

The Netherlands, Belgium and Luxembourg have already ratified the EDC agreement. In Italy, the Parliament discussed the project and found no major obstacles. However, in France, the country on whose behalf Monnet and Schuman proposed the project to the others, the text has not yet been subject to debate.

The French Assembly is scheduled to hold the first-reading vote on 30 August. Amongst politicians there are all kinds of opinions, so the result is unpredictable and the constant changes of government in France only add to the uncertainty. This instability is incomprehensible to the German people, who begin to lose confidence in the European project. Mendès France listens carefully to Adenauer's words but cannot make concessions. He came to Brussels with a well-defined plan and will not even alter a comma.

An hour later, the leaders enter the meeting room with circumspect gesture. Mendès France presents his new version of the Treaty. It introduces radical changes, including a derogation of eight years of the supranational institutions. The other five members listen to him astonished.

Adenauer explains as calmly as he is capable of, that the new French demands would mean that everything would have to be renegotiated and, depending on the outcome, potentially a restarting of the ratification process. He wants him to be aware of the problems and risks that this would entail.

Mendès France apologises and explains his situation: seven parliamentary committees have spoken out against the EDC treaty and against the political union. In such circumstances it is impossible to approve the treaties as they stand. If he tries he will lose not only that vote, but also the government. This would lead to a victory of the extreme-left coalition of the Popular Front and therefore jeopardise not only the EDC, but also NATO.

Spaak is disappointed. He thinks that Mendès France would rather sacrifice Europe than lose the government. He regrets his lack of historical vision. There are moments in life when one must take risks, convince the others and energetically defend one's convictions in an attempt to change an adverse situation. It saddens him to see that Mendès France has already thrown in the towel.

Despite his efforts over four days, Spaak's diplomatic and conciliatory skills don't work, due to the intransigence of Mendès France. At least, this is Spaak's view, even though the story that the French minister tells back home is quite different. According to his version, the failure is due to the manoeuvres of the Belgian, who isolated and despised Mendès France at the conference.

Beyond any allocation of blame, the fact is that the conference ends on 22 August and each and every participant leaves Brussels with a strong feeling of sorrow. The chancellor returns to the Bühlerhöhe thermal spa in Baden-Baden to conclude his holidays. He feels absolutely dispirited. The plan designed to accomplish the reconciliation between France and Germany ended up having the opposite effect and now there seems to be an insurmountable fracture between them. To make matters worse, De Gasperi's death has deprived the project of a great defendant of the federation, and Schuman is offside in French politics.

Schuman attends as a regular MP the French Assembly debate on the EDC, starting on Friday 27 August. From his seat he listens saddened by the words of Mendès France as he abandons defence of the European Army. During the three-day debate he is stranded in a neutral position between the heated speeches of both defenders and detractors. As if it had nothing to do with him. As if the future of peace with the German neighbour was not at stake.

When a majority in the Assembly rejects even to vote on the proposal – by 319 votes to 264 –, Schuman's mind flies to Bonn. What will Adenauer think? He will probably feel betrayed by France. These are the inherent risks to democracy. If only Schuman had continued in the Foreign Affairs Ministry!

This is, indeed, the worst day in Adenauer's political life. He is still on vacation in Baden-Baden when he hears the news. In the evening, shortly before 9 pm, the German embassy in Paris telephones the chancellor's office, who then sends a message to the hotel. Adenauer can already guess the content of the note. He impassively reads the paper at the front desk, and rushes up to his room. He does not want to give any chance to the curious onlookers to read the undisguised anger and disappointment in his face.

The foundations of the ECSC wobble. Without continuity, without a solution to the defence of West Germany, Europe is meaningless. Adenauer does not wish to anticipate events, but he reviews one after another all the possible alternatives to the project of European integration. His main support will now once again be the United States. Germany's entry into NATO should be accelerated.

Even more upset is Spaak. He is also vacationing with friends at Lake Maggiore in the Italian town of Cannobio, close to the Swiss border. The beauty of nature, the good food and the hosts' attempts to appease him do not calm his anger. Mendès France has not only killed the EDC but he is also blaming Spaak, saying that his wicked arts pushed the other participants to look at the French with suspicion and antipathy.

As Spaak does not want to spoil the party, he retires to his room that evening shortly after dinner. He finds some relief in writing a letter to Simonne. Since they met in exile in London they have never separated, even if they do not live together. Spaak was already a husband and a father, so after the London hiatus he returned to his family in Brussels. His marriage survived, at least in appearance. Simonne remains his intellectual and emotional support, the depository of his secrets and desires. With her he can be sincere about Mendès France:

"Never in my life have I found such a proud man and, what is worse, so unfair," he writes in his letter. "What he is saying after the meeting is a monument of half-truths and deliberate lies."

He can no longer enjoy the holidays, being anxious for the fate of Europe after the EDC fiasco. He goes back home earlier than expected and on his way he stops by in Paris to speak with Monnet. They must discuss this together. He foresees the pressure that he will receive from Monnet, whose frustration with the slow reaction by politicians is blatant. The problem is that Jean never experienced the ruling of the polls or the parliamentary rejection – a democratic and legitimate decision – that conditions those governing. But at this point in time they need each other to rescue the fledgling Community and, to Spaak, that is more important than any personal disagreement.

Jean Monnet is recovering and does not attend the debate in the National Assembly. He was at the Trianon palace, near Versailles, when he heard the news. He has settled there with his family for a few weeks while his Houjarray house is undergoing renovations. He will not tell his Belgian friend, but he was alone when he found out about the defeat – Silvia and the girls were out for a walk –, and he collapsed. Contrary to his usual fighting and optimistic spirit, he wondered for the first time whether his dream was worth it, whether all his efforts over the years for a united Europe were but a pipe dream. Fortunately, Spaak's call to prepare a joint response brings him back to his usual mood.

According to Spaak, it is essential to unlink German rearmament from European integration. The EDC has proved to be an obstacle to the integration project by cause of the military carrying a strong symbolic and patriotic charge, and therefore it is not the best foundation on which to build a mechanism for the transfer of sovereignty; especially at the beginning. The integration will be a slow process, while solving Germany's defence is pressing.

Monnet agrees. The question now is choosing between two options: the integration of Germany into NATO or trying to recover the EDC treaty. They make a round of telephone consultations with their partners: Rome, Bonn, The Hague and Luxembourg. Except for Italy, everyone thinks it is better to abandon the EDC. Monnet and Spaak, who have excellent relations with the US administration and with the British government since the Second World War, start to work on a consensus solution.

The formula accepted by all and proposed both to Mendès France and to Adenauer, is that Germany will join NATO with certain obligations. Although Mendès France is a tough nut to crack, he eventually compromises. The main condition is that the German arms production is managed from the common ECSC institutions, while the size and shape of military units belong to the scope of NATO.

The solution to the EDC disaster somehow reassures participants that the integration process is here to stay. It is a sliver of hope to reopen the door. Now the problem is that France and Germany seem to have given up on solving their problems within the European framework and prefer a bilateral dialogue or sponsorship of the United States and the United Kingdom. They are about to solve their dispute on the Saar with a bilateral agreement. Spaak and Monnet fear that Europe is less relevant for Paris and Bonn than it was a few months ago.

In late September, at the Council of Europe's Assembly in Strasbourg, Spaak delivers a passionate defence of integration. He will not give up on Europe despite the EDC defeat. The fight continues, because unity is the natural destiny of a continent that already shares the same values. Although Spaak is not a believer, he thinks that the spiritual roots are an anchor for coexistence and unity: "We share the same civilisation, which is a Christian civilisation."

He encourages members to banish their fear of Germany, to grant it its place among the peoples of Europe, and also to defend a free Europe capable of defending itself:

"A memory comes to my mind: the memory of a woman of the resistance who died in prison during the war. Before she died she wrote with blood on the wall of her cell a phrase from Revelations; 'I have opened a door for you that no one can close: nothing: no person, no old tradition, no selfish nationalism, no *chauvinism*'."

The vibrant emotion in his words is not pure declamatory rhetoric this time. Images of the wars flood into his head; the First World War, when he ran away from home to fight for freedom and was imprisoned in Germany. Then the second big war, a conflict he survived unlike his sister-in-law, Suzanne. She was the wife of his brother Claude and worked as a musician playing in the so-called "Red Orchestra" for their leftist political views. She was shot dead in Fresnes during the war. She is the one who wrote that sentence with her blood.

Those who have not lived through such experiences are unaware of the strength, the resilience that these memories imprint on the soul. Spaak shares such memories with Schuman and Adenauer. This bond, stronger than flags and acronyms, unites them in their ceaseless effort to which it is worth dedicating one's life, like De Gasperi.

A few days later, Adenauer congratulates Spaak on his speech and reiterates his full support. He will not give up. Over the following months, in October and November, they often talk on the phone to prepare the counterattack.

What is clear is that the EDC defeat has left France and Germany offside. Spaak considers that Benelux must take the initiative, so he summons Joseph Bech and Johan Willem Beyen in order to study a common position. As they already share a long friendship, Spaak frankly expresses his concern about France, which seems to have lost its way and fallen into a state of confusion about its role in Europe.

The three men came together for the first time during their exile in London in 1943, when Spaak and Bech officially represented their government in exile and Beyen advised the Dutch government. Each one belonged to a different political family: Joseph Bech, who is ten years older than Spaak, is a conservative; Spaak is a socialist, and Beyen a liberal economist without any political affiliation. However they risked their promising careers for a crazy plan: to create a common customs union, to set a stable exchange rate between their currencies and to coordinate their trade policy.

Until then, the three small countries harboured historical grudges against each other. But the atmosphere of freedom and courage that was felt in the political circles of the London exile created strong ties among its leaders. Taking some distance from home, they realised that they shared the same problems and that only together could they solve them.

The three then convinced the Dutch Foreign Minister Van Kleffens. The minister did not think it was very realistic. He accepted because he thought – like many others – that the plan would be just thrown into the dustbin after the war and would never be implemented. He almost gets away with it, given the initial reluctance of public opinion. In Belgium the project was renamed "Spaakistan" after the war, mocking what many regarded as the behaviour of a flamboyant politician. But the three held their nerve and went ahead.

Ten years later, they have not only achieved the customs union between the three countries but are willing to enlist other European partners in their adventure. Spaak, Bech and Beyen meet in late November and promise to give new impetus to integration. Time is short. What will happen in Germany when Adenauer is no longer there? He is 78 years old and may soon retire. For decades his nickname is "the Old One", because he has been involved in politics for many years. He has seen everything and has no interest other than ensuring a better future for the next generations. "We need to bring to fruition the project while we can still count on him," Spaak says.

In Luxembourg, Monnet is still mulling over the European Army. He somehow blames himself for having failed to pull the strings behind the scenes. If instead of becoming chair of the High Authority he had used his contacts and invested the time to privately explain the meaning of the EDC to journalists and politicians, perhaps it would have gone through.

Now it's too late to think of what could have happened. That is why Monnet wants to act quickly, to give a new direction to the integration process: instead of the army, he believes that the European Coal and Steel Community must broaden its scope to other areas such as transport and energy. And to fully engage in that task Monnet needs to be free from any official responsibility.

This is what he tells Spaak in a visit to Belgium. They meet for lunch at the usual restaurant, at the Astoria, one of the finest hotels in the centre of Brussels. Spaak is also eager to talk to Monnet and coordinate a response, but there are two things about the Frenchman that make him nervous: the first one, his criticism of politicians for not being strong enough to defend the EDC, and the second one is Monnet's frugality. He always eats a salad, a grilled sole and a glass of wine. Every time they eat together the stocky Spaak is still hungry! So this time he has a hearty snack before leaving home.

The conversation flows cordially: both agree on Mendès Frances' disastrous management of the negotiation and the ratification process. But now they must look to the future. Monnet communicates to Spaak his intention to quit the High Authority and focus on sowing the seeds of "Europeanism" in the public opinion, discretely and patiently. To the surprise of the Frenchman, Spaak is not particularly upset and instead of asking him to remain in office, he encourages Monnet to engage in this new mission.

Monnet explains that before leaving office on 15 February, he will write a paper with his proposal for the next phase of integration. They agree they should go slowly in small stages before calling for a political federation.

On 9 November, during an ECSC ministerial meeting, Monnet officially announces that he will not continue as president of the High Authority when his term expires. The statement is not followed by any nostalgia or regret. On the contrary, it immediately unleashes manoeuvres by the six governments to find a replacement. In late January, they all put several names on the table. By then Monnet has reflected over his own decision and discreetly tells Spaak that he could reconsider. "Did he think we were going to beg him to stay?" Spaak wonders. The Belgian has no problem for Monnet to continue, although he believes that it is now too late to take back his decision.

Spaak consults with Adenauer, who says that it would be better to have a non-French president of the High Authority this time. Of course the chancellor asks Spaak to keep his opinion secret to avoid any antagonism with Monnet. Adenauer does not want a German for that position either, because it seems that everything revolves around these two countries. It would be refreshing to have someone from Benelux, he says.

Thinking that he still has a chance to stay as head of the High Authority, Monnet invests money in creating an institution that could "lobby" for Europe even if he holds a public office position: It is the Action Committee for the United States of Europe, based in Paris. The vision that he wants to promote through this lobby is to expand the powers of the High Authority to other economic sectors. In the long term the goal is a confederation following the Swiss model, where different communities live together in democratic system without domination. He hopes that this committee will work as an engine for gradual integration, through a grassroots action of addressing civil society, political parties and unions.

On 6 February, a week before the expiry of Monnet's mandate, the French pro-Europeans receive with optimism the fall of Mendès Frances' government. This political crisis has nothing to do with Europe: the censure motion is due to a crisis in North Africa. However, this change opens a door to hope in Europe. Edgar Faure forms a new government and is surrounded by several of the people who launched the European project, such as Robert Schuman and Pierre-Henri Teitgen.

In Belgium, Spaak welcomes the changes, not only for his animosity toward Mendès France, but because his friends are back. He and Monnet discuss the latest news by phone and then call the foreign ministers of Germany (Adenauer), France (Antoine Pinay) and Italy (Gaetano Martino) for a meeting to address Monnet's proposal.

The date is 2 April, and the agenda includes a twofold proposal: to expand the ECSC powers to the energy sector (electricity, gas and fuel) and transport (railway, river and road transport). Monnet also wants a shared management of the development of atomic energy for peaceful purposes. The powers of the High Authority would be extended to take the new responsibilities, and Monnet could reconsider seeking a second term as president.

The ministers of Germany, France and Italy support the proposal, but are reluctant to let Monnet continue. Even though they cannot say it aloud, almost all the leaders would prefer him to leave. They are already mulling over the name of René Mayer. When Monnet finds out he is shocked. Not because he dislikes René Mayer, who he has known since they met in Algiers in 1943, but because he questions his ability for the post, and also because he feels that ministers have forgotten that he inspired the whole process when he wrote the Schuman declaration.

On his side, Beyen writes a memorandum to Spaak and Bech stating his point of view: Monnet is mistaken in his insistence to integrate different economic sectors vertically (starting with energy and transport). Beyen advocates instead creating a common market at once, copying the model of Benelux: start by a customs union and move horizontally towards the economic union:

"Any partial integration tends to resolve difficulties in a sector with measures that can affect other sectors or the interests of consumers, and may lead to the exclusion of foreign competition. That is not the way to increase European productivity. Moreover, sector integration does not contribute to strengthening the sense of solidarity and unity of Europe in the same degree as a full economic integration."

Bech replies in writing that he fully agrees with Beyen, while Spaak does not want to choose. It feels he is caught between two opposing positions: one from Monnet and one from Beyen. He wants to know what Konrad Adenauer and Gaetano Martino think, so he explains to them the difference between the sectoral and progressive plan advocated by Monnet and the common market proposed by Beyen. He invites them to discuss this issue in person and they arrange for a meeting in Luxembourg on 25 April. The idea is that Monnet will chair the meeting, so that despite not being a government representative he can explain his point of view and then start drafting a text for a new treaty.

However, as soon as Spaak sends out the invitation he starts receiving contradicting messages. Pinay accepts the invitation but not without warning Spaak that "we must go step by step, not to gallop." The French suggests that it could be convenient to postpone the summit so that they have enough time to prepare the documents for the negotiation. The Italian minister, Martino, is in agreement with Pinay: before accepting to engage in the adventure of a new treaty, they need to thoroughly study the different options.

To make matters worse, Spaak has health problems and is hospitalised between 8 and 20 April. But even from his sick bed he does not stop working. He refuses to cancel the upcoming meeting for fear that it would linger indefinitely. He calls Beyen to have his advice, and he proposes a compromise-formula: they should accept the principle of sectoral integration advocated by Monnet to please the French, but link this short-term goal to a medium-term horizon of full economic integration. Spaak thinks that the compromise solution is worth trying and decides to postpone the meeting in order to prepare a good presentation of both lines of action.

When Spaak leaves the hospital he spends some days convalescing at home, where he receives Monnet's visit. He comes to see how Spaak is doing… and also to submit a draft declaration that he has written with the help of his faithful collaborator Pierre Uri. The text includes sectoral integration in atomic energy and transport, as well as the start of a customs union with a view to economic union. It includes both proposals; although Monnet himself remains unconvinced that Europe is mature enough for a common market.

The next day, 23 April, Spaak travels to The Hague with Monnet's text to discuss it with Beyen and Bech. In an intense day of work, they draft a document combining Monnet's proposal and their own views. They call it the Benelux Memorandum. Once all the loose ends are tied up, they send it to all six foreign offices on 20 May.

So there is already a document to take as the basis for the negotiation, as requested by Pinay and Martino. However, they still have only the date – 1 June –, but not the place, since the original meeting in Luxembourg was postponed. Gaetano Martino wants them to meet in Messina, Sicily. Beyen is taken aback: the city has poor connections and it would take ages to get there. It would also give a bad image to the project because it is a town with beach and sun, more suitable for a holiday. Monnet shares Beyen's opinion. But Martino is not discouraged and insists. There will soon be elections in Sicily, and the presence of international leaders comes in handy for his campaign, as he is running for this constituency. Moreover, he cannot leave his town during the campaign.

In the end the others agree for the sake of a friendly atmosphere for the difficult decisions which lie ahead. Also Beyen and Spaak think that by making Martino happy it will be easier to count on his support for the Benelux plan. To sweeten the pill for the public opinion and explain why they are spending a few days at a luxurious sea front resort, they tell the press that they are returning "to the Greco-Roman past of Europe to build a common future".

Spring 1955, Messina

On 31 May, Beyen arrives in a bad mood. He was right. It took him and Spaak an eternity to finally get there: first a flight to Rome, then by car to Naples, and from there by boat to Palermo. Finally on 1 June, early in the morning they reach Taormina. Martino is exultant when he welcomes them at the fantastic San Domenico hotel, in the small town famous for its Greek theatre. He can barely disguise his pleasure as he shows them the palm trees in the garden and the balustrade overlooking the sea. To enjoy the sunny day after the long trip Spaak, Bech and Beyen take off their jackets, roll their sleeves up, and sit on the terrace to prepare the negotiation.

The conference officially begins at 5 pm in the city of Messina, about 45 kilometres from Taormina. Bech, Hallstein, Pinay, Beyen and Spaak immediately set to work in a relaxed atmosphere... that soon becomes twisted. Just when everyone thought that the appointment of René Mayer was a closed issue, the German minister, Walter Hallstein, says that he disagrees. With his negotiating skills, Spaak manages to convince Hallstein in exchange for having a German as deputy president of the High Authority. Then each minister explains his vision of the next step in European integration.

Discussions continue the following day, this time about the future of Europe. Before addressing the choice between the Beyen and the Monnet's paths, Spaak reminds the participants about the meaning of a united Europe, and why having a clear agenda is necessary: it is all about peace, shared prosperity, solidarity and unity of peoples. After this introduction, he goes into the full details of a common market and a monetary policy. The atmosphere gradually heats up until they reach a point in the afternoon when the negotiation stagnates.

Then they are asked to leave the room, for there is a break to attend a dinner and a show arranged by Gaetano. Although at first the other ministers found this side activity a frivolous entertainment, it turns out to be a very stimulating input: with the dances and the drinks the politicians relax and when they come back to the hotel, at 2 am, they feel at ease to resume the negotiation. They go to a meeting room and now it seems easier to reach agreements. Shortly after 4 am Spaak looks through the window and sees the sun rising behind the Etna volcano. They are close to reaching a deal and the Belgian will always remember this moment. Finally at dawn, the general terms for a new treaty are accepted and they go to sleep. They are all tired and cranky except Spaak, who feels the beauty of a historic moment in a unique setting. He steps out to the balcony of his room. Staring out to the sea he starts singing *O sole mio*, provoking the fury of Pinay, who had already gone to bed and bangs on the wall to make his neighbour shut up.

Summer 1955, Val Duchesse

Following the Messina conference, a committee of national experts must prepare the documents for the ministers to discuss two new European treaties: One for atomic energy (to be called Euratom) and another for a common market. Spaak is charged with chairing the working committee, which must submit a draft by October.

Experts from the six ECSC countries and a British representative get together in the Belgian capital on 9 July. They break into three working groups: one with experts for the common market, another one with experts on atomic energy, and a third one of lawyers who will draft the articles of the treaties.

In early September, the experts move to Val Duchesse. This castle, a former medieval priory near Brussels, is used by the Belgian government to accommodate international leaders and to hold big conferences and receptions. The place is suitable for walks in the garden and the environment favours a good atmosphere for the negotiators. The fact that most of them already know each other, because they have already drafted the Benelux, the OEEC, the ECSC , the European Defence and the Political Community treaties, also helps. Monnet would be happy with the atmosphere that has been created, as he strongly believes that this is a crucial element of his "method".

Spaak jokes with the participants about their forced monastic life: getting up very early to attend the meetings, having lunch together – often reading documents and discussing their content during the meal –, then returning to their desks in the afternoon, again dining all together... and sometimes even staying up late into the night to finish work. Their only rest is during the sporadic walks around the gardens of Val Duchesse to clear their minds.

During the weekends the negotiators return home. In addition to seeing their families they take the opportunity to meet with their respective ministries and to update their negotiating mandates. Spaak doesn't mind. Experience has shown him that it is better to consult with governments during the process and to know in advance which red lines cannot be crossed in order to avoid last minute surprises.

In November the technical studies are finished, and shocking news gives an unexpected boost to the supporters of integration: On 4 November, Soviet troops enter Budapest and any hope of a rapprochement between Moscow and Western Europe fades away. Before the eyes of the helpless West, Poland, Czechoslovakia and Hungary were not able to free themselves from Soviet tyranny, despite Stalin's absence. The expectations raised by his death in 1953 have vanished and left instead a new wave of fear that another world war breaks out. Those who criticise the economic and political integration of Western Europe for being a provocation to the Soviet bloc lose arguments, as well as those opposed to NATO and to a European defence system.

Also in public opinion favourable winds are blowing for closer cooperation in the field of energy. Egypt's unilateral decision to nationalise the Suez Canal the previous summer exposed the fragility of the European industry and its dependence on energy imports. Jean Monnet intensifies his contacts to advance the project of a common administration of the atomic energy for peaceful purposes.

After a long Christmas break, experts resume in February. When a deal is practically closed, it comes to Spaak's ears that the British are going to block the single market, because they fear that it will harm their products. Spaak speaks with Anthony Eden to placate him. The British minister is afraid that Europe aspires to becoming a third power between the USSR and the United States. Spaak clears all his doubts: the military alliance NATO will remain, and the common market in no way intends to turn its back on the UK or the US; they are key partners of the Europe that is developing. Furthermore, Spaak reminds Eden that the doors of the ECSC and of the new organisations to be created are always open to London.

However the Belgian also makes it very clear to Eden that the British intention to create a free trade area with the Nordic countries and Switzerland within the OEEC framework is totally unacceptable for the six ECSC member states. When Eden, annoyed, asks why they are so insistent on the political union, Spaak smiles and states diplomatically that they will not give up that. The political union is the ultimate goal and despite the failure of the European Defence Community and the European Political Community they will keep pursuing it.

Happy for having resolved the crisis with Britain before it broke out, Spaak must now face a new conflict, this time between France and Germany. Their positions are growing increasingly apart, because the French are concerned about the negative effects that the common market may have on their colonies, and Germany is not convinced that an atomic energy agency should be set up. Spaak must also address urgent

175

problems of Belgian foreign policy, to the extent that he has to delegate the presidency of the European meetings to Baron Jean-Charles Snoy et d'Oppuers, a high ranking official in the Ministry of Economy.

What at first seems like a drawback ends up being a very useful tool for negotiations: every time Snoy notices that talks get stuck on some controversial point, he calls Spaak to go to Val Duchesse. Then Spaak makes one of his stellar appearances. With the dramatic skills that he has inherited from his family and extensively exploited in his youth, he does not object to making a scene that often leaves experts stunned. National officials from the ECSC countries remain petrified when the Belgian spits at them phrases like "I'd rather ask advice to my cook than to you".

Snoy also plays the game. At the right time, Spaak enters the meeting room faking a fit of anger at the inability of experts to agree on technical minutiae. After walking up and down in the room spouting expletives, he asks to see the papers and leaves the room slamming the door. He just goes to an adjoining office where, sitting quietly in his chair, he waits for Snoy to come to tell him the solution they have found. The strategy of good cop, bad cop gives very good results!

It seems easier to Spaak to broker a compromise on topics he is not familiar with. Sometimes experts get blocked in the detail, unable to see the forest for the trees. On such occasions he asks explanation of what he does not understand and proposes the idea that comes to his mind in light of the different elements. "Sometimes an innocent and ignorant opinion can more easily find a sensible solution," he thinks.

Once there is a technical agreement, then he behaves in an affable and open way with the ministers when they meet to wind up the loose ends. He listens to all and patiently seeks practical solutions. Out of all the experts, the most difficult one to get along with is Pierre Uri. Spaak is exasperated by his arrogance and self-centredness, but admits that he is an invaluable aid to finding imaginative solutions and consensus.

At the Paris summit on 19 and 20 February, the ministers find a deal. The key to the dispute between Paris and Bonn lies in the hands of Belgium, and Spaak does everything possible to please his neighbours: although Belgium does not want the Congo to be included in the treaties; it accepts that France joins the common market with its overseas territories. Belgians also have the key to the functioning of Euratom – because they have the uranium from Congo –, and they agree that the new organisation for the atomic energy, Euratom, is the owner of the fissile material.

Throughout the negotiations France insists on having Belgian uranium for its own national defence. For now, the only uranium ever used for military purposes was obtained from mines in Congo by the Belgian government and Spaak himself sold it to the US during the Second World War. Spaak and Van Zeeland negotiated with Washington and London an agreement on the use of uranium and on a research training program in 1955. Now Belgium must change that agreement to create Euratom and to share its uranium with the five ECSC partners.

The US opposes the French having uranium and developing nuclear weapons. For their part, Germans argue that there is no need for a common management in this area, because they dislike the idea of using nuclear energy, even for peaceful purposes. The problem is that the French are not willing to accept the common market if the other partners do not accept the Euratom.

Finally Spaak pleases everyone by ensuring the Americans that France will not go it alone in the use of uranium whilst telling the French that in the future France may use the uranium for military purposes. It is the only way not to let the common market derail.

The first version of the "Spaak Report" is ready on 8 April. After some minor changes, Spaak makes it public on 23 April. It will be the basis on which foreign ministers will negotiate a new treaty when they meet in a final summit.

Spring 1956, Venice

This time the appointment is in Venice, in late May. If the background of the previous meeting, Messina, was idyllic this one is just as impressive: a former convent on the island of San Giorgio Maggiore, opposite of St Mark's Square. The small island is accessible only by boat and has one of the most beautiful buildings by the architect Palladio who, in the 16th century, built an abbey for a community of monks.

The participants are the same as in Messina: Spaak, Hallstein, Martino, Bech and Beyen. Only the French minister changes: Christian Pineau has replaced Antoine Pinay. Pineau lands in Italy directly from a long trip to Asia and arrives exhausted, but he finds the energy to chair the meeting. His role as chairman poses a problem for consensus, precisely because the French delegation is the most sceptical about the common market. Yet the other ministers notice immediately that Pineau is more pro-European than his predecessor. While defending the French interest he contributes to seeking common positions.

During their spare time the ministers visit the abbey church, which houses works by Tintoretto. The bravest among them dare to climb the 60-metre tall tower to enjoy one of the most breathtaking views in Venice. They also walk around St. Mark's square and the canals, while Bech films the beautiful city with his new camera. As they loosen up, it looks like it will be easy to find an agreement.

In the afternoon, from his bedroom, Spaak writes to Simone: "I think it is enough that a small group of men have a firm will. That's enough to engage the masses." He is aware of the historical importance of the step they are about to take: to voluntarily relinquish sovereignty as a means to create a community of peace and progress that unites people. "If this goes well, my grandchildren will read my biography in the Larousse [encyclopaedia] and perhaps even with my portrait. What selfishness in the face of such greatness!" he says to himself sardonically.

The summit in Venice winds up with unbeatable news: the treaties are finalised and there is already a date for the signature: It will be on 25 March, in Rome.

February 1957, Belgium

At the last moment, and despite all efforts by Spaak, Belgian public opinion turns against the treaties. Belgians do not like French colonies being part of the deal. They think that it is an unnecessary concession to France because Paris has many problems with its colonies, while the Congo gives many benefits to Belgium.

They also feel discriminated against regarding each member's contribution to an investment fund for the colonies out of which the Netherlands will receive as much money as Belgium, even though Belgians have far more territory overseas. Spaak despairs at people's short-sightedness when they criticise the project's trifling details and compare their own gain against their neighbour's without understanding the spirit behind it. He gets even more discouraged when he learns that King Baudouin is reluctant to delegate new elements of national sovereignty to the common institutions. Spaak suddenly realises that he made a mistake by letting himself be dragged into hyperactivity in the Foreign Office and at Val Duchesse, forgetting to inform the monarch and the Belgian government of each step so that they could fully understand the ultimate meaning of the treaties. He will have to explain it now.

The straw that broke the camel's back for Spaak is a conversation with the Belgian Prime Minister Achille Van Acker who complains that the French always abuse Belgium, and therefore they should not be involved in an economic union with them. The evidence is that the French want to impose high custom rates to endives, which is a typical product in Belgian gastronomy. The endives crisis is too much for Spaak. He cannot believe it. So he threatens to resign. Van Acker had not expected such a virulent reaction, and in the middle of a government crisis… so he begs Spaak to continue.

Monnet launches his own campaign to ensure the success of the treaties. He writes letters to every minister to remind them that it is of utmost importance to ratify them as soon as possible. They must avoid another fiasco like the EDC or it would be a mortal blow to integration. He urges them to act before 6 July 1957, when the Bundestag will be dissolved for elections. At every election campaign there is always a risk that the European issue will be used against the government, and they don't know if Adenauer will revalidate his leadership. It is better to ensure ratification while he is still chancellor.

Furthermore, Monnet pushes political leaders to take two fundamental decisions that they have left unanswered because they are too thorny: who will chair the new institutions – something he is concerned about because the first leadership will stamp a certain style – and where the final seat of Europe's government will be. Of course on both issues Monnet tries to impose his own criteria.

He would like to make the staff selection, to make sure that candidates share the European spirit. The institutions ought to defend the common good, and not any particular national interest. Hiring the wrong person could destroy the project. Monnet speaks unofficially with Adenauer, who tells him that he will support Hallstein's candidacy. Monnet can sleep easy, as he has known Hallstein for a long time now and is confident that he is a true "Europeanist". So he continues his lobbying trying to convince the French government to accept Hallstein.

Regarding the seat of the institutions, Monnet finds it essential to group them in one place and give the designated location a special European status, a federal district independent from member states. They had already tried to agree on the place for a European capital in 1952, but the long discussions were unsuccessful. They all wanted to feather their own nests and did not accept the proposals of the others. So they only managed to find an agreement which Monnet found absurd and ineffective: to split the ECSC institutions between Luxembourg and Strasbourg, with the highest authority in the Grand Duchy and the Assembly in the Alsatian capital. It was supposed to be a provisional arrangement, and Monnet hoped that once the treaties were ratified the politicians would come to their senses and elect a single seat. But now, when the time for a permanent decision comes, they propose the addition of new cities to the list of institutional headquarters instead of choosing only one. Bech is not willing to give up the ECSC, which has given new life to Luxembourg. But neither does he want all institutions to be installed in the Grand Duchy, because the country is too small and it could lose its identity.

He tells the minister that time has come to give the united Europe a capital of its own, falling outside the national sovereignty of any member state. Having one seat would not only facilitate the work and enhance the independence from any country. It would also send a message of unity to the world.

Monnet organises a panel in the Committee for the United States of Europe charged with preparing a plan for the single seat, with the hope that the heads of government will accept a proposal before the treaties are ratified.[1]

---

[1] Monnet did not succeed and today EU's institutions have several seats. The European Commission (heir of the ECSC High Authority) has two seats, in Luxembourg and Brussels. Luxembourg hosts the Court of Justice; the Court of Auditors, and the General Secretariat of the European Parliament. The official seat of the European Parliament is in Strasbourg although it meets in Brussels for the daily work. Brussels hosts the Council of the EU, the Committee of Regions and the European Economic and Social Committee.

Paul-Henri Spaak, a Master on the Political Scene

Paul-Henri Spaak looking at a model of the "House of Europe"
that would host the Consultative Assembly of the Council of Europe
and the ECSC Common Assembly (© Council of Europe)

The weeks preceding the signing of the treaties are hectic for Spaak. Both King Baudouin and the prime minister are suspicious of the agreement to create a single market and Euratom. Although it was forged at Val Duchesse, not far from the royal palace, the government and the King were not fully informed and now Spaak faces their bewilderment. Belgium cannot ratify without the King's signature, and the whole project risks collapsing.

The young Baudouin, who is 27, is afraid to transfer sovereignty to the European institutions, and Spaak doesn't know how to persuade him. He asks Baron Snoy et d'Oppuers for help. He belongs to the Catholic aristocracy of the country, close to the monarchs, and could enlighten the King about the ultimate goal of the project: beyond all the technical and economic details, the final aim is to achieve peace and solidarity. Spaak needs to know that the King will support the ratification to have some peace of mind when he goes to Rome to sign the treaties.[2]

The second task taking up Spaak's time is the speech to be delivered on the day of signing. It may seem trivial, but the Belgian has a reputation in international political circles and he does not want to disappoint his admirers. The 25th of March will be a historic day, the beginning of a peaceful revolution by which the European peoples come together and blur their borders. No doubt he will start by remembering those who are absent.

Locked in his office he strives to find the words and the tone that will convey his emotion, imagining the cadence of his address. It will be a short but intense speech, enhanced by his acting skills. Spaak would like his intervention to be remembered in the coming years, just like his now famous "speech of fear" which he made in Paris to the UN General Assembly in 1948. The Russian leader Vichinsky had accused Belgium of mounting a defence organisation – the Brussels Pact – along with Luxembourg, the Netherlands, the United Kingdom and France to attack the Soviet Union. Far from showing any signs of being daunted, Spaak replied bluntly to the Russian. He denied the accusation of promoting "warmongering campaigns" and said:

"Do you think that my country has the intention of a military aggression? Or the Netherlands and Luxembourg for that matter? The Soviet delegation should not look for complex explanations for our policy. Our policy is based on fear. Fear of you. We get together to defend ourselves because we are afraid."

His direct and poignant plea unleashed a standing ovation because everyone – except the Russians – felt represented by his speech. Spaak let the people applaud and waited a bit before delivering the punch-line: "It is not too late. It is not too late," he said slowly but in a loud and strong voice. "But it's about time."

Eloquence and rhetoric are in Spaak's genes, because he has both political and theatrical lineage. On the paternal side the Spaak name was well known among the literary and cultural elites of Brussels. His father, Paul, although qualified as a lawyer, worked as a professor of

---

[2]   Baron Snoy et d'Oppuers finally convinced King Baudouin I before the signature of the Rome treaties. In recognition of his help, Spaak insisted that Snoy et d'Oppuers went to Rome with him to sign the treaties.

French literature and as director of the Royal Theatre *La Monnaie*. Spaak and his three siblings grew up in an artistic and literary environment. Charles works as a screen-writer and Claude in the theatre. Paul-Henri is passionate for French literature, but in his case the mother's side has outweighed the father's and he has chosen to follow the political saga of the Jansons. He has also inherited his thin lips and sly eyes from his mother's side of the family.

The Janson's patriarch was Spaak's grandfather Paul, a lawyer and MP for the Liberal Party for seven years. Later he founded the Progressive Federation. He was a freethinker who fought for universal suffrage, fair working time and free and compulsory schooling for all. Two of his six children continued in his steps: Paul-Émile (Paul-Henri's uncle) would be prime minister, and Marie (mother of Paul-Henri) became the first female senator in Belgium in 1921, two decades before women achieved the right to vote.

Marie met her future husband through grandfather Janson, when the young Paul Spaak started his internship at Mr Janson's law firm. The odd couple attracted people's attention: Marie was tiny, sweet and cheerful... notwithstanding her strong character and determination. What a contrast with the young lawyer! He was tall, stout and had a thick black beard. Both were passionate in different ways: her for politics and him for literature. He ended up quitting law and devoted himself to writing and teaching French literature. Paul and Marie married, and by the time Paul-Henri was born in January 1899, his father had already become a renowned author and university professor.

He was not the firstborn, but the second of four children: Madeleine, Paul-Henri, Charles and Claude, all born in the neighbourhood of Schaerbeek, although they spent their childhood and adolescence in Saint-Gilles, in a house on rue Jourdan. Belgium was going through good times with a cultural explosion in architectural and decorative developments marked by the *Art Nouveau* movement. The opera house, *La Monnaie*, became the epicentre of a renewal of the opera. From childhood, he rubbed shoulders with politicians, artists and intellectuals who came to his home for gatherings and dinners.

Paul-Henri Spaak loved school, where the flexible educational system left space for independence and freedom. He stood out in rhetoric but was hopeless at mathematics, like the other Spaak brothers. After school he played football with friends or saw his grandfather Janson, with whom he had a very special relationship. That old man, scholar in law and philosophy, was able to charm the masses, and even children.

Paul Janson often invited his grandson for lunch. He would tell him stories about his political life and in exchange he asked the child to recite the poems that he had learned at school. He also encouraged Paul-Henri when he started writing his own poetry.

The death of grandfather Janson, when Paul-Henri was 14, was the first blow to the adolescent's life. He would never forget the funeral. That is when he realised what his grandfather meant to the city and to his country. More than 400,000 workers interrupted their activities when they learned of the death of "Father of universal suffrage" and went to the family house to show their support to the relatives.

In his last eccentricity and challenge to the Church, Paul Janson had ordered that he be cremated, something that was forbidden in Belgium.[3] The family had to take the body to Paris by train. First they carried the coffin from his house to the station, the *Gare du Midi*. Dozens of workers volunteered to carry the coffin through the streets. All along the route neighbours had placed black ribbons in the windows and balconies to show respect for old Janson.

Only three years later the *Belle Époque* that Paul-Henri had enjoyed was cut short when the First World War broke out. At first his own family and his youthful optimism were not affected. He continued his secondary education at the *Athénée* in Saint-Gilles while his mother was engaged in social action and decided to leave the Liberals and join the Socialist Party.

In 1916 they began to suffer the effects of the war, the economic depression and a growing fear. After completing his schooling Spaak wanted to contribute to the defence of his country, but he was only 17. His parents refused to give him permission to go to the front.

They had strong arguments but Paul-Henri did not budge. So, without parental consent he contacted underground fighters and left. He lied about his age to the military authorities and enlisted in the army.

It was not easy to leave Belgium, as the country was occupied by the German army. He prepared an ambitious plan: he would go north to reach the Netherlands and from the Dutch coast he would cross by boat to the UK. From England he would then take a ship back to Normandy, in France, and join the Belgians fighting there. He did not speak a word of English and his knowledge of Dutch was quite scarce. But that should not be a problem. His goal was to reach the Belgian training camps in France. His dream did not last very long. He did not even have the chance to cross the border: German soldiers captured him in May, only a few miles east of

---

[3] Around 1870 an Italian professor developed a cremation system and some groups started promoting it as opposed to a traditional burial. The Catholic Church banned cremation in 1897, because it saw anti-Catholic organisations (particularly Freemasons) behind its promotion, as a way to deny the afterlife.

Antwerp, while attempting to cross the Campine canal which links Liège and Maastricht.

First he was locked alone in a cell for three months in the Flemish city of Turnhout. There he befriended the prison librarian and a young German soldier. They both gave him a hand to contact his family, and on 15 June he wrote a letter to his grandmother Janson, playing down his captivity with a sense of humour.

After three months he was sent to the Sennelager prison camp, in North Rhine-Westphalia in Germany. His guardian was a German soldier with whom he could not exchange a single word. He spent two years there. That period helped him to mature, and the experience did not leave horrible memories: the officers behaved properly, there were interpreters, and inmates were allowed to organise their social lives.

Spaak spent most of the time reading and arranging theatre performances. Every Saturday evening and Sunday afternoon he offered a play from his extensive repertoire: drama, comedy, vaudeville... he learned to enjoy the moment and not to complicate life too much with negative thoughts or by holding grudges. He came to the conclusion that under extreme situations the human being is capable of anything from radical generosity to extreme selfishness.

Upon release in November 1918 he returned home and started studying law in a special fast track programme offered to young ex-combatants by Brussels Free University. He graduated in 1921 and quickly became engaged in politics. He first stepped into the circles of the Liberal Party, although he finally joined the Belgian Labour Party (POB), which aroused in him more passion and enthusiasm than the gentrified image he had of the Liberals. His name and family connections opened many doors, but he soon forged his own reputation, mostly of being a radical. At 22, he did not believe in a socialist economic plan as implemented in Russia but nonetheless he knew he wanted to be close to the workers. He wrote articles in the press and developed his personality in political circles.

A year after graduating in 1922 he married Marguerite Malevez, the daughter of a family of industrialists from Namur. Even though she was aware of his political activism before marriage, it took Marguerite time to realise that her husband would not be at home much, as he was always attending meetings and travelling around the country with the party people. It was particularly hard following the birth of their first son, Ferdinand, in the summer of 1923. But Paul-Henri amused her so much, always making her laugh, that she forgave his absence.

The couple would often take the tram to go to Brussels city centre, just like any other couple. On one occasion, Paul-Henri kissed his wife passionately on the tram, and then got off while she continued. Then from the street he shouted to the astonishment of the passengers and to the amusement of Marguerite: "And greetings to your husband!"

In 1925 Spaak entered a cabinet, against all odds. In the April elections the Socialists won over the Catholic Party by a single seat in the Parliament. The new government appointed Joseph Wauters as Industry Minister and he asked Paul-Henri to join as deputy chief of cabinet. Besides being a politician Wauters ran a newspaper and was a bon-vivant, with whom Paul-Henri had an enjoyable time and learned a lot. They worked together for a year, until another government crisis broke out and Wauters had to quit.

Spaak resumed his work as a lawyer in the firm of Paul-Émile Janson. Although he had a great appreciation for his uncle, it soon became obvious that they did not understand each other professionally. So he moved to another firm and chose to defend controversial cases like that of some Communist party activists accused of endangering state security. Around that time he contributed to the emergence of a group of young progressive lawyers who met occasionally to discuss social issues and provide legal advice to trade unionists.

Although he was still a member of the POB he felt increasingly estranged from the official line. With the 1929 financial crash the Belgian economy plunged into a depression and it triggered a deep social divide. Spaak expected more action and less talk from politicians.

He went to Russia and for four weeks travelled around talking to people to learn more about Soviet socialism. However, he came back very disenchanted. As he reported in the pages of *Le Soir* newspaper, he realised that communism was not the way. In Russia he had seen some positive examples in different areas, but none of them worth the ruthless dictatorship. Nevertheless he was convinced that socialism should get closer to the masses, mobilise them and provide real solutions to their problems. If socialism failed to provide solutions the masses would be attracted by extremist populisms like fascism and communism.

He travelled around Belgium talking to the workers, delivering fiery harangues against capitalism and advocating equity and a moral regeneration. By then he already had three children – after Ferdinand, Marie and Antoinette were born – so his wife thought that he should spend more time at the law firm and less in politics. However in October he would become fully engaged in politics and quit the firm when he was elected Member of Parliament for the POB in the 1932 elections.

He delivered his first speech in January 1933. His mother listened to him from the gallery and his uncle from his seat in the Liberals' rows. He wanted to arouse the emotions of the members. At the end of his speech he declared in a melodramatic tone: "Given that capitalism does not allow for a living by working, we will have to die fighting." There was applause from the left and complaints from the right. He was not satisfied with his speech, though his mother told him that she felt very proud.

The next day he was criticised in the press. While admitting that the criticism was right, it hurt and he thought he would prepare a better speech next time. Journalists gave him the nickname "the Bolshevik in tuxedo", because after haranguing factory workers he could be seen at the opening of an opera directed by his father.

His political thinking evolved, and this change was reflected in the articles he wrote for the newspaper *L'Action Socialiste* (Socialist Action). He criticised the POB apparatus, its bureaucracy and some members' opportunism. So he earned many enemies in the party.

On top of the struggle of the working class, he was interested in political theories advocating the integration of the continent. He was inspired by Aristide Briand's famous speech to the League of Nations calling for a united Europe. A group of young Belgians organised meetings to discuss the feasibility of the United States of Europe. The promoter was Edouard Didier, owner of a printing press and editor of a magazine called *Jeune Europe* (Young Europe), which sought to become a citizen's movement in Europe. Many young Belgians and foreigners passing through Brussels would attend these gatherings.

Spaak was a regular, and there he met future leaders of other parties. Among them was Paul Van Zeeland, six years older than Paul-Henri and with a very different personality. He came from a family of provincial bourgeoisie and was a member of the Catholic party, but he shared with Spaak the outgoing personality and sense of humour. And yet Van Zeeland was always discreet, nothing at all like the extravagant Spaak. But the young man was curious to meet this Bolshevik he had heard so much about. He went up to him and, by chatting, he realised that behind the excessive appearance there was an energetic man, willing to defend his values and his passion for politics.

Thus, when in 1935 King Leopold III commissioned Van Zeeland to form a government, he offered the Transport and Communications portfolio to Spaak. It came as a great surprise to many, also to Spaak. Even more shocked were some in the POB when the revolutionary Spaak accepted. *L'Action Socialiste* considered it a political suicide. "Men pass, but ideas survive", was the mournful headline. Spaak's father rejoiced, because he disliked any radicalism.

For Spaak, it was an opportunity to serve his countrymen. Despite criticism from friends and colleagues he admired Van Zeeland and was determined to be a loyal minister. The experience started well, and Spaak showed restraint and realism in his decisions. The prime minister must have been happy, because a year later in the first remodelling of the government he confirmed Spaak as minister and gave a much more relevant portfolio: foreign affairs. Spaak was puzzled. He had barely travelled, except to France and the Netherlands, and that exploratory trip to the Soviet Union. He didn't speak any foreign languages, nor had he any international contacts.

Some MPs thought that the appointment was merely a tactic of Van Zeeland to exert his direct control over foreign policy. But Spaak was not willing to be a puppet. He wanted to be efficient and learn the task. With his friendliness and people skills he soon earned the appreciation of the diplomats.

Once he felt comfortable in the ministry, he explained the principles of his foreign policy to the press. He followed the guidelines outlined by King Leopold III based on the country's independence: a "fully Belgian" foreign policy, no alliances and with an army focusing exclusively on defence. The threat of nazism was already looming over Europe, and he thought that by not allying with Germany's foes he would not challenge Berlin and thus would prevent Belgium becoming the battlefield between the French and the Germans. This was the opinion of the King and the minister fully agreed.

Until then Spaak had always declared himself a pacifist, and perhaps in his new capacity he would have to make difficult decisions. In that sense his thinking evolved from absolute pacifism – which had led him to defend several conscientious objectors as a lawyer – to the acknowledgment that organising the national defence was crucial for the country.

Many foreign ministries interpreted that declaration of independence as a rejection of the efforts of the League of Nations to establish a system of international law. Spaak took pains to show that he supported the new international system, but sometimes the law is not sufficient to guarantee peace. He thought that the conditions agreed at Versailles in 1919 after the First World War were certainly consistent with the law, and yet the Treaty aroused irreconcilable hatreds.

In his travels to the League of Nations headquarters in Geneva, he met the Luxembourgian Minister Joseph Bech. They shared geo-strategic concerns, as both came from small countries squeezed between France and Germany, two large states in permanent conflict. And through their discussions on how to maintain peace they became friends.

Spaak was then 37 years old, energetic and had the full confidence of Leopold III, who was 35. The death of Queen Astrid in a car accident in 1935 during a visit to Switzerland brought the King and the politician closer. Spaak was the newly appointed transport minister and was deeply saddened by the death of the Queen and the solitude into which the young King was plunged. He wrote a personal letter to Leopold III. It was addressed to the man, not to the King, speaking to the broken heart of a widower.

The King took the gesture as a sign of spontaneous and sincere affection that led to a friendship. They chatted about the world, international politics, about the Congo... and in addition to addressing official issues they sometimes played golf together. Leopold III appreciated the minister's sense of humour and his laughter. Occasionally he would invite Paul-Henri and Marguerite to spend Sunday afternoon with his family at the Laeken palace.

Things could not have been going better for him, and in May 1938 Spaak was appointed prime minister. He was the first Socialist prime minister in Belgium and the youngest in the history of the country. But soon his decisions as head of government would end up ruining the friendship. He thought that his honest aspiration to serve the state would suffice in securing the sympathy of the King, but in the face of nazism many good intentions turned out to be historical mistakes that changed the fate of governments, countries and royal houses.

As military tensions rose, Spaak's relations with the King gradually became complicated. In September 1939 a national-unity government led by the Catholic Conservative Hubert Pierlot was formed, and Spaak stayed in the cabinet as foreign minister. The situation was confusing: in the first six months there were two false warnings that Germany had invaded Belgium. Pierlot tried to keep everyone's nerves under control, and he was in constant communication with the Belgian ambassadors in Germany and in the Netherlands. He also spoke with the Dutch royal family and government, since their neighbours would suffer the same fate as Belgium if the German Army advanced towards France.

Spaak accompanied Leopold III to The Hague to meet Queen Wilhelmina. The royal houses of the Netherlands and Belgium wanted to mediate between France and Germany. This short trip filled Spaak with sadness, because he understood that the monarchs lacked a clear view of what was happening and had no idea how to manage the crisis.

On his return to Brussels in November, Spaak summoned the German ambassador Vico von Bülow-Schwante, with whom he was on friendly terms. The German did not seem to sympathise with the Nazi regime but of course he had to toe the official line, and if his country ever declared war on Belgium, he would be the one to announce it.

In the afternoon of 7 November von Bülow-Schwante went to the Foreign Ministry. Spaak wanted to tell him about the Belgian and Dutch monarchs' offer to mediate. While they were chatting, Spaak received a call from his ambassador in Germany. So he apologised, left the ambassador alone for a moment and went to his office to talk in private. In Germany an intense press campaign had just been unleashed against the Belgians and the Belgian ambassador was calling to reassure Spaak that the German government had promised to put an end to it.

When he came back he found von Bülow-Schwante nervous, altered. Spaak explained that the call was from the ambassador in Berlin. Still Bülow-Schwante's expression did not change. Spaak thought that he was uncomfortable due to the anti-Belgian press campaign and tried to reassure him saying: "Tomorrow it will be over." The German jumped from his seat, grabbed the minister's arm with deep emotion and asked: "So it will be tomorrow?"

In the confusion of the conversation the German believed that the Belgian ambassador had told Spaak about the day of the Nazi invasion. Suddenly it was obvious to Spaak that the ambassador knew that there would be an invasion of Belgium, but he just didn't know when. The German government was keeping the secret in the hope of finding the Belgian and Dutch armies unprepared!

Spaak was quick to tell Leopold III. The country should prepare for the worst without sparking social alarm. In the evening of 9 May rumours were circulating that the Germans had entered Belgium. A crisis cabinet was set up with the prime minister and four ministers who were in permanent contact with the Netherlands and Luxembourg. The next day Germany declared war against Belgium, Netherlands and Luxembourg, and the Queen of the Netherlands announced that she would go into exile to England.

What should Leopold III do? He wished to stay with his people and fight. He wanted to send the army to the north of the country, where they could organise the defence. He told Spaak that he was ready to be taken prisoner. The minister advised him to divide the army into two: one part would stay in Belgium and the other part would go to the south of France, as he considered that the Belgian troops would only be able to resist the German assault very briefly. Regarding the King himself, Pierlot and Spaak believed that, rather than having a prisoner king, it would more useful for him to go into exile, like other royals.

This is how these two men, so different from each other, found themselves as allies trying to persuade the King: Pierlot was a Conservative politician and a strict Catholic, and Spaak had the impression that the cold prime minister was not very gifted with social skills. At that particular time all they had in common was their strong loyalty to the monarch: Pierlot out of tradition and Spaak out of friendship. Afterwards they would share adventures that would create a bond of respect and affection forever.

The King would not give in, even after most of the ministers had fled Belgium and settled in France. Only four ministers stayed, including Spaak. He paid blind allegiance to the King and so his disappointment was great when he realised that Leopold III was conducting his own diplomatic manoeuvres behind his back. The monarch did not gladly accept his role in a democracy. He thought that his capacity as chief of the armed forces was above the government's decisions when it came to the defence of the country.

So while Spaak, as foreign minister, gave instructions to embassies and diplomats, the King was making parallel contacts and deciding on strategies without consulting the government. Slowly Spaak's eyes were opened to this deception. He tried to talk to him, to advise him, but he had the impression that the King had swapped his trust in Spaak for other secret advisers. Sometimes after a discussion Spaak left him, apparently persuaded to go into exile, and then the following day he would out rightly rejected the idea.

The situation became increasingly dramatic. It was urgent to take action. When Leopold III decided to give in to the Third Reich, Spaak's instinct was to stay at his side for the sake of their friendship. So he informed Pierlot, who strongly opposed. The prime minister said that it was an unacceptable decision. Spaak would not stay because the government could not give up: they had to go abroad to defend Belgium's freedom and honour.

Spaak will always recall with sadness his last interview with the King in the Wynendaele palace. Even then, about to leave, the minister wondered if it was the right decision and how history would judge each of them. He failed to persuade the monarch to leave with them, and a few days later the last members of the government departed leaving their King behind.

Their plan was to establish themselves in Paris, as they believed that the French would stop the Nazi troops. To Spaak, France was his second home, and he hoped to work closely with the French government. However what Pierlot and his ministers found was very different from what they had imagined.

It took them two days to reach Dunkerque, which was already under shelling, and then they took a boat to Britain. In the afternoon of 26 May they finally landed in Paris, where the other ministers were waiting for them. By then the Belgian Army had surrendered, although Pierlot and Spaak didn't know. Upon arrival, they were summoned by the French President Paul Reynaud.

Pierlot began his account of their last hours in Brussels and about the King's attitude. Reynaud abruptly interrupted him and said: "Your King bowed to German command," and went on ranting against the Belgian Army to the extent that Pierlot had to stop him and beg for some respect. Reynaud was furious. He only calmed down when Pierlot said that his government intended to keep up the fight beside the French.

That night Pierlot woke up Spaak at 2 am. Reynaud wanted to see them, this time at his home. He wanted them to know that he would address the French people on the radio the following day to announce the Belgian surrender. He warned that it could spark some aggressive reactions against the Belgian refugees in France. Spaak was hurt and deeply humiliated. It was as if Reynaud blamed them for the dire situation they were in: in confrontation with the King, defeated militarily and with the Belgian ministers separated in exile between France and the UK. The next morning, Spaak listened to Reynaud's speech at the Belgian embassy, with tears in his eyes. He felt shame and sorrow for the suffering of his countrymen.

All Pierlot and Spaak could do was to reassure Belgians and try to restore their dignity. They took paper and pencil to write a speech to read on the radio on the morning of 29 May. They explained that they were still responsible for the Belgian government and for the defence of the country from their exile in Paris. Army officers owed them allegiance, and from that moment they were released from their duty to obey the King. What was really hard for Pierlot and Spaak was to learn that, contrary to what they expected, most Belgians supported the King and disliked the ministers acting on their own.

Shortly afterwards they had even worse news: France had also called for an armistice and its government split between those who accepted the Nazi occupation and those who wanted a government in exile. Belgian ministers moved to Poitiers and on 15 June held a council to decide on their next move. The UK offered an 18-seat aircraft to take them, but they did not all fit. It would take off in a few hours, time was pressing. Finally they decided not to separate and declined the invitation.

These were moments of solitude and incomprehension for Spaak. Their best option was moving to London. And then another problem came up: the new French government, the Vichy regime, asked Pierlot and Spaak to sign a document before they were allowed to leave France. They had to swear that they would not go to the UK. Spaak saw no problem in this, because an oath by coercion is void, but the prime minister didn't find it appropriate. They discussed it and Pierlot decided to stand up to the authorities. Spaak could not believe it and considered this fuss a folly in such a situation! Pierlot told the officials that asking them for an oath was a lack of respect for him and for the state he represented. They had come to France freely and they wanted to leave to wherever they wished. The French authorities agreed and the prime minister won Spaak's admiration.

Despite not having a visa, Spaak, Pierlot and all his family – his wife, seven children and the governess – left to Perpignan, in the south of France, on 27 August. Spaak's family had accompanied him to Paris but returned to Brussels after the change of government in France. After much paperwork and many telephone conversations with Vichy, their two cars went from Perpignan to the Spanish border. There, Pierlot and Spaak left the group in order to not arouse suspicion. So the family crossed the border in two cars on the 28th at 8 pm and arrived at the Spanish town La Junquera.

Pierlot and Spaak appeared before the Civil Guard in La Junquera. The former introduced himself in a very dignified manner as the prime minister of Belgium. Spaak could hardly contain his laughter, but managed to restrain himself and followed his example, introducing himself as the foreign minister. The officials serving the Franco Regime were not impressed, and they began making phone calls to find out what to do with them. At first they tried to send them back to France, but after several days they received instructions to place them under house arrest in Girona.

The prime minister delegated all executive powers to the ministers in London. He and Spaak settled in the Peninsular Hotel, although they changed hotels several times while they were under the Civil Guard's surveillance.

They spent the spring and summer of 1940 in Barcelona. At least the guards let them go out to see the city. Pierlot took long walks in the Tibidabo mountain. Spaak was crestfallen, his usual optimism clouded by boredom. His friends in London sent them plots to escape, but it felt unsafe. The event that pushed them to take the risk was learning that Serrano Suñer – brother-in-law of the dictator Franco and a Hitler supporter – would become the foreign minister in Spain. Their goal was to reach Portugal as soon as possible, where they hoped to join Mrs Pierlot. The guards were quite friendly, and the Spanish government did not seem to care about the Belgians. Spain already had enough problems trying to recover after its civil war. When they requested to contact the Belgian consul, Mr Jottardno, the guard did not object.

The consul turned out to be a brave man who agreed from the outset to come up with an escape plan. They did not know exactly when it would happen, but they should be ready. Jottardno prepared a van with a false bottom with space for two people to hide. He sought a trusted driver who would take them to the western border.

The days went by and the life of the prisoners passed peacefully. Pierlot asked permission to go to church on Sundays, and of course it was granted to him. They were also allowed to run errands or buy food. The guards only complained on Saturday evenings: they could not see the football match because they were on duty. So one October afternoon Pierlot encouraged them to go to the stadium. He promised that they would not run away that evening.

He kept his word, and his captors got into the habit of leaving them alone on Saturday afternoons. After a few weeks they prisoners seized their opportunity. Around 4 pm they got into the van leaving all their personal belongings in the hotel room. The driver was a Belgian chauffer living in Catalonia.

They started their journey on 19 October and had to travel non-stop for 24 hours until they reached the border. As soon as they curled up in their seats, Pierlot pulled a rosary from his pocket and asked Spaak if he mind his praying. Not only didn't he mind, but he encouraged him to go ahead! In his mind Spaak went through all the gods and prophets he could think of... "Mohammed, Confucius, Buddha, and even the Roman gods... if we need some life insurance I prefer the comprehensive coverage!"

The guards did not go back to the hotel after the match, and only showed up on Sunday morning. When they did not find the Belgians they thought that they were probably at church. They waited for a couple of hours before they contacted the consul. By then the fugitives were already half way to their destination.

The consul appeared at the hotel. He pretended to be worried that an accident may have happened. In the evening they were still missing. The Civil Guard passed the warning to the police, but the police chief could not be disturbed because he was at the bullring watching a bullfight. By the time the police alert was issued the fugitives were already close to the Portuguese border, which they reached around 5 am on 20 October.

They held their breath as the car went through the border control, until they arrived safely on Portuguese soil. Mrs Pierlot awaited them very calmly. After the hugs, Spaak asked her if she was not surprised to see them there. Nobody except them knew about the escape day. "Not at all – she replied – this morning in church, when I opened my prayer book I read a passage that begins with these words: 'The prisoner is soon to be set free'. So I was expecting you." Spaak froze. "It was amazing, so simple and so true," he would remember. At that particular moment, he wished he could share her faith.

After resting briefly in Lisbon they took a seaplane to London. The British capital had become the heart of the free Europe. Joseph Bech was already there, and very soon also Paul Van Zeeland also joined them. Spaak stayed at the Carlton hotel, and despite the German shelling, he felt comfortable. One night the wall of his room collapsed with an explosion. He was in his pyjamas and just had time to put on his trousers and slippers before going out in the street! He admired the British phlegm, and how people went in an orderly way to the shelters and kept their lives as normal as possible. His time in London took him out of his tiny Brussels world and introduced him to the cosmopolitan life of an open and dynamic metropolis.

The British gave them a warmer welcome than the French. One morning during his first days in London, Churchill received Pierlot and Spaak in his office. Spaak was impressed from the outset by the determination and security that his words expressed. Pierlot, however, was not impressed. The prime minister found the Brit too aggressive, eccentric and sarcastic. They definitely did not get along. In that first meeting, Churchill told Spaak that he hadn't liked his first speech as minister announcing the neutrality of Belgium. By now Spaak had understood his mistake and accepted the criticism.

The Belgian government was reconstituted in London – even though it was not officially recognised – and Spaak regained confidence in the future of their country. He worried that the King might call another government in Belgium, because that would derail the efforts of the government in exile.

A few weeks later, when British planes were bombing Germany, Churchill invited Pierlot and Spaak for lunch. Trying to be polite, Pierlot said that he was glad that the British aviation had instructions to bomb only military targets. Churchill replied in French with a strong British accent: "Yes, we do not have enough ammunition. And you know it is business before pleasure." Spaak could not hide a smile and a look of admiration: he loved the British dark humour. Pierlot was appalled.

The British government tried to ease the lives of exiles and helped to create a network between the governments established in London. Spaak met with Foreign Minister Anthony Eden, whom he had briefly met in Geneva at the Assembly of the League of Nations. Eden had established links with leaders from Poland, Czechoslovakia, Norway, the Netherlands, Luxembourg and Greece. Representatives from these countries met regularly to discuss their contribution to the allied effort and to sketch the future of Europe. Van Zeeland accompanied Spaak to these meetings.

Cocktails and receptions animated London's social life. However, Spaak missed his ordinary life. The first weeks he suffered for not hearing from his family. Finally, on 7 November his aunt sent him a telegram saying that they were all right. A month later he received the first letter from Marguerite. In addition to reassuring him about their situation, she begged him to be cautious. Despite the distance between them, she acknowledged that his place was in London with the other ministers. What Marguerite did not mention was how much it hurt her the way many in Belgium talked about her husband and Pierlot as traitors. Meanwhile, Spaak feared that his family could suffer reprisals for his political activities. He encouraged Marguerite to move with the children into an apartment in the same building as her mother.

To distract himself he would go to the cinema and to see football matches, and whenever he could, he went for a walk in the countryside on weekends. But the person who would bring him the stability he craved was Simonne Dear, whom he met at a cocktail party in March 1941. She was intelligent and attractive, and despite being ten years younger than Paul-Henri she showed a maturity that soothed the minister. With her he could share his longings for Europe.

Meanwhile, he and Marguerite were still writing letters and managed to skip controls through friends in Lisbon who received the correspondence from one spouse and forwarded it to the other one. They used false names and code words to refer to the political situation, to the attitude of the King, and above all they spoke about their children. She also told him about his siblings and about his elderly mother. Spaak's heart was divided between his new life in London and the family he missed. In 1942 the eldest son, Fernand, moved to London with him and then to Oxford to attend university.

With his charisma and sense of humour, Spaak became one of the key figures in exile. In 1942, the British government launched an initiative for diplomatic collaboration. The Polish General Władysław Sikorski took the lead and proposed laying the foundations for a European community among the eight governments established in London. The only tangible result of this cooperation – apart from networking and declarations – was that in October Van Zeeland was commissioned with setting up a committee to study the economic rebuilding of Europe. He created a committee with all foreign ministers, but it never came up with any specific proposal. Some, like the Poles and Czechs, perceived problems in Europe from a perspective different from that of Van Zeeland and Spaak, because on top of nazism they had to face the Soviet Union.

Belgium, the Netherlands and Luxembourg decided to move forward together. "What has been happening in Europe for the last 20 months proves that it is essential that European countries join," said Van Zeeland. Our safety depends on each other. As it happened in the First World War,

European nations came together to defend themselves. He believed that this time they should keep that bond when the war ended. "The formula 'solidarity for war but isolated for peace' did not survive yesterday and does not have a chance to survive tomorrow," he wrote.

Like Jean Monnet, he thought that nations should give up their right to veto for the League of Nations to work. "From now regional and international organisations are doomed to impotence if participants do not accept the idea that the collective body is superior to the individual members," he said. "No system presents only advantages. Always, to some extent, order involves a limitation of freedom. One must learn to choose and especially to accept the consequences of the choice."

He was confident that the UK, the cradle of parliamentary democracy, would lead the union. In his view, small countries should play a supporting role. They could not afford to waste any time: the representatives of Belgium, the Netherlands and Luxembourg chose to link their destinies.

Belgium and Luxembourg already had a customs and economic union in place since 1921.The Dutch Finance Minister Johannes Vandenbroek suggested enlarging this union to his country. It would be the only way to end a long economic conflict between Belgium and the Netherlands. He urged his partners to adopt the agreement before the end of the war, while they were away from the pressure from industry and farmers. The Dutch Foreign Minister Eelco Van Kleffens, a pragmatic and prudent man, did not find it a good idea. He would have preferred a military alliance with the UK and France.

Bech alleged that his union could later be joined by other partners. "The organisation of Western Europe can only be achieved by gradual enlargement," he told the Dutchman. Their three-country project would be the first step towards a wider union. Once Van Kleffens was on board, they began to deal with figures. They worked for two years, and after tough negotiations the financial experts closed an interim monetary agreement. On 21 October 1943 they fixed the official exchange rate between the Belgian-Luxembourg franc and the Dutch guilder. They abolished all internal customs duties and adopted a common tariff for trade with third parties. To ensure the effectiveness of their financial and foreign trade policies they created several coordination and communication councils between the three governments.

Despite the political activity and the illusions sown in London, the long wait to go back home was unbearable for Spaak. In autumn 1943, the Germans imprisoned his uncle Paul-Emile Janson who did not resist very long and after a few months died of exhaustion. On 31 October, Marguerite and her sister Madeleine were arrested and locked up in a prison in Brussels. Spaak's friends took care of his daughters Marie and Antoinette while Marguerite was imprisoned. Fortunately those friends managed to have both Marguerite and Madeleine released quickly. His sister-in-law Suzanne's fate was darker. She was tortured and shot in a concentration camp. His brother Charles, who had already become a famous screenwriter, left the country.

Spaak dreamed of the day they could all go back to "living humanely". Finally in September 1944, the long-awaited liberation of Belgium took place. Before leaving London, the three Benelux governments sealed their common destiny. On 5 September they announced the customs integration between the Belgo-Luxembourg Economic Union and the Netherlands. In principle it was a provisional agreement and it aimed at facilitating the post-war economic recovery, but in the longer term it should be the basis for a permanent union.

The flight home was difficult for Spaak. The experience in London had changed him both on a personal and a political level. Simonne stayed in England and with her the life that he did not yet want to relinquish. And yet, he was also looking forward to seeing Marguerite and the children. Back in Brussels, he resumed his family life and always attended public events with Marguerite, though he would never break the tie that bound him to Simonne.[4]

Nor was it easy to face the Belgian political scene. On the one hand, addressing "the royal question" would be tough. Leopold III and his family had been released, but the regent Charles – the King's brother – remained neutral between supporters and critics of his brother. Some thought that he could not retake the crown after having surrendered to the Nazis. Also, many Belgian people could not forgive him for getting married in 1941, and holding a celebration whilst the population was enduring so much suffering during the war. At the same time, however, many in the country had a tarnished image of the ministers who exiled in London, and this criticism found Spaak off guard.

Gone were the days of his isolationist theories. Now more than ever he saw the need for international cooperation and for rules to solve the world's problems. In the fall of 1944 the victorious powers – the US, the UK, the Soviet Union and China – drafted the Charter for the "new" League of Nations. Despite its failure to prevent the Second World War, Spaak defended the efforts to rebuild the organisation:

"Great scientific experiments fail dozens of times before they succeed. Why should great human experiments succeed in the first attempt? It is by

---

[4]   Spaak and Simonne Dear married in April 1965, one year after Marguerite passed away.

repeating them, by studying the cause of their failure that we will finally find the successful formula."

Following the signing of the Charter to create the United Nations, at a conference held in San Francisco in April 1945, Spaak was elected as the first president of the UN General Assembly. "If one day we create a universal organisation powerful enough to set international law, and especially to enforce it, relations between peoples will enter into a new era", he wrote. "Peace will be certainly assured in the world."

He managed his UN responsibilities alongside those of the Belgian government, whilst continuing with his determination to pursue the adventure of European unity. But the implementation of the Benelux union was delayed *sine die*. In late 1946 Spaak travelled to the Netherlands to meet with Willen Schermerhorn, Prime Minister, and ask him whether his country still backed the decisions taken in London. He answer was positive, so the two governments gave an ultimatum to the officials charged with preparing the documents: the technical problems should be solved within six months. On 14 March 1947 the three countries signed in The Hague an additional protocol to the convention on the customs union that they had already signed in London.

Spaak defended the treaty in the Belgian Parliament on 1 July 1947: "I believe that this agreement between Belgium, the Netherlands and the Grand Duchy is a good thing for our country and an example for the world."

1957

The Signature of the Treaties in Rome

Signature of the Rome Treaties (© European Commission)

On the Campidoglio, Rome's ancient sacred hill where the armies thanked Jupiter for their victory, a modern epic is achieved on Monday 25 March. This time without bloodshed. Chroniclers pass the baton to new technologies: RAI TV channel covers it live and broadcasts to the world how representatives of six European countries freely bind their destiny together.

The dark clouds threatening rain have not intimidated the Romans, many of whom have been waiting around the Campidoglio since morning for the arrival of the signatories. Young people roam the stairs, as local schools and institutes have declared a holiday so that students can attend the celebration.

Posters around the city recall the reason: "Six peoples, one family, for the good of all," is the sentence printed on a background in which six female silhouettes, each one dressed in the colours of one of the six countries, hold hands and dance in front of a map of Europe.

It is the dream of several generations of men and women, from Aristide Briand and Bertha von Suttner to Coudenhove-Kalergi and Spinelli. De Gasperi would also have been very happy to host to his partners today. The Italian Foreign Minister Gaetano Martino couldn't stop thinking about him during the preparations. The other participants as well, so the official programme includes a tribute to him early in the afternoon.

Although the curious onlookers crowd on to the steps designed by Michelangelo on the Campidoglio hill, leaders are already inside. In the morning, they finalise the last details of the two treaties, the European Economic Community (EEC) that provide the basis of a single market and Euratom. Many annexes and accompanying statements must be added to the treaties. Overall there are two volumes: one of 157 pages for the EEC and 158 more pages on the joint management of atomic energy for civilian use. After 22 months of negotiations on highly technical and sometimes difficult questions, the result is a legal tangle that national experts will have to unravel. The most problematic task is to compare translations, since the texts are now available in French, German, Italian and Dutch. But the political will is clear, and that's what matters. If any minor problem or misunderstanding comes up, it will be dealt with later. Politics is the art of the possible, and Spaak's mediation facilitated consensus.

They don't stay too long drinking their coffee after lunch, because the six ministers and their assistants join the Italian authorities to pay tribute to De Gasperi. The memorial begins with a holy mass in the Basilica of San Lorenzo, where the president is buried. Afterwards, they inaugurate the mausoleum that holds his remains. A few steps behind Francesca, ministers approach the coffin, which lies in the narthex of the church. One by one they leave a bunch of flowers. When it is his turn, Adenauer thinks of Schuman, who in the distance must be sharing with emotion this moment and also cherishing the memory of their friend.

Shortly before six o'clock, the procession of cars returns to the Campidoglio, where the City Hall stands. The imposing equestrian statue of Marcus Aurelius dominates the square where nearly a thousand Italians crowd to listen to the speeches through strategically placed large speakers. People wait patiently despite the rain, protected by umbrellas and raincoats.

Ministers go up to the first floor of the Curators' Palace through a monumental staircase embellished with azaleas and primroses. Down the corridor leading to the signature hall, flags of the six states hang on the walls. Journalists, officials and experts involved in the negotiations are already waiting in the Hall of the *Horatii* and *Curiatii*.

The first to enter is Adenauer, with his usual seriousness and grim figure, followed by the host, Antonio Segni, Italian Prime Minister. The German walks slowly and takes a seat at the huge table covered with a luxurious scarlet cloth. Just behind him, a painting of a battle scene reflects the history that they seek to leave behind today: the use of violence to resolve conflicts. The four walls of the magnificent hall are decorated with frescoes, imitating tapestries, depicting the legendary origins of Rome. All the battles to control the Seven Hills of Rome were steeped in blood.

This scene, after which the hall is named, recounts the war between Rome and Alba Longa (now Albania) in the seventh century B.C. According to the legend, the key battle for the Roman victory was between three Roman brothers (*Horatii*) against three Albanian brothers (*Curiatii*). The sequence also includes the mythological wolf with Romulus and Remus and the Rape of the Sabines.

"We Italians feel the need to give special thanks to two names: Alcide de Gasperi and Carlo Sforza, whose spirits are felt in this room today," declares the host. We are here to inaugurate a new stage in the history of peoples. We must turn our eyes to the future and not the past."

And he adds: "It is a new family, a large new family that we are creating and, as members of the same family, they will all feel united in a life-long bond, as our Latin ancestors used to say, united in a common destiny."

Adenauer, Spaak, Bech and the Dutch Foreign Minister Joseph Luns also praise the new project and the window of peace and prosperity that is opening for all Europeans, because they insist that "Little Europe" is born with the aim of growing to the east and west, north and south, also noting that the union has no enemies. Adenauer cannot forget the East Germans: he wishes that someday a united Germany will contribute with all its energy to the material and spiritual progress of the European community that is taking its first steps today.

The only person who adds a discordant note is the French Foreign Minister Christian Pineau. He describes all the difficulties and obstacles to be overcome before a united Europe can be brought about. He wonders how the overseas territories will be associated with the project. It remains to be seen, he says. The same applies to the participation of the British, still a matter to be resolved, because "without them the construction would be incomplete". As he closes his speech, a French journalist asks whether the French Assembly will ratify these treaties. Pineau wants to show his determination and answers: "Tomorrow I will present it to the Assembly for an early endorsement." He knows he will face strong opposition from the Gaullists and the Communists.

When the time comes to sign, the documents are not ready. Because they finalised the last details in the morning, there was no time to complete the translations, print copies and bind them for everyone. Largely unnoticed, government representatives end up signing a volume of blank pages! No one can tell as every copy is beautifully bound. The signatories don't mind. They have followed the negotiations for so long that they understand that such last-minute incidents happen. The attractive cover and the signature page suffice. There will be time to fill out the other pages before ratification.

The first one to sign is Paul-Henri Spaak. Comments are unanimous among experts and ministers: it has been an honour to share with him the last two years of intense work. Adenauer says out loud what they all think: "He deserves Europe." Spaak ceremoniously sits down, takes a pen and without anyone noticing, he slightly turns the H in his name into an S. He wants his beloved Simonne to be part of History with him. Then he raises his eyes in satisfaction.

There is general happiness in the room, the smiles reflecting the complicity of the leaders. The treaties are more than just a political agreement. Affection has grown between them, especially between those who shared so many battles over the years, like Adenauer, Spaak and Bech.

Nearly 500 photographers from all over the world want to capture the moment. Journalists do not miss any detail and the correspondent for the French daily *Le Figaro*, Paul Chalze, tells his colleague: "It is surprising to see this harmony between Socialists and Christian-Democrats."

After Spaak, Jean-Charles Snoy et d'Oppuers signs on behalf of Belgium. The Germans follow: Adenauer and his Secretary of State for Foreign Affairs, Walter Hallstein. For France, Minister Christian Pineau and Undersecretary Maurice Faure, the youngest signatory; the President of the Council Antonio Segni and Minister Gaetano Martino for Italy; Joseph Bech and Lambert Schaus on behalf of Luxembourg; Minister Joseph Luns and the head of the Dutch delegation Johannes Linthorst Homan; and Joseph Bech, who is at the same time Luxembourg Prime Minister and Foreign Minister.

At 6.50 pm a bell tolls in the Capitoline tower announcing that the signing is done and a United Europe is born. The youth movement of *Democrazia Cristiana* performs a symbolic celebration that they have been preparing for weeks: throwing paper butterflies of all colours from the rooftops in the square. Torrential rains have soaked the paper, so instead of flying, the butterflies plunge to the ground. The carpets hung on the facades of the *Capitolio* buildings are also wet. But the rain does not dampen the spirits of the audience or the message written on the main tapestry: *Roma, communis patria* (Rome, common homeland.)

The Italian authorities offer dinner to delegations and ambassadors at Villa Madama. In the same place as where Mussolini hosted Hitler a few years earlier, the flamboyant partners now celebrate the new Europe and discuss outstanding details. The fundamental decision has been taken, but some small decisions still give them a headache. The main one is where to establish the European institutions. Despite pressure from Jean Monnet, politicians refused to address this issue before signing. Everyone knows that Monnet advocates an autonomous Federal District that will bring all the institutions of the three communities – the ECSC, Euratom and the common market – but there is no quorum.

Luxembourgers defend their capital because they are already adapted to host the ECSC, and yet they don't want to have all the institutions, because their country is too small and they would lose their identity. The Belgians want Brussels, where the treaties were negotiated. Italians propose Stresa, near Switzerland. The French are divided: unofficial sources in Strasbourg indicate that French diplomats argue for the outskirts of Paris (Saint-Germain, Dijon or Chantilly), but Alsatians feel really offended that Strasbourg is not the obvious choice. The mayor of Strasbourg, Pierre Pfimlin, has complained to Pineau. While they take the final decision, the Interim Commission of the common market will be installed in Brussels, without that temporary decision determining the future permanent seat.

Over dinner, ministers prefer to leave the issue aside, or the celebration could be ruined. After eating at the Baroque palace of Villa Madama they attend a reception at the Palace of Piazza Venezia, where Mussolini declared war and stirred up the crowds with slogans of war. This time the palace witnesses how a thousand guests seal a long term project for brotherhood among the peoples of Europe, in the eternal city.

Bibliography

Books

ADENAUER, Konrad. *Mémoires* (1945-1953). Translation from German into French by Denise Meunier. Librairie Hachette, 1965.

ADENAUER, Konrad. *Mémoires* (1953-1956). Translation from German into French by Geneviève Teissèdre and Georgette Chatenet. Librairie Hachette, 1967.

ANTA, Claudio Giulio. *Les pères de l'Europe: sept portraits.* Brussels: P.I.E. Peter Lang, 2007.

AUDISIO, Giuseppe, CHIARA, Alberto, KOHL, Helmut et PRODI, Romano. *Les fondateurs de l'Europe unie selon le projet de Jean Monnet: Robert. Schuman, Konrad Adenauer, Alcide De Gasperi.* Paris: Salvator, 2004.

BITSCH, Marie-Thérèse. *Histoire de la construction européenne de 1945 à nos jours.* Brussels: Complexe, 1999.

BORELLA, François, PAPIN, Jean-Louis. *Robert Schuman: homme d'Etat, citoyen du ciel: actes de la journée d'étude du 20 novembre 2004.* Paris: Ed. François-Xavier de Guibert, 2006.

CANEVARO, Alfredo. *Alcide de Gasperi. Cristiano, democratico, europeo.* Rubettino Editore, 2003.

CHENAUX, Philippe. *De la chrétienté à l'Europe.* Tours: CLD Editions, 2007.

CHENAUX, Philippe. *"Humanisme Intégral" de Jacques Maritain.* Paris: Editions du Cerf, 2006.

DE GASPERI, Alcide. *Cara Francesca. Lettere.* Ed. Morcelliana, 2000.

DE GASPERI, Alcide. *Scritti e discorsi politici. Vol. IV: "Alcide de Gasperi e la stabilizzazione della Repubblica 1948-1954."* A cura di Sara Lorenzini e Barbara Taverni. Bologna: Il Mulino 2009.

DUJARDIN, Vincent, DUMOULIN, Michel et PLASMAN, Pierre-Luc. *Snoy-Spaak.* Brussels: Le Cri Editions, 2007.

DUMOULIN, Michel. *Spaak.* Brussels: Racine, 1999.

GIOVANNINI, Francesco. *Suor Lucia De Gasperi. Disarmata di sé.* San Paolo Edizioni, 2012.

GUIEU, Jean Michel and LE DRÉAU, Christophe. "'Le Congrès de l'Europe' à La Haye (1948-2008). Brussels: P.I.E. Peter Lang, 2009.

MADARIAGA, Salvador de. "Bosquejo de Europa. Estudio introductorio de José María Beneyto". Colección Raíces de Europa. Madrid: Instituto Universitario de Estudios Europeos y Ediciones Encuentro S.A., 2010.

MONNET, Jean. *Mémoires*. Paris: Fayard, 1976.

PREDA, Daniela. *Alcide de Gasperi federalista europeo*. Bologna: Il Mulino, 2004.

RICCARDI, Andrea. *Pio XII e Alcide De Gasperi. Una storia segreta*. Editori Laterza, 2003.

ROTH, François. *Robert Schuman. Du Lorrain des frontières au père de l'Europe*. Paris: Fayard, 2008.

ROUSSEL, Eric. *Jean Monnet*. Paris: Fayard, 1996.

SCHIRMANN, Sylvain (dir.). *Robert Schuman et les pères de l'Europe: cultures politiques et années de formation*. Brussels: P.I.E. Peter Lang, 2008.

SCHUMAN, Robert. *Pour l'Europe*. Paris: Fondation Robert Schuman, 2010.

SPAAK, Paul-Henri, *Combats inachevés I. De l'indépendance à l'Alliance*. Paris: Fayard, 1969.

WEYMAR, Paul. *Konrad Adenauer. Souvenirs, témoignages et documents*. Paris: Plon, 1956. Translated from German to French by Jacques Delpeyrou.

Pour une communauté politique européenne: Travaux préparatoires (1952-1954). Préface de Leo Tindemans. (Bibliothèque de la fondation Paul-Henri Spaak). Brussels: Bruylant, 1984.

Pour une communauté politique européenne: Travaux préparatoires (1955-1957). (Bibliothèque de la fondation Paul-Henri Spaak). Brussels: Bruylant, 1987.

Articles

DURCERF, Laurent. "Les jeunes des Nouvelles Équipes Internationales, entre jeune Europe et nouvelle chrétienté," *Histoire@Politique* 1/2010 (No. 10), p. 6-6. URL: www.cairn.info/revue-histoire-politique-2010-1-page-6.htm.

GEHLER, Michael and KAISER, Wolfram. "Transnationalism and early European integration: the Nouvelles Équipes Internationales and the Geneva Circle 1947-1957," *The Historical Journal*. Volume 44, Issue 03, September 2001, pp. 773-798.

KAISER, Wolfram. "Christian Democracy and the origins of the European Union," University of Portsmouth. November 2007

LE LORRAIN, Georges, "MM. Adenauer, Bech et Robert Schuman affirment à leur tour la nécessité de l'Europe unie: A la tribune des Grandes

Conférences catholiques," *Le Monde*, 27 September 1956, No. 3 632, p. 5. Translated by the CVCE.

Official Web Pages

European Movement: http://www.europeanmovement.eu

Council of Europe: http://hub.coe.int/

Museums, institutes and foundations linked to the "Founding Fathers"

Network of the Houses-Museums of the "Founding Fathers": http://www. peresdeleurope.eu/

Fondation Robert Schuman: http://www.robert-schuman.eu

Konrad Adenauer Stiftung: http://www.konrad-adenauer.de/

Konrad Adenauer's House: http://www.adenauerhaus.de/

Fondazione De Gasperi: http://www.degasperi.net/

Fondazione Trentina Alcide De Gasperi and Casa Museo: http://www. degasperitn.it/it/

Fondation Paul-Henri Spaak: http://www.fondationspaak.org/

Paneuropa Foundation: http://www.paneuropa.org/index.html

Historical Digital Archives

Centre Virtuel de la Connaissance sur l'Europe : http://www.cvce.eu/

European Commission: http://ec.europa.eu/historical_archives/links_en.htm

European University Institute: http://www.eui.eu/Research/HistoricalArchivesOf EU/Index.aspx

Etienne Hirsch's archives: http://www.eui.eu/Documents/Research/Histo ricalArchivesofEU/PublicationsAbouttheFonds/HIRSCH2.pdf

Cahiers européens de Houjarray: http://www.cahierseuropeens.net/

Toute l'Europe (about the signing of the Treaties in Rome): http://www. traitederome.fr/fr/histoire-du-traite-de-rome/25-mars-1957-signature-du-traite-de-rome/les-negociations.html

Cercle d'études Jacques & Raïssa Maritain de Kolbsheim (France): http:// maritain.sharepoint.com/Pages/default.aspx

Interviews

Paul Collowald. Journalist covering the first European meetings in Strasbourg for *Le Monde*. Afterwards spokesperson of Commission Vice-President Robert Marjolin. President of the Robert Schuman Association in Scy-Chazelles. (Brussels. 25 February 2009).

Antoinette Spaak. Daughter of Paul-Henri Spaak and former member of the European Parliament. (Brussels, 5 March 2009).

Jacques-René Rabier. Head of the Private Office of Jean Monnet at the French National Planning Board from 1947 to 1952. (Brussels, 2 March 2010).

Father Bernard Ardura. President of the Pontifical Council of Historical Sciences and postulator of the beatification cause of Robert Schuman (Rome, 16 May 2010).

Konrad Adenauer Jr. Grandson of Konrad Adenauer. (Brussels, 6 May 2010).

François Danis. Spaak's grandson and secretary general of the Fondation Paul-Henri Spaak. (Brussels, 6 August 2012).

Michel-Armand Dear, son of Simonne Dear. (Brussels, 2 April 2014).

Visits and interviews at the houses of Jean Monnet in Houjarray (France), Robert Schuman in Scy-Chazèlles (France), Konrad Adenauer in Rhöndorf (Germany), Alcide de Gasperi in Pieve Tesino (Italy) and the Centre Jacques Maritain in Kolbsheim (France).

Memories of an Evolving Europe

Memories of an Evolving Europe is a collection devoted to highlighting the historical memory of European integration. It aims to ensure that citizens of the new Europe have a better understanding of the values, goals and methods behind their common destiny. There are four different categories of work in this collection. First, there are biographies, memoirs and portraits of the "actors" personally committed to contributing towards construction of the new Europe. Second, there is analysis of the "events" that shaped the future and changed the course of history. Third, there are stories of the conception, development and achievements of the "institutions and associations" that participated in transforming the attitudes and awareness of European citizens. There is also a presentation and analysis of the "themes" that marked the original evolution of European society towards a new way of doing things. This collection, inspired by recent history, aims to be all-encompassing, diverse, original and dynamic, just like the Europe it wants to help create.

Published Books

N° 1 – Daniel MARGOT, *L'acteur européen Jean-Pascal Delamuraz. De l'usage d'une Suisse rétive mais pas chétive*, 2009

N° 2 – Johan VAN MERRIËNBOER, *Mansholt. A Biography*, 2011

N° 3 – Pierre DUCHÂTEAU, *Mon aventure européenne. Images et souvenirs*, 2011

N° 4 – Françoise JURION-DE WAHA, *Fernand Herman. La passion de l'Europe*, 2014